TRANS- METRO- POLITAN:

LUST FOR LIFE

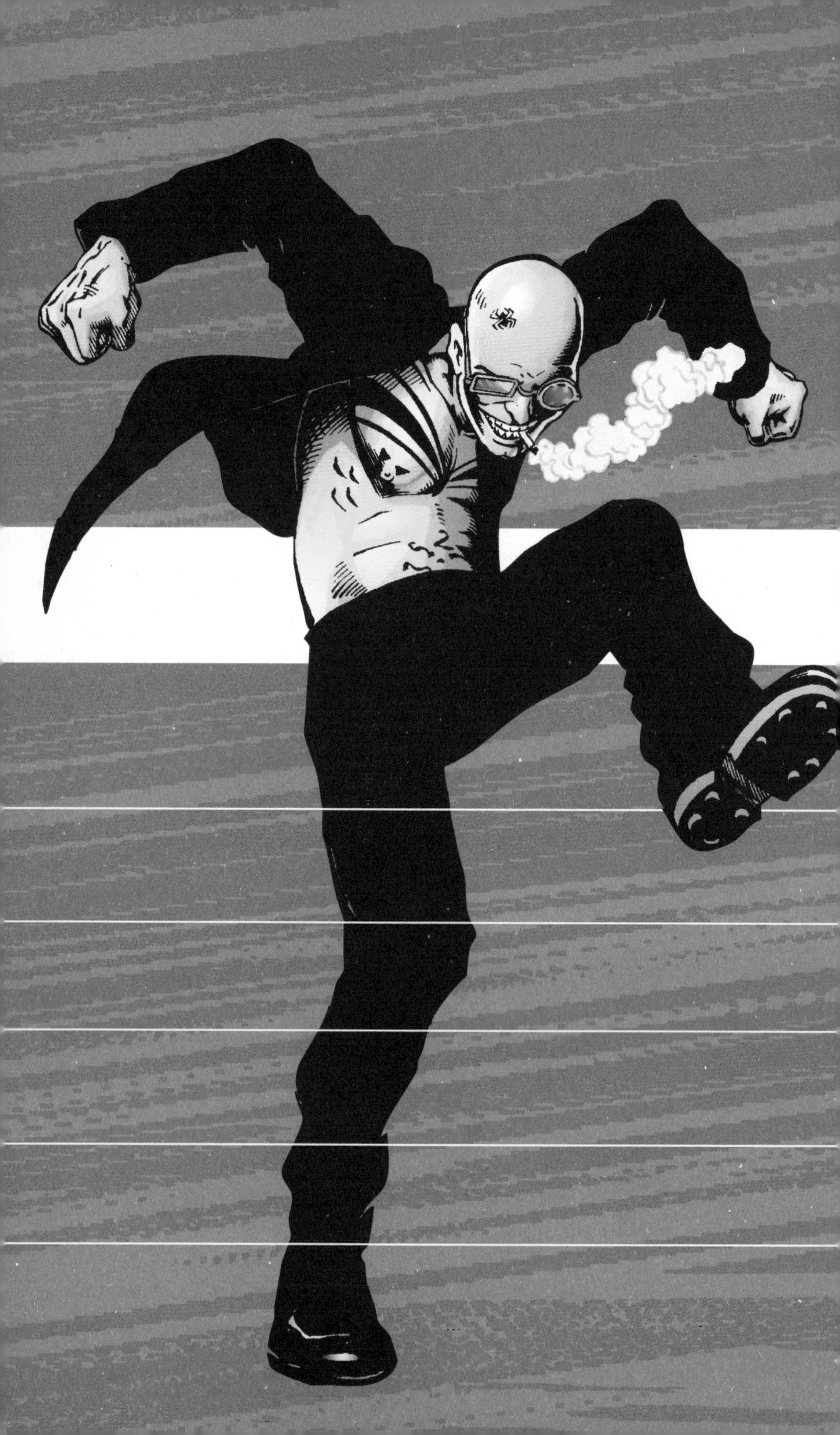

TRANS-
METRO-
POLITAN:
LUST FOR LIFE

Warren_Ellis
Writer

Darick_Robertson
Penciller

Rodney_Ramos
Inker

Nathan_Eyring
Colorist

Clem_Robins
Letterer

Darick_Robertson
Original Series Covers

TRANSMETROPOLITAN created by Warren_Ellis and Darick_Robertson

Special thanks to Janice Corfield-Ricciardi, Andre Ricciardi, Mike O'Brien, Larry Young, and Meredith Miller.

Dedicated to Tibor Sardy, with appreciation.

— **Darick_Robertson**

For Niki, for Lilith, and for my father.

— **Warren_Ellis**

Stuart Moore Editor – Original Series Cliff Chiang Assistant Editor – Original Series Jeb Woodard Group Editor – Collected Editions
Scott Nybakken Editor – Collected Edition Steve Cook Design Director – Books Louis Prandi Publication Design
Shelly Bond VP & Executive Editor – Vertigo Diane Nelson President Dan DiDio and Jim Lee Co-Publishers Geoff Johns Chief Creative Offic
Amit Desai Senior VP – Marketing & Global Franchise Management Nairi Gardiner Senior VP – Finance Sam Ades VP – Digital Marketing
Bobbie Chase VP – Talent Development Mark Chiarello Senior VP – Art, Design & Collected Editions John Cunningham VP – Content Strate
Anne DePies VP – Strategy Planning & Reporting Don Falletti VP – Manufacturing Operations
Lawrence Ganem VP – Editorial Administration & Talent Relations Alison Gill Senior VP – Manufacturing & Operations
Hank Kanalz Senior VP – Editorial Strategy & Administration Jay Kogan VP – Legal Affairs
Derek Maddalena Senior VP – Sales & Business Development Jack Mahan VP – Business Affairs
Dan Miron VP – Sales Planning & Trade Development Nick Napolitano VP – Manufacturing Administration Carol Roeder VP – Marketing
Eddie Scannell VP – Mass Account & Digital Sales Courtney Simmons Senior VP – Publicity & Communications
Jim (Ski) Sokolowski VP – Comic Book Specialty & Newsstand Sales Sandy Yi Senior VP – Global Franchise Management

Cover illustration by Darick Robertson.
Cover color by Nathan Eyring.

TRANSMETROPOLITAN: LUST FOR LIFE

DC Comics, 2900 W. Alameda Avenue, Burbank, CA 91505. Printed by Transcontinental Interglobe Beauceville, Canada. Seventh Printing.

ISBN: 978-1-4012-2261-1

PEFC Certified
Printed on paper from
sustainably managed
forests and controlled
sources
PEFC/01-31-106   www.pefc.org

Library of Congress Cataloging-in-Publication Data

Ellis, Warren.
  Transmetropolitan. Vol. 2, Lust for life / Warren Ellis, Darick Robertson, Rodney Ramos.
    p. cm.
  "Originally published in single magazine form as Transmetropolitan 7-12."
  ISBN 978-1-4012-2261-1 (alk. paper)
  1. Graphic novels. I. Robertson, Darick. II. Ramos, Rodney. III. Title. IV. Title: Lust for life.
  PN6728.T68E4427 2012
  741.5'973–dc23
                    2012025423

by **Spider Jerusalem** [author of "waving and drowning"]

I HATE IT HERE

—Yesterday, here in the middle of the City, I saw a wolf turn into a Russian ex-gymnast and hand over a business card that read YOUR OWN PERSONAL TRANSHUMAN SECURITY WHORE! STERILIZED INNARDS! ACCEPTS ALL CREDIT CARDS to a large man who wore trained attack cancers on his face and possessed seventy-five indentured Komodo Dragons instead of legs. And they had sex. Right in front of me. And six of the Komodo Dragons spat napalm on my new shoes.

Now listen. I'm told I'm a FAMOUS JOURNALIST these days. I'm told the five years I spent away from the City have vanished like the name of the guy you picked up last night, and that it's like I never left. (I was driven away, let me remind you, by things like Sickness, Hate and The Death of Truth.)

So why do I have to put up with this shabby crap on my front doorstep? Now my beautiful new apartment stinks of wet fur and burning dragon spit, and I think one of the cancers mated with the doormat. It keeps cursing at me in a thick Mexican accent. I may have to have it shot.

If you loved me, you'd all kill yourselves today.

— SPIDER JERUSALEM

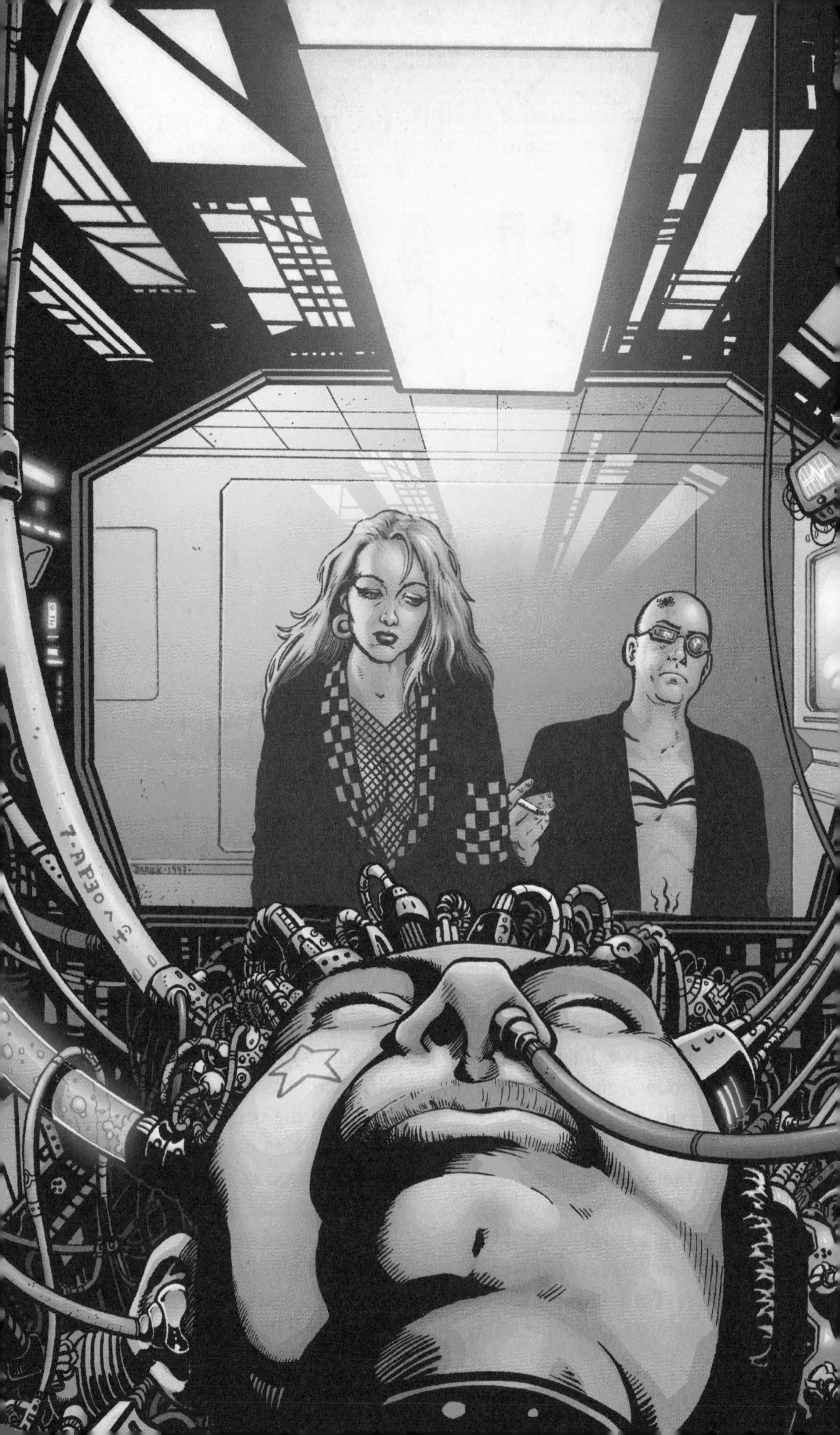
DARICK·1997·

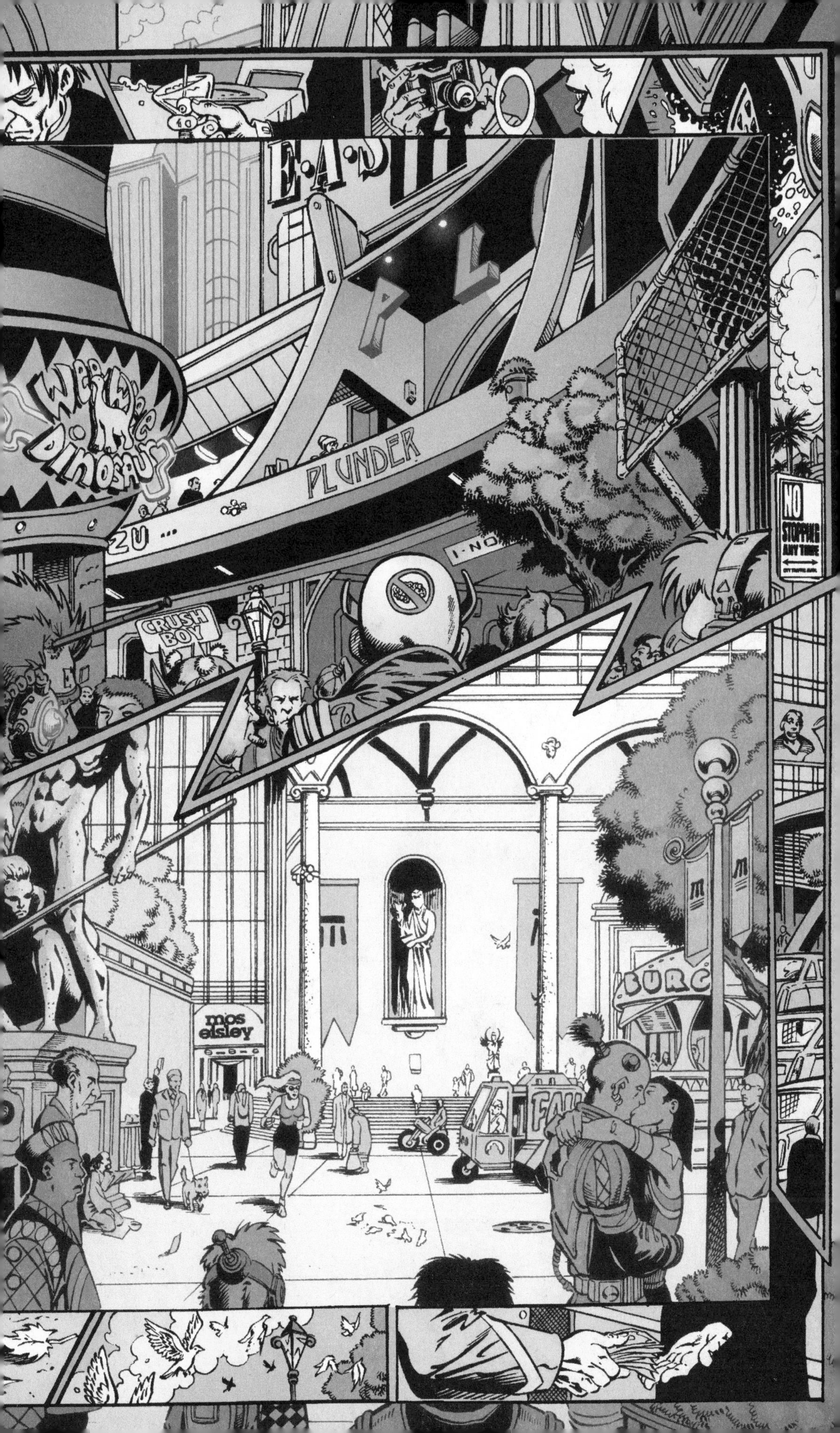

PLUNDER
NO STOPPING ANY TIME
CRUSH BOY
mos eisley

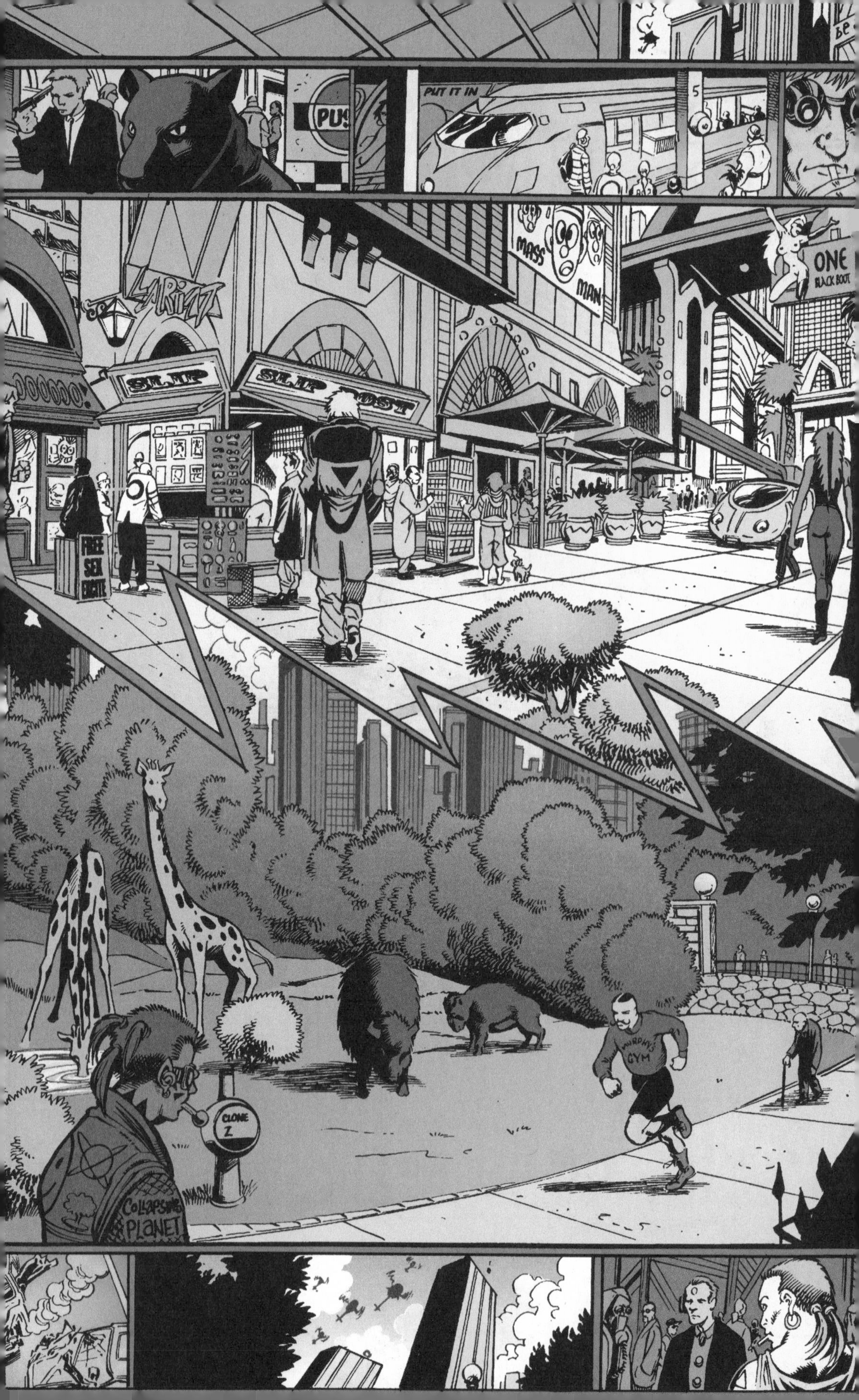

PUT IT IN
5
MASS
MAN
ONE
BLACK BOOT
SLIP
SLIP POST
FREE
SEX
EXCITE
GYM
CLONE
Z
COLLAPSING
PLANET

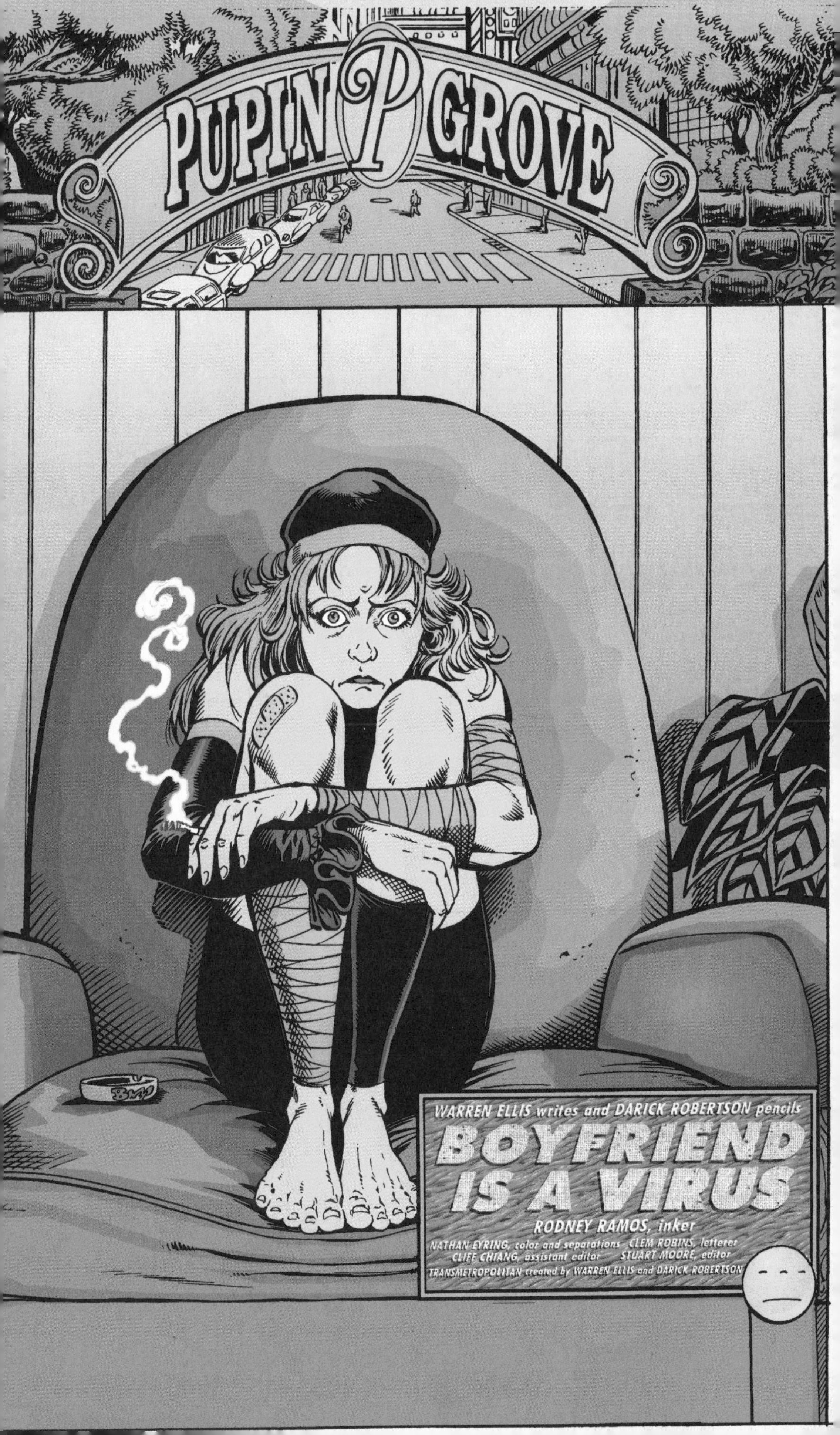
PUPIN P GROVE
WARREN ELLIS writes and DARICK ROBERTSON pencils
BOYFRIEND IS A VIRUS
RODNEY RAMOS, inker
NATHAN EYRING, color and separations CLEM ROBINS, letterer
CLIFF CHIANG, assistant editor STUART MOORE, editor
TRANSMETROPOLITAN created by WARREN ELLIS and DARICK ROBERTSON

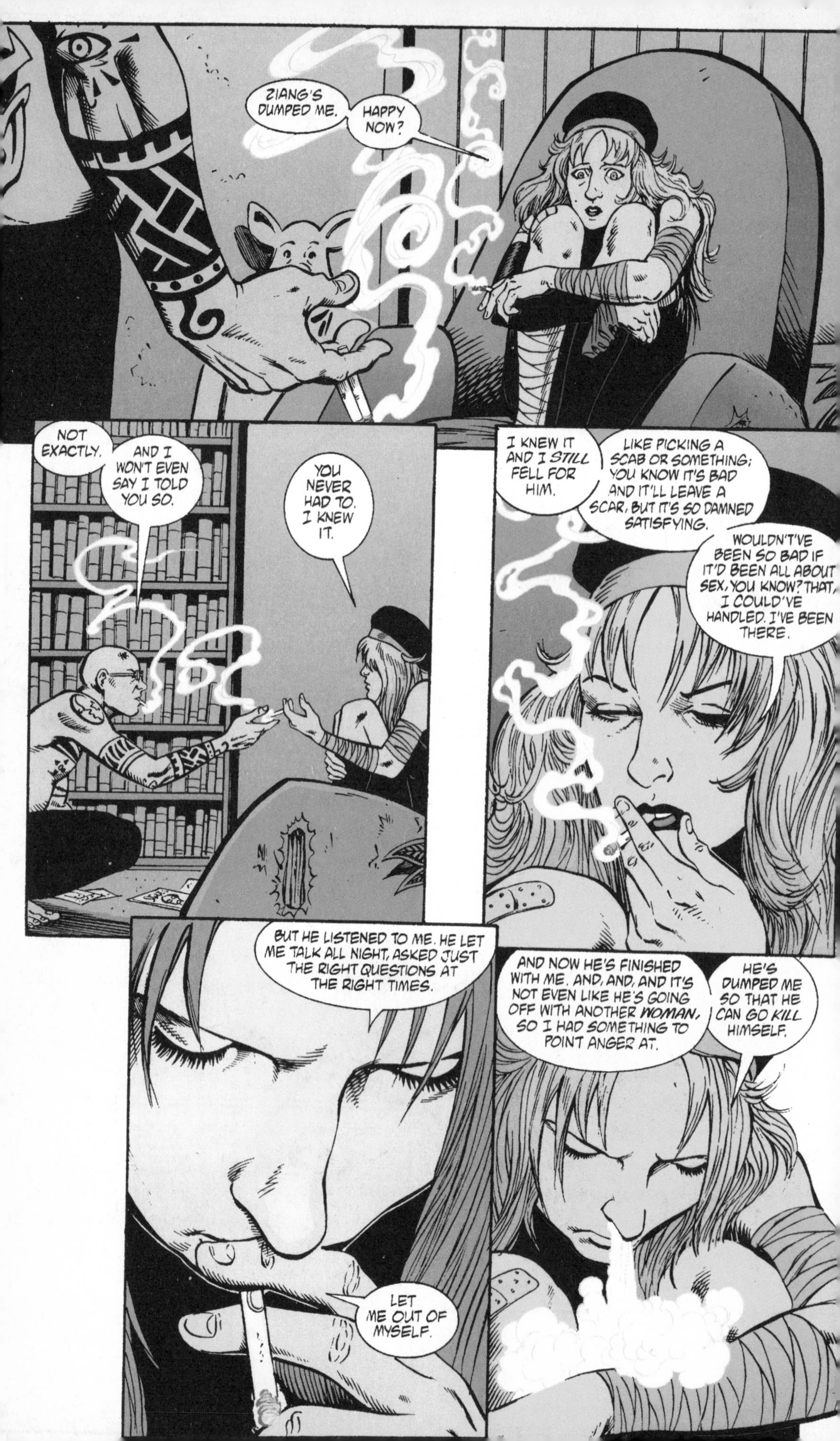
ZIANG'S DUMPED ME.
HAPPY NOW?
NOT EXACTLY.
AND I WON'T EVEN SAY I TOLD YOU SO.
YOU NEVER HAD TO. I KNEW IT.
I KNEW IT AND I STILL FELL FOR HIM.
LIKE PICKING A SCAB OR SOMETHING; YOU KNOW IT'S BAD AND IT'LL LEAVE A SCAR, BUT IT'S SO DAMNED SATISFYING.
WOULDN'T'VE BEEN SO BAD IF IT'D BEEN ALL ABOUT SEX, YOU KNOW? THAT, I COULD'VE HANDLED. I'VE BEEN THERE.
BUT HE LISTENED TO ME. HE LET ME TALK ALL NIGHT, ASKED JUST THE RIGHT QUESTIONS AT THE RIGHT TIMES.
LET ME OUT OF MYSELF.
AND NOW HE'S FINISHED WITH ME. AND, AND, AND IT'S NOT EVEN LIKE HE'S GOING OFF WITH ANOTHER WOMAN, SO I HAD SOMETHING TO POINT ANGER AT.
HE'S DUMPED ME SO THAT HE CAN GO KILL HIMSELF.

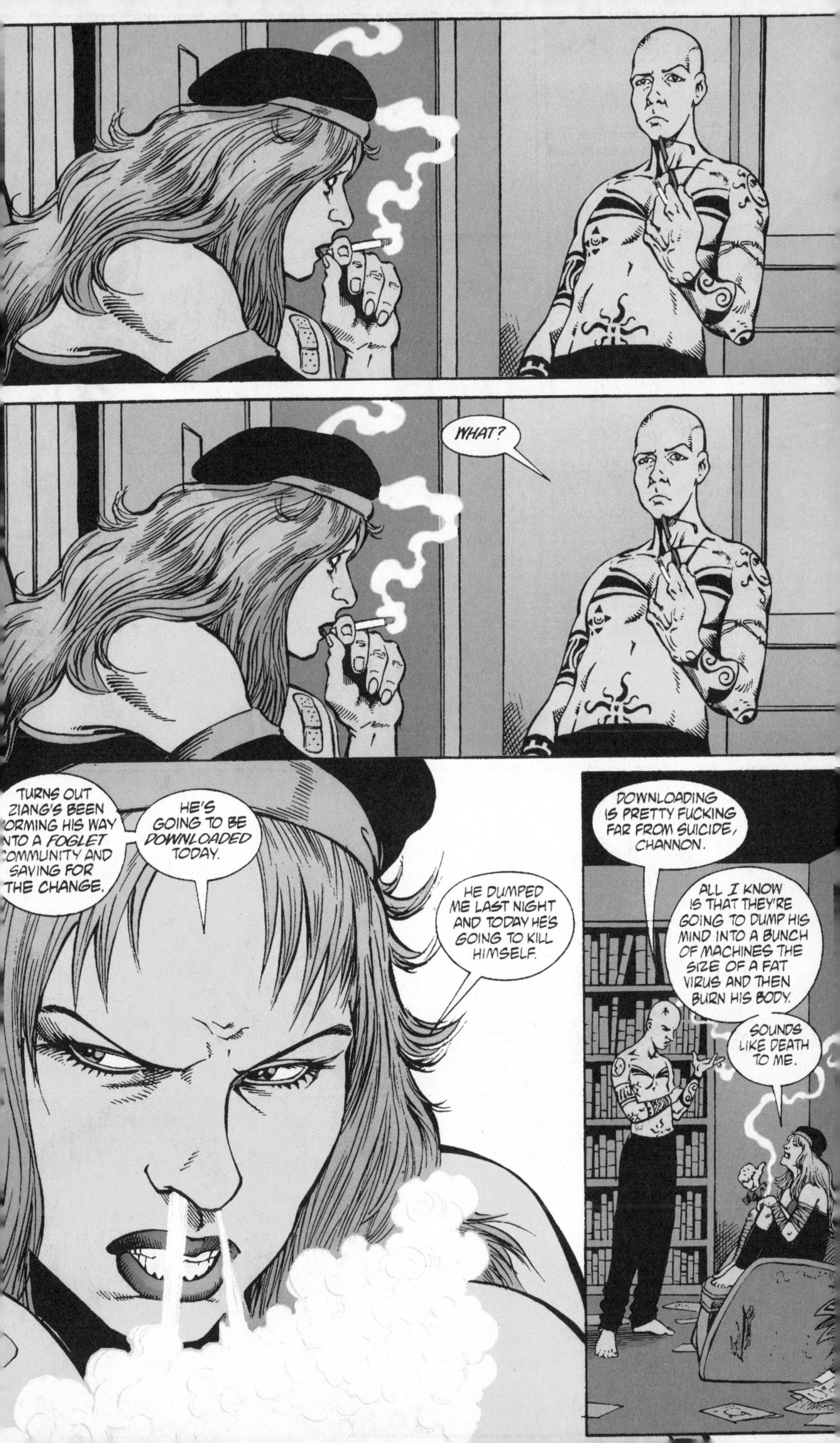
WHAT?
TURNS OUT ZIANG'S BEEN WORMING HIS WAY INTO A FOGLET COMMUNITY AND SAVING FOR THE CHANGE.
HE'S GOING TO BE DOWNLOADED TODAY.
HE DUMPED ME LAST NIGHT AND TODAY HE'S GOING TO KILL HIMSELF.
DOWNLOADING IS PRETTY FUCKING FAR FROM SUICIDE, CHANNON.
ALL I KNOW IS THAT THEY'RE GOING TO DUMP HIS MIND INTO A BUNCH OF MACHINES THE SIZE OF A FAT VIRUS AND THEN BURN HIS BODY.
SOUNDS LIKE DEATH TO ME.

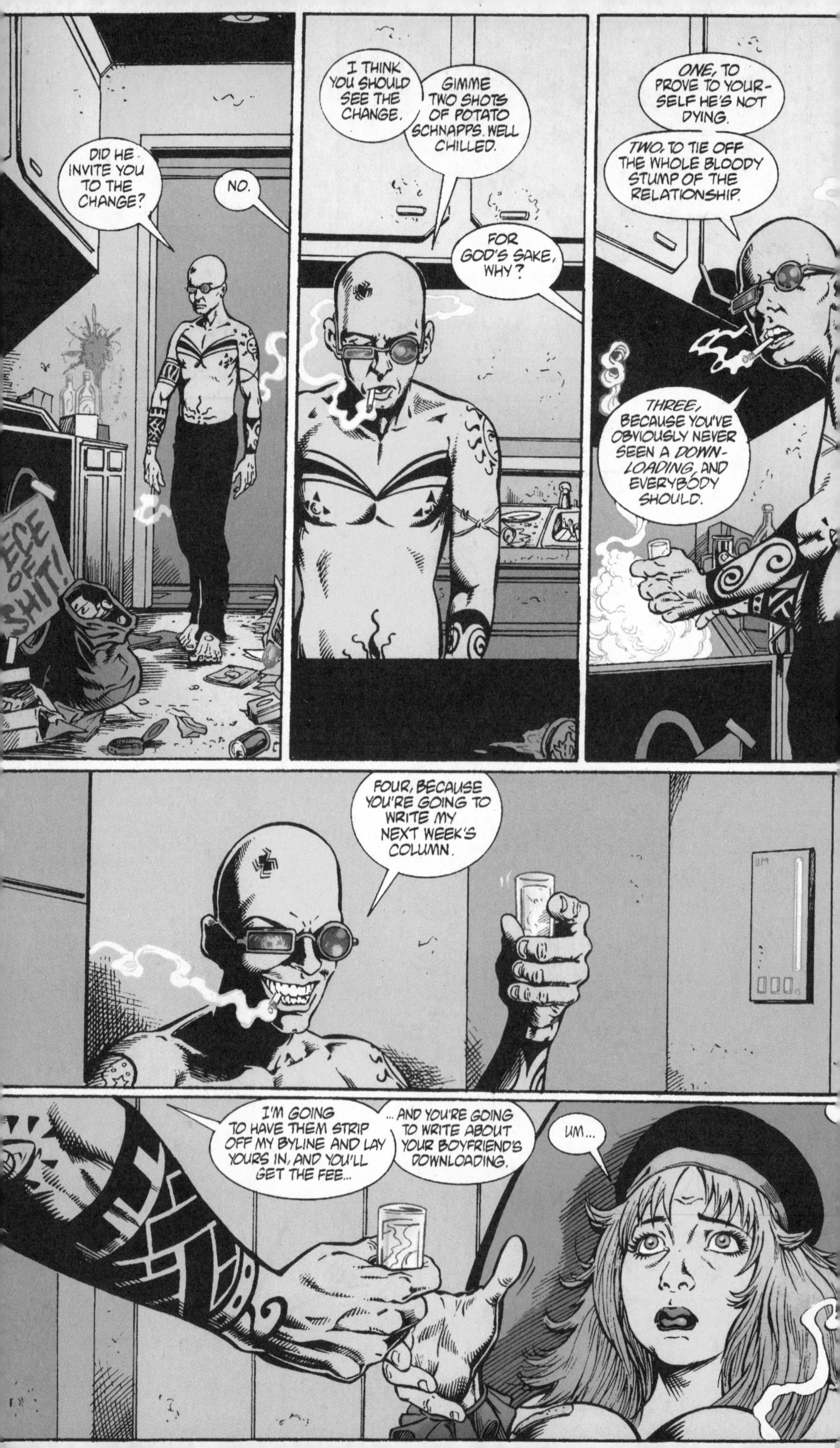
DID HE INVITE YOU TO THE CHANGE?
NO.
I THINK YOU SHOULD SEE THE CHANGE.
GIMME TWO SHOTS OF POTATO SCHNAPPS. WELL CHILLED.
FOR GOD'S SAKE, WHY?
ONE, TO PROVE TO YOURSELF HE'S NOT DYING.
TWO, TO TIE OFF THE WHOLE BLOODY STUMP OF THE RELATIONSHIP.
THREE, BECAUSE YOU'VE OBVIOUSLY NEVER SEEN A DOWNLOADING, AND EVERYBODY SHOULD.
FOUR, BECAUSE YOU'RE GOING TO WRITE MY NEXT WEEK'S COLUMN.
I'M GOING TO HAVE THEM STRIP OFF MY BYLINE AND LAY YOURS IN, AND YOU'LL GET THE FEE...
...AND YOU'RE GOING TO WRITE ABOUT YOUR BOYFRIEND'S DOWNLOADING.
UM...

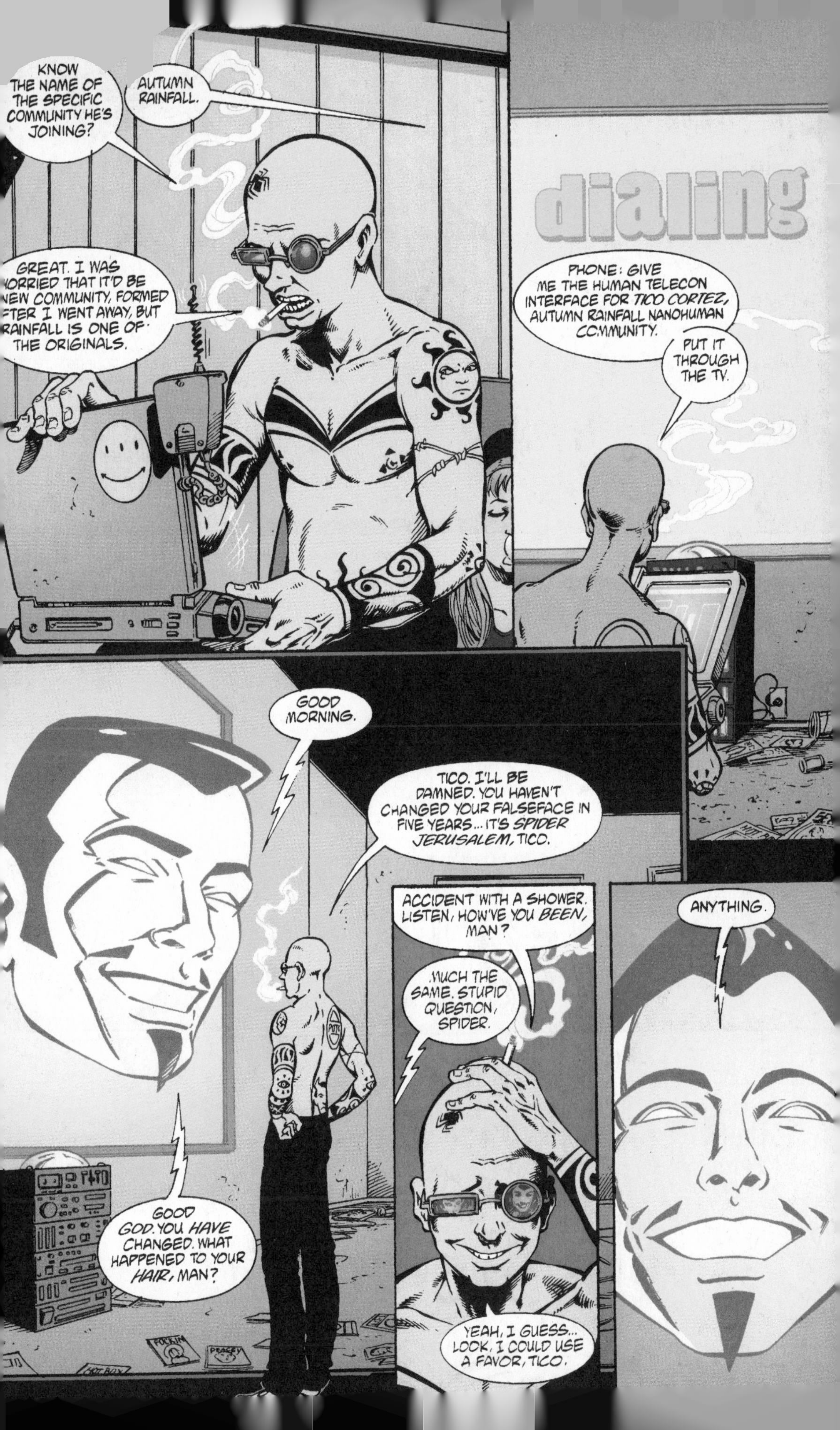
KNOW THE NAME OF THE SPECIFIC COMMUNITY HE'S JOINING?
AUTUMN RAINFALL.
GREAT. I WAS WORRIED THAT IT'D BE NEW COMMUNITY, FORMED AFTER I WENT AWAY, BUT RAINFALL IS ONE OF THE ORIGINALS.
dialing
PHONE: GIVE ME THE HUMAN TELECON INTERFACE FOR TICO CORTEZ, AUTUMN RAINFALL NANOHUMAN COMMUNITY.
PUT IT THROUGH THE TV.
GOOD MORNING.
TICO. I'LL BE DAMNED. YOU HAVEN'T CHANGED YOUR FALSEFACE IN FIVE YEARS... IT'S SPIDER JERUSALEM, TICO.
GOOD GOD. YOU HAVE CHANGED. WHAT HAPPENED TO YOUR HAIR, MAN?
ACCIDENT WITH A SHOWER. LISTEN, HOW'VE YOU BEEN, MAN?
MUCH THE SAME. STUPID QUESTION, SPIDER.
YEAH, I GUESS... LOOK, I COULD USE A FAVOR, TICO.
ANYTHING.

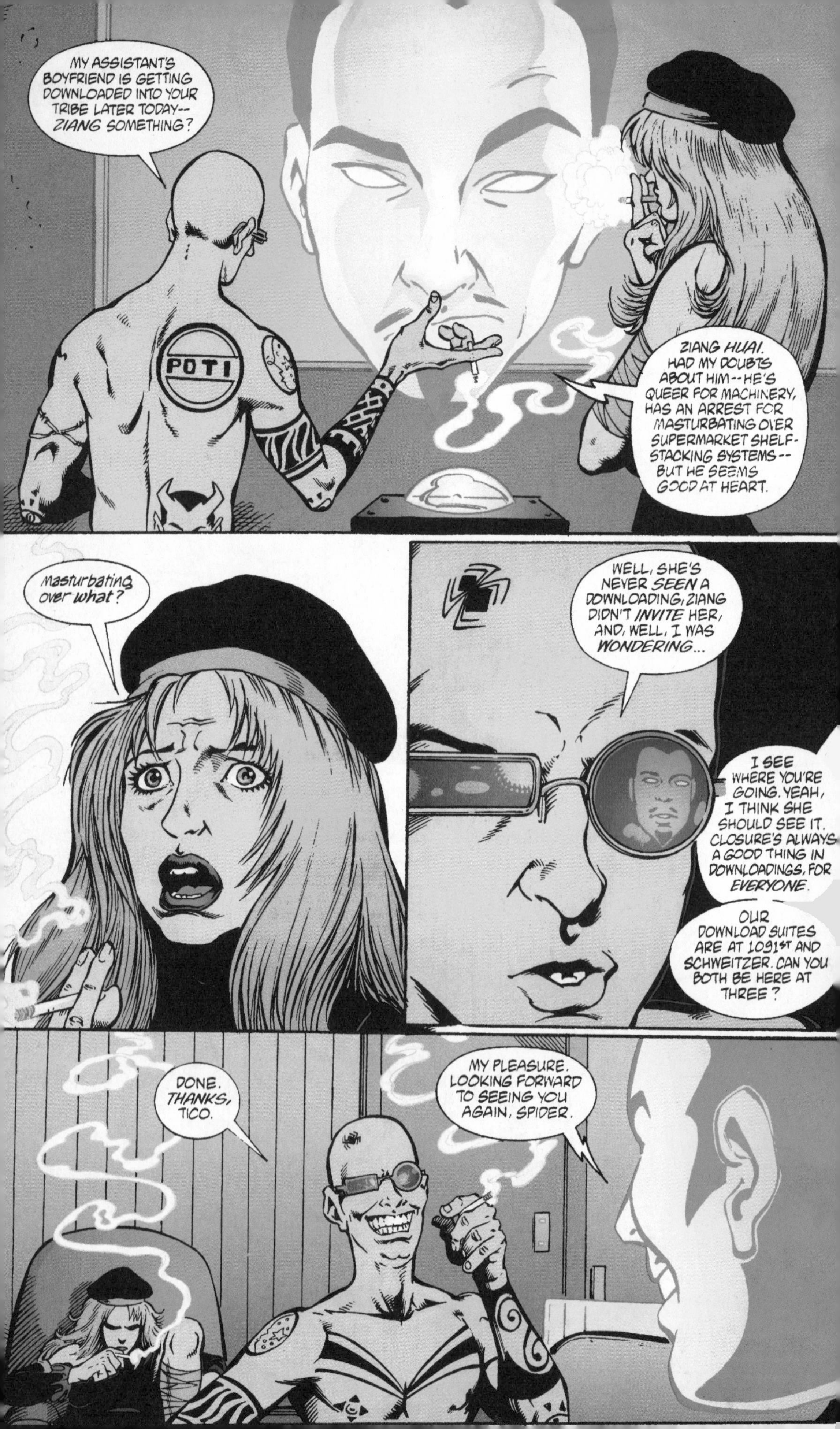
MY ASSISTANT'S BOYFRIEND IS GETTING DOWNLOADED INTO YOUR TRIBE LATER TODAY-- ZIANG SOMETHING?
POTI
ZIANG HUAI. HAD MY DOUBTS ABOUT HIM--HE'S QUEER FOR MACHINERY, HAS AN ARREST FOR MASTURBATING OVER SUPERMARKET SHELF-STACKING SYSTEMS--BUT HE SEEMS GOOD AT HEART.
Masturbating over what?
WELL, SHE'S NEVER SEEN A DOWNLOADING, ZIANG DIDN'T INVITE HER, AND, WELL, I WAS WONDERING...
I SEE WHERE YOU'RE GOING. YEAH, I THINK SHE SHOULD SEE IT. CLOSURE'S ALWAYS A GOOD THING IN DOWNLOADINGS, FOR EVERYONE.
OUR DOWNLOAD SUITES ARE AT 1091ST AND SCHWEITZER. CAN YOU BOTH BE HERE AT THREE?
DONE. THANKS, TICO.
MY PLEASURE. LOOKING FORWARD TO SEEING YOU AGAIN, SPIDER.

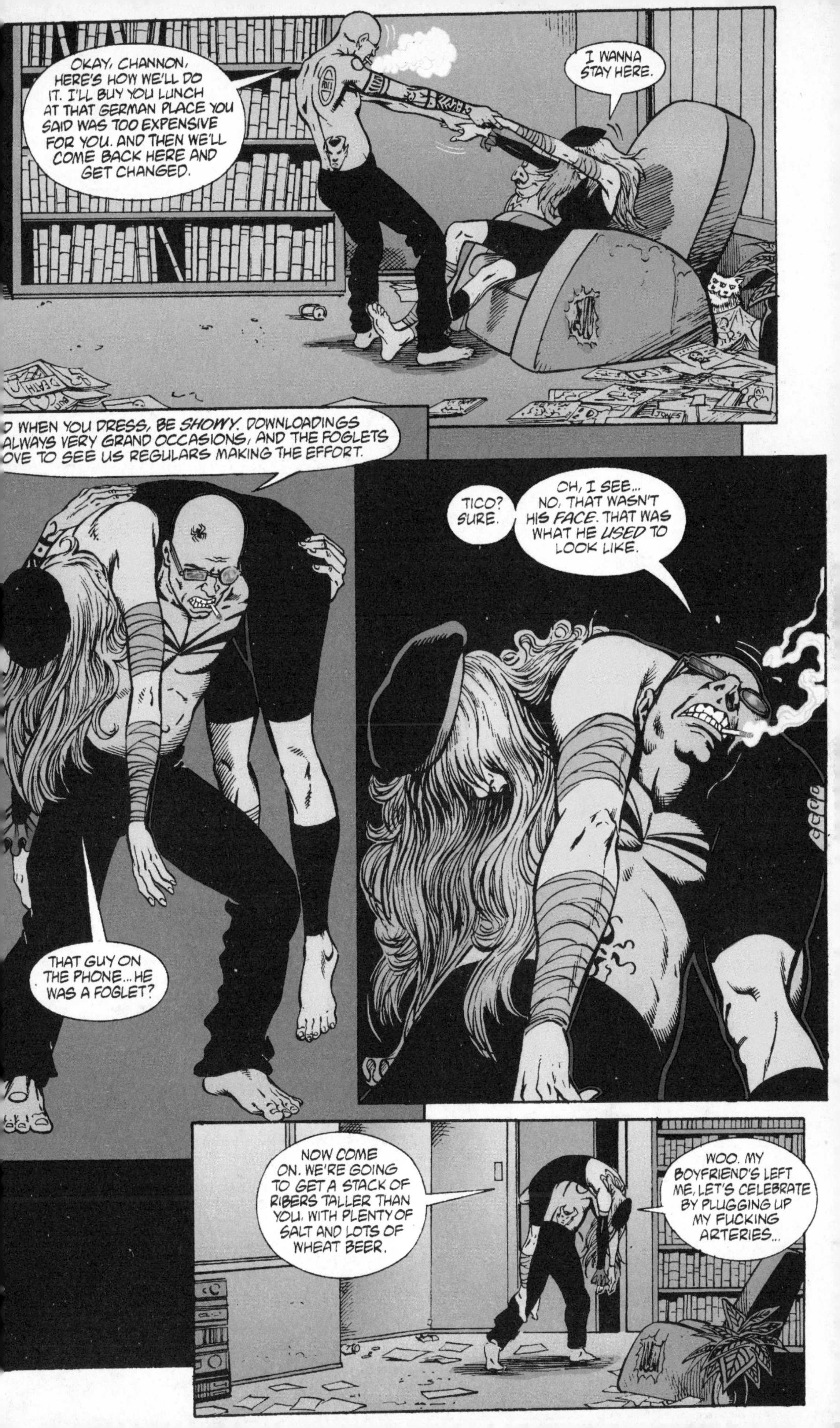
OKAY, CHANNON, HERE'S HOW WE'LL DO IT. I'LL BUY YOU LUNCH AT THAT GERMAN PLACE YOU SAID WAS TOO EXPENSIVE FOR YOU. AND THEN WE'LL COME BACK HERE AND GET CHANGED.
I WANNA STAY HERE.
D WHEN YOU DRESS, BE SHOWY. DOWNLOADINGS ALWAYS VERY GRAND OCCASIONS, AND THE FOGLETS OVE TO SEE US REGULARS MAKING THE EFFORT.
THAT GUY ON THE PHONE... HE WAS A FOGLET?
TICO? SURE.
OH, I SEE... NO, THAT WASN'T HIS FACE. THAT WAS WHAT HE USED TO LOOK LIKE.
NOW COME ON. WE'RE GOING TO GET A STACK OF RIBERS TALLER THAN YOU, WITH PLENTY OF SALT AND LOTS OF WHEAT BEER.
WOO. MY BOYFRIEND'S LEFT ME, LET'S CELEBRATE BY PLUGGING UP MY FUCKING ARTERIES...

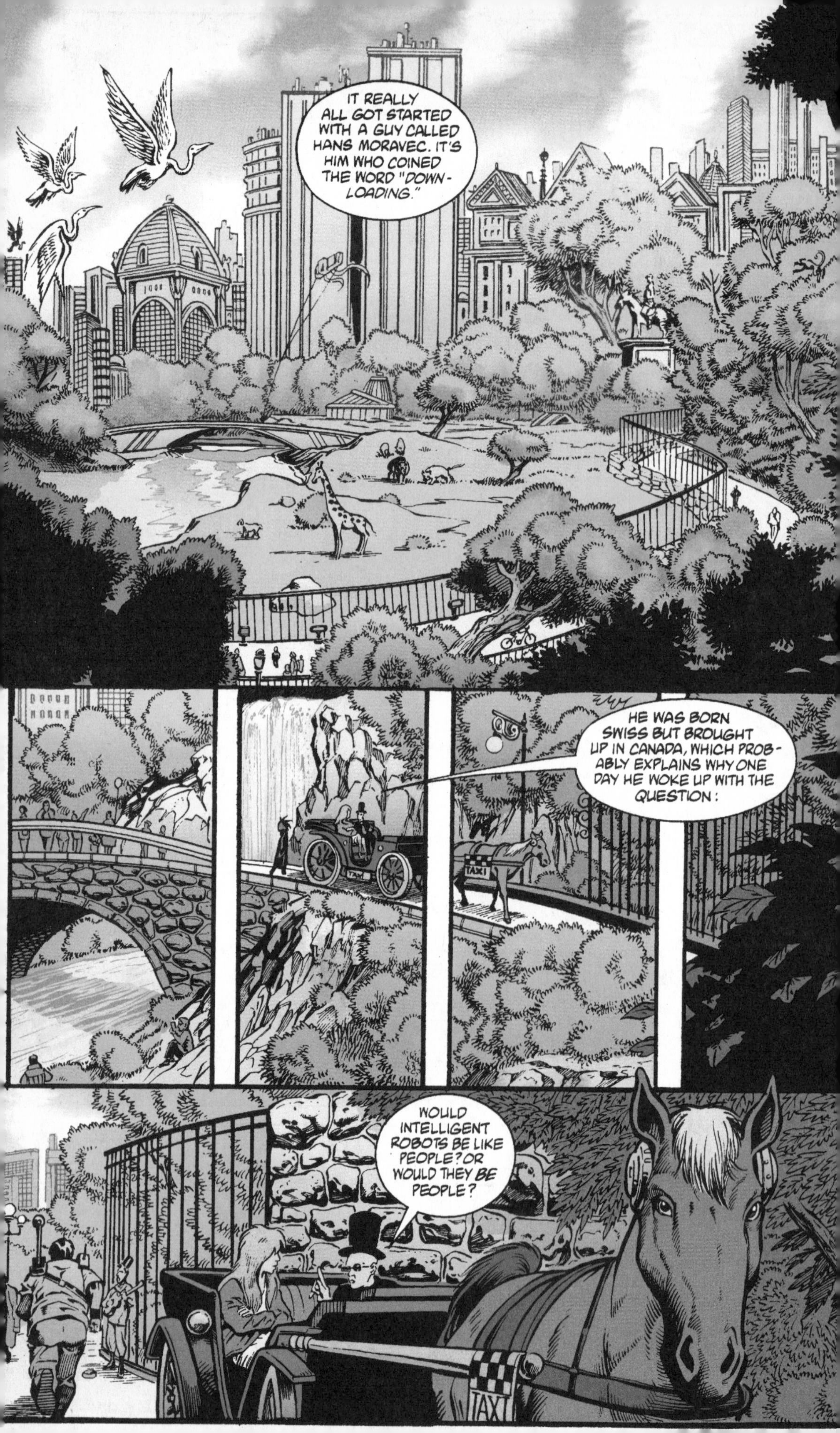
IT REALLY ALL GOT STARTED WITH A GUY CALLED HANS MORAVEC. IT'S HIM WHO COINED THE WORD "DOWN-LOADING."
HE WAS BORN SWISS BUT BROUGHT UP IN CANADA, WHICH PROB-ABLY EXPLAINS WHY ONE DAY HE WOKE UP WITH THE QUESTION:
TAXI
WOULD INTELLIGENT ROBOTS BE LIKE PEOPLE? OR WOULD THEY *BE* PEOPLE?
TAXI

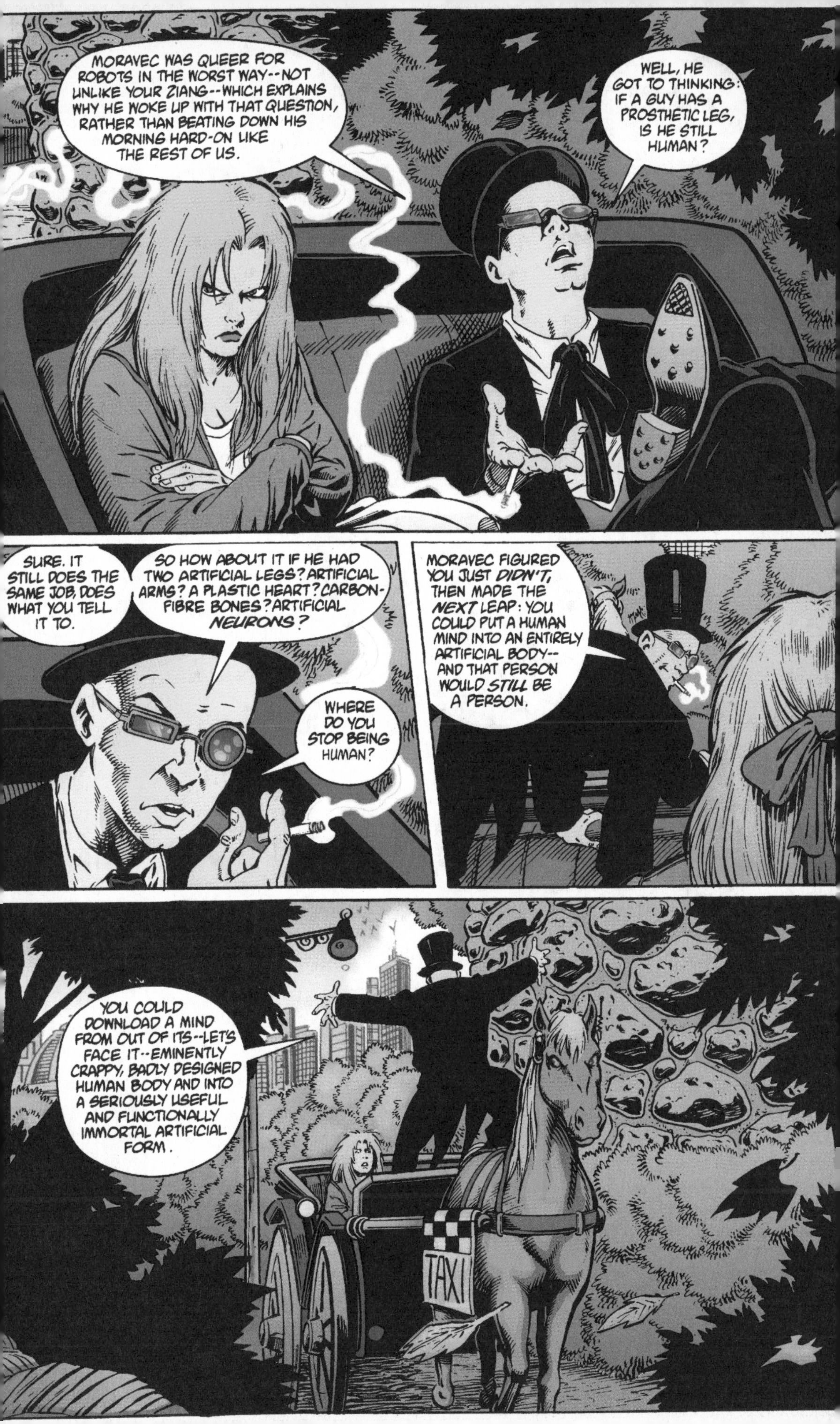
MORAVEC WAS QUEER FOR ROBOTS IN THE WORST WAY--NOT UNLIKE YOUR ZIANG--WHICH EXPLAINS WHY HE WOKE UP WITH THAT QUESTION, RATHER THAN BEATING DOWN HIS MORNING HARD-ON LIKE THE REST OF US.
WELL, HE GOT TO THINKING: IF A GUY HAS A PROSTHETIC LEG, IS HE STILL HUMAN?
SURE. IT STILL DOES THE SAME JOB, DOES WHAT YOU TELL IT TO.
SO HOW ABOUT IT IF HE HAD TWO ARTIFICIAL LEGS? ARTIFICIAL ARMS? A PLASTIC HEART? CARBON-FIBRE BONES? ARTIFICIAL NEURONS?
WHERE DO YOU STOP BEING HUMAN?
MORAVEC FIGURED YOU JUST DIDN'T, THEN MADE THE NEXT LEAP: YOU COULD PUT A HUMAN MIND INTO AN ENTIRELY ARTIFICIAL BODY--AND THAT PERSON WOULD STILL BE A PERSON.
YOU COULD DOWNLOAD A MIND FROM OUT OF ITS--LET'S FACE IT--EMINENTLY CRAPPY, BADLY DESIGNED HUMAN BODY AND INTO A SERIOUSLY USEFUL AND FUNCTIONALLY IMMORTAL ARTIFICIAL FORM.
TAXI

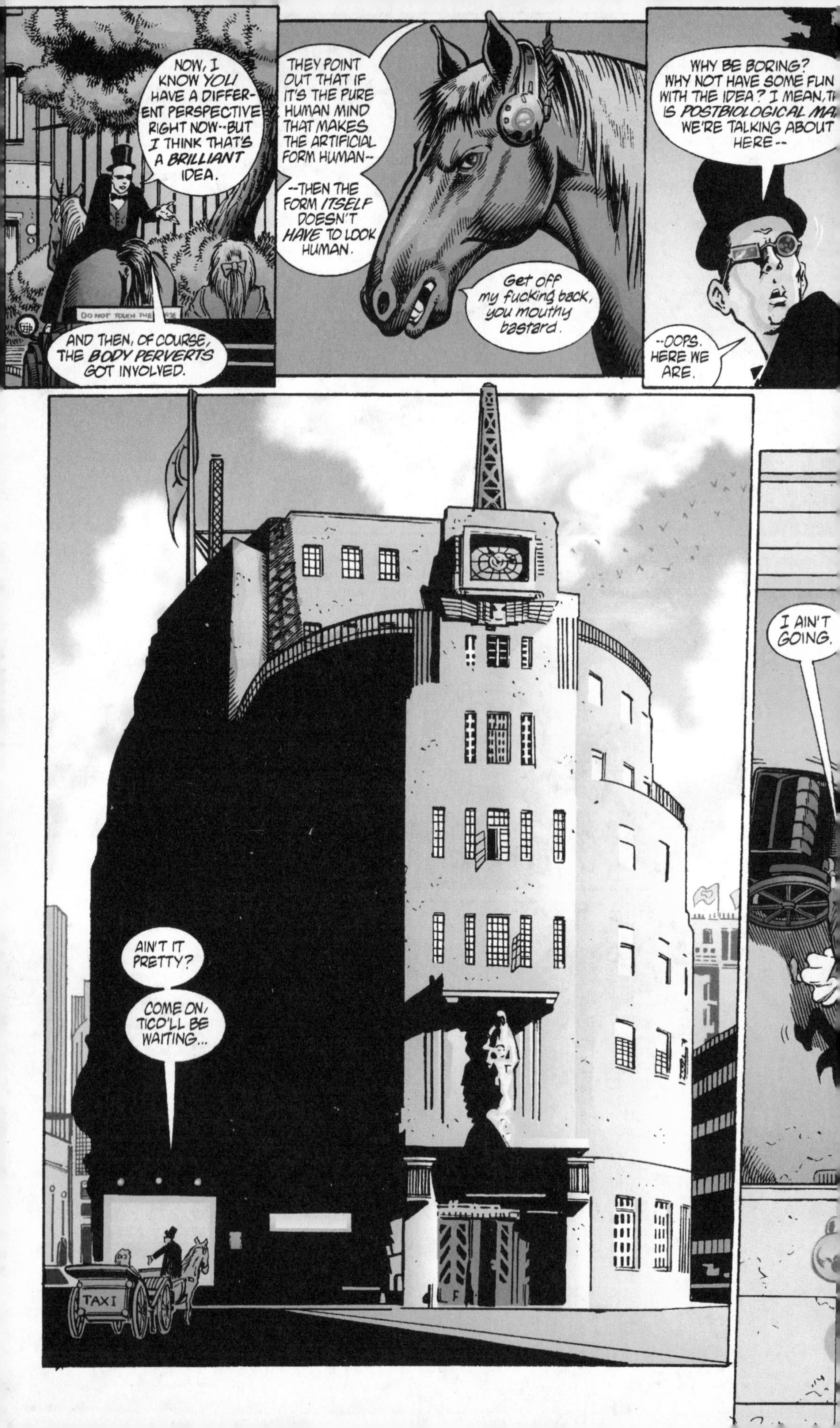
NOW, I KNOW YOU HAVE A DIFFERENT PERSPECTIVE RIGHT NOW--BUT I THINK THAT'S A BRILLIANT IDEA.
DO NOT TOUCH THE HORSE
AND THEN, OF COURSE, THE BODY PERVERTS GOT INVOLVED.
THEY POINT OUT THAT IF IT'S THE PURE HUMAN MIND THAT MAKES THE ARTIFICIAL FORM HUMAN--
--THEN THE FORM ITSELF DOESN'T HAVE TO LOOK HUMAN.
Get off my fucking back, you mouthy bastard.
WHY BE BORING? WHY NOT HAVE SOME FUN WITH THE IDEA? I MEAN, TH IS POSTBIOLOGICAL MA WE'RE TALKING ABOUT HERE--
--OOPS. HERE WE ARE.
AIN'T IT PRETTY?
COME ON, TICO'LL BE WAITING...
TAXI
I AIN'T GOING.

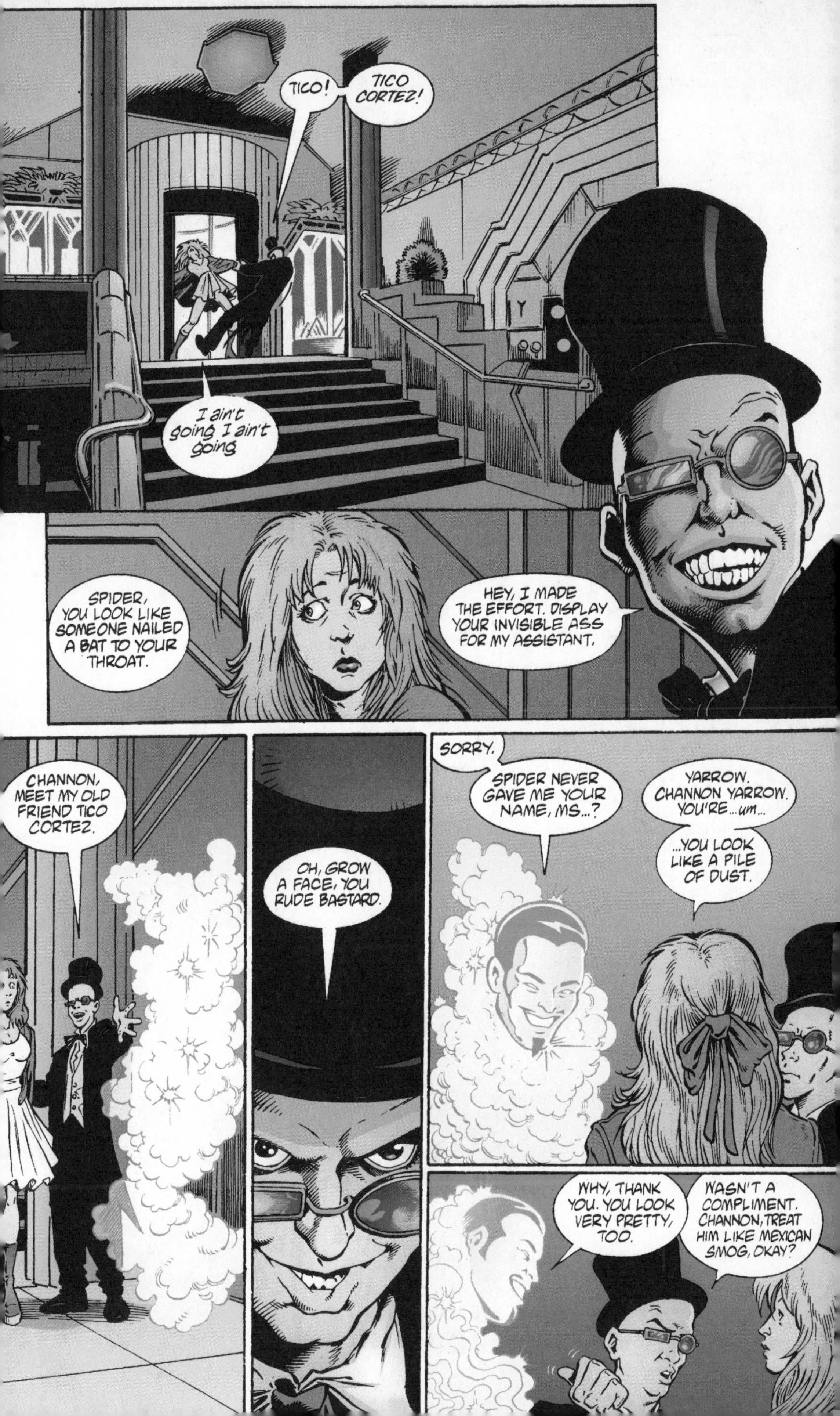
TICO!
TICO CORTEZ!
I ain't going I ain't going
SPIDER, YOU LOOK LIKE SOMEONE NAILED A BAT TO YOUR THROAT.
HEY, I MADE THE EFFORT. DISPLAY YOUR INVISIBLE ASS FOR MY ASSISTANT.
CHANNON, MEET MY OLD FRIEND TICO CORTEZ.
OH, GROW A FACE, YOU RUDE BASTARD.
SORRY.
SPIDER NEVER GAVE ME YOUR NAME, MS...?
YARROW. CHANNON YARROW. YOU'RE...um...
...YOU LOOK LIKE A PILE OF DUST.
WHY, THANK YOU. YOU LOOK VERY PRETTY, TOO.
WASN'T A COMPLIMENT. CHANNON, TREAT HIM LIKE MEXICAN SMOG, OKAY?

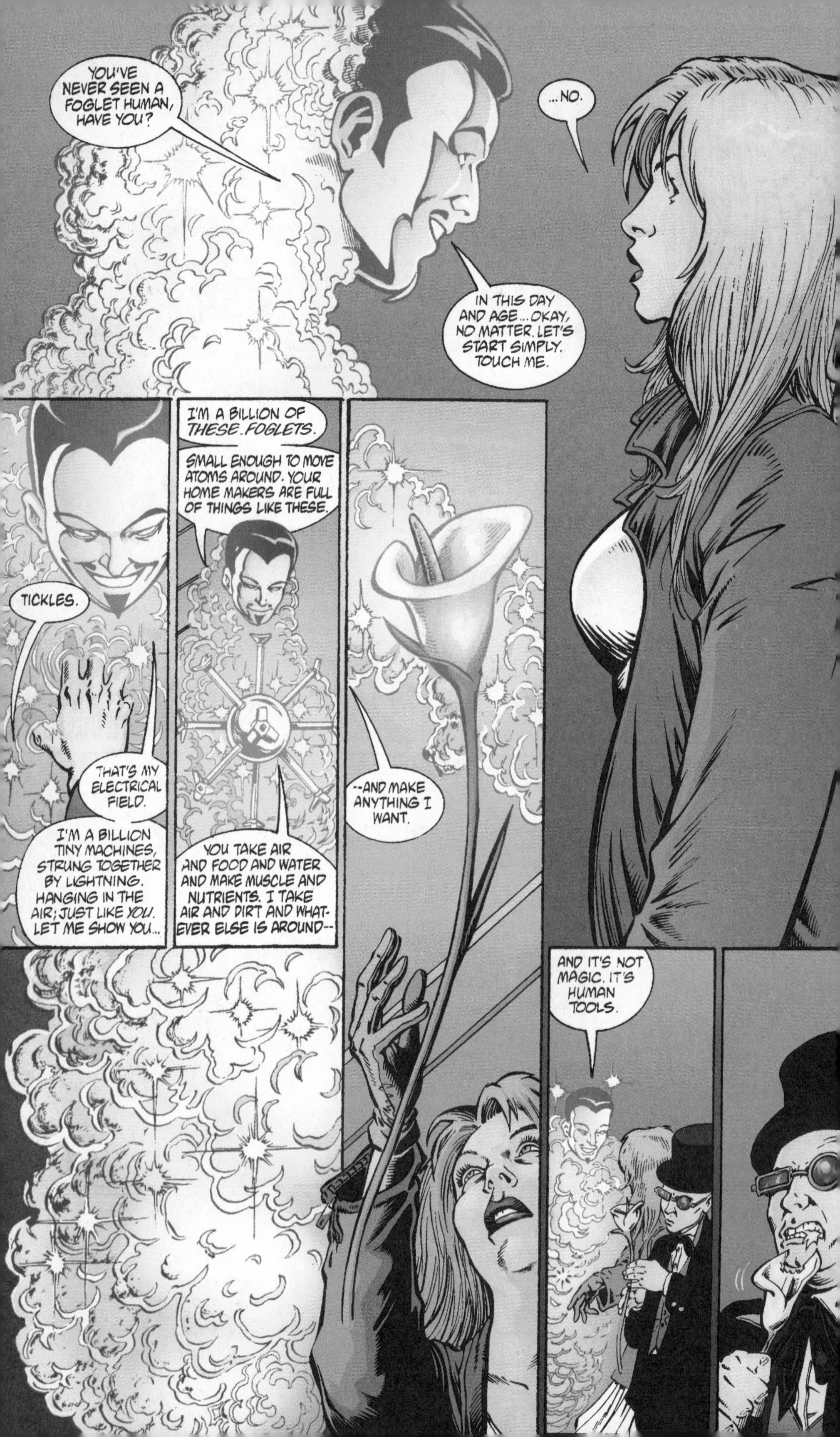
YOU'VE NEVER SEEN A FOGLET HUMAN, HAVE YOU?
...NO.
IN THIS DAY AND AGE... OKAY, NO MATTER. LET'S START SIMPLY. TOUCH ME.
TICKLES.
THAT'S MY ELECTRICAL FIELD.
I'M A BILLION TINY MACHINES, STRUNG TOGETHER BY LIGHTNING. HANGING IN THE AIR; JUST LIKE *YOU*. LET ME SHOW YOU...
I'M A BILLION OF *THESE. FOGLETS.*
SMALL ENOUGH TO MOVE ATOMS AROUND. YOUR HOME MAKERS ARE FULL OF THINGS LIKE THESE.
YOU TAKE AIR AND FOOD AND WATER AND MAKE MUSCLE AND NUTRIENTS. I TAKE AIR AND DIRT AND WHATEVER ELSE IS AROUND--
--AND MAKE ANYTHING I WANT.
AND IT'S NOT MAGIC. IT'S HUMAN TOOLS.

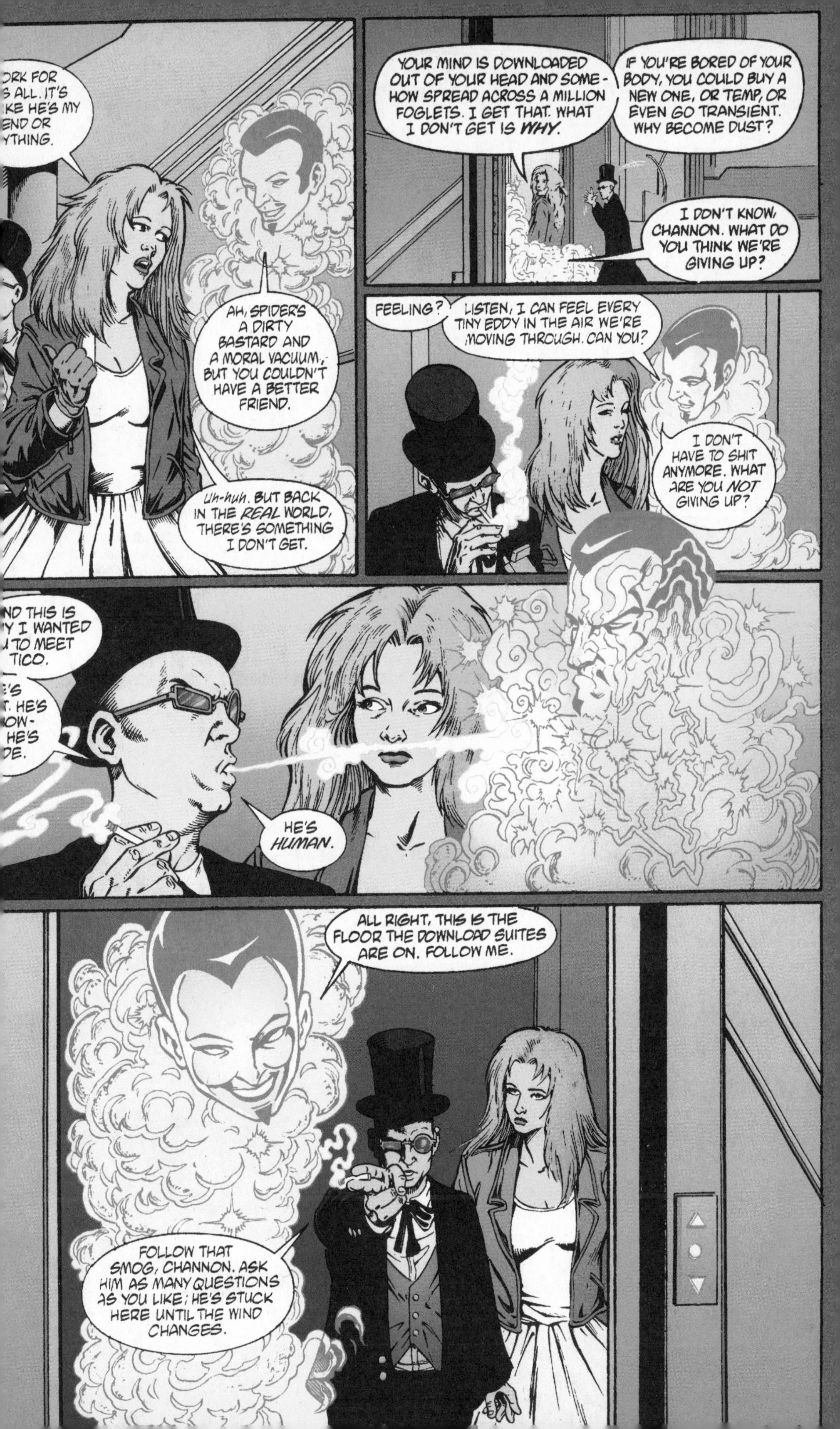
ORK FOR
S ALL. IT'S
KE HE'S MY
END OR
THING.
AH, SPIDER'S A DIRTY BASTARD AND A MORAL VACUUM, BUT YOU COULDN'T HAVE A BETTER FRIEND.
UH-HUH. BUT BACK IN THE *REAL* WORLD, THERE'S SOMETHING I DON'T GET.
YOUR MIND IS DOWNLOADED OUT OF YOUR HEAD AND SOME-HOW SPREAD ACROSS A MILLION FOGLETS. I GET THAT. WHAT I DON'T GET IS *WHY*.
IF YOU'RE BORED OF YOUR BODY, YOU COULD BUY A NEW ONE, OR TEMP, OR EVEN GO TRANSIENT. WHY BECOME DUST?
I DON'T KNOW, CHANNON. WHAT DO YOU THINK WE'RE GIVING UP?
FEELING?
LISTEN, I CAN FEEL EVERY TINY EDDY IN THE AIR WE'RE MOVING THROUGH. CAN YOU?
I DON'T HAVE TO SHIT ANYMORE. WHAT ARE YOU *NOT* GIVING UP?
ND THIS IS
Y I WANTED
U TO MEET
TICO.
HE'S *HUMAN*.
ALL RIGHT, THIS IS THE FLOOR THE DOWNLOAD SUITES ARE ON. FOLLOW ME.
FOLLOW THAT SMOG, CHANNON. ASK HIM AS MANY QUESTIONS AS YOU LIKE; HE'S STUCK HERE UNTIL THE WIND CHANGES.

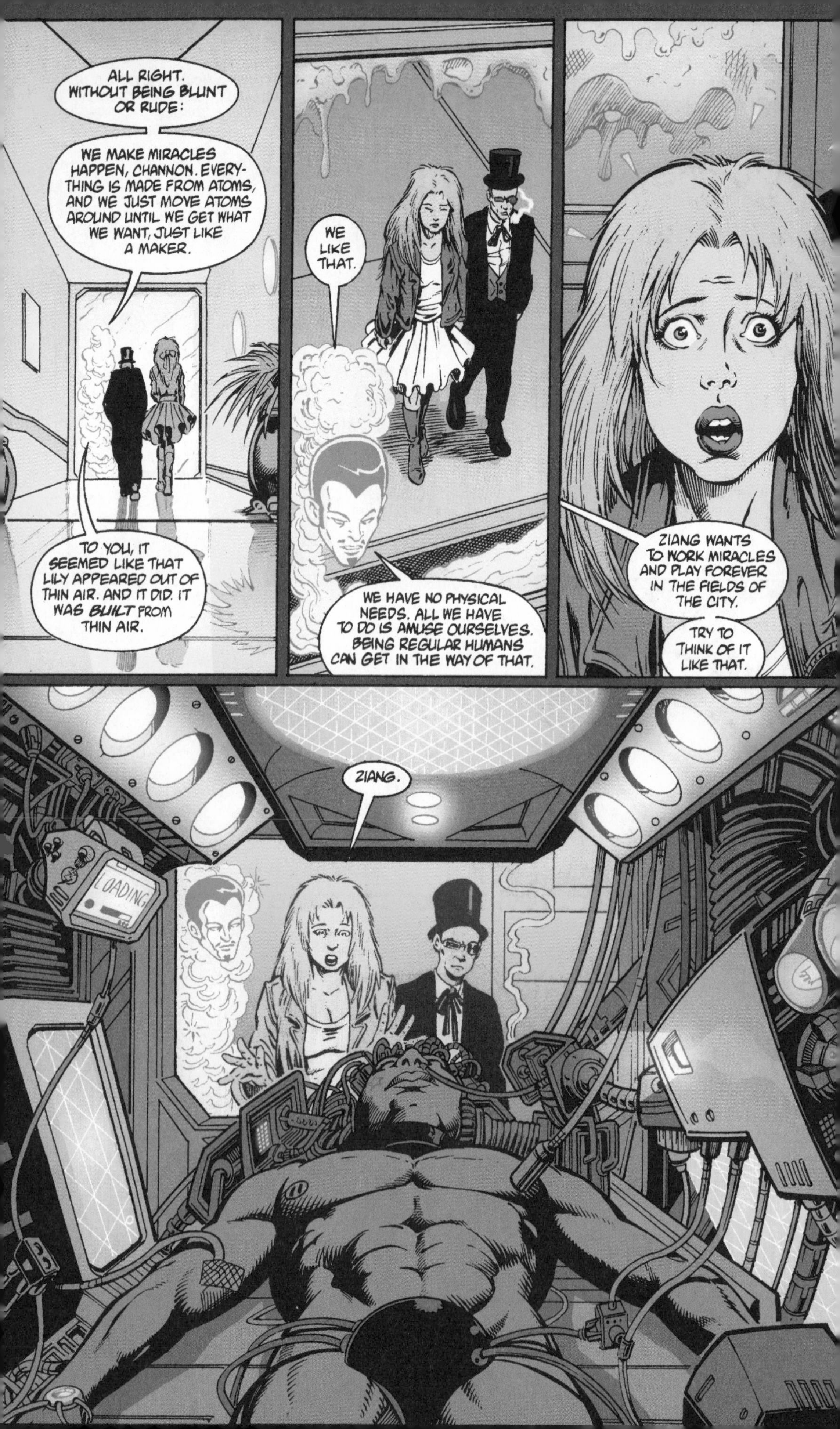
ALL RIGHT. WITHOUT BEING BLUNT OR RUDE:
WE MAKE MIRACLES HAPPEN, CHANNON. EVERY-THING IS MADE FROM ATOMS, AND WE JUST MOVE ATOMS AROUND UNTIL WE GET WHAT WE WANT, JUST LIKE A MAKER.
TO YOU, IT SEEMED LIKE THAT LILY APPEARED OUT OF THIN AIR. AND IT DID. IT WAS BUILT FROM THIN AIR.
WE LIKE THAT.
WE HAVE NO PHYSICAL NEEDS. ALL WE HAVE TO DO IS AMUSE OURSELVES. BEING REGULAR HUMANS CAN GET IN THE WAY OF THAT.
ZIANG WANTS TO WORK MIRACLES AND PLAY FOREVER IN THE FIELDS OF THE CITY.
TRY TO THINK OF IT LIKE THAT.
ZIANG.
LOADING

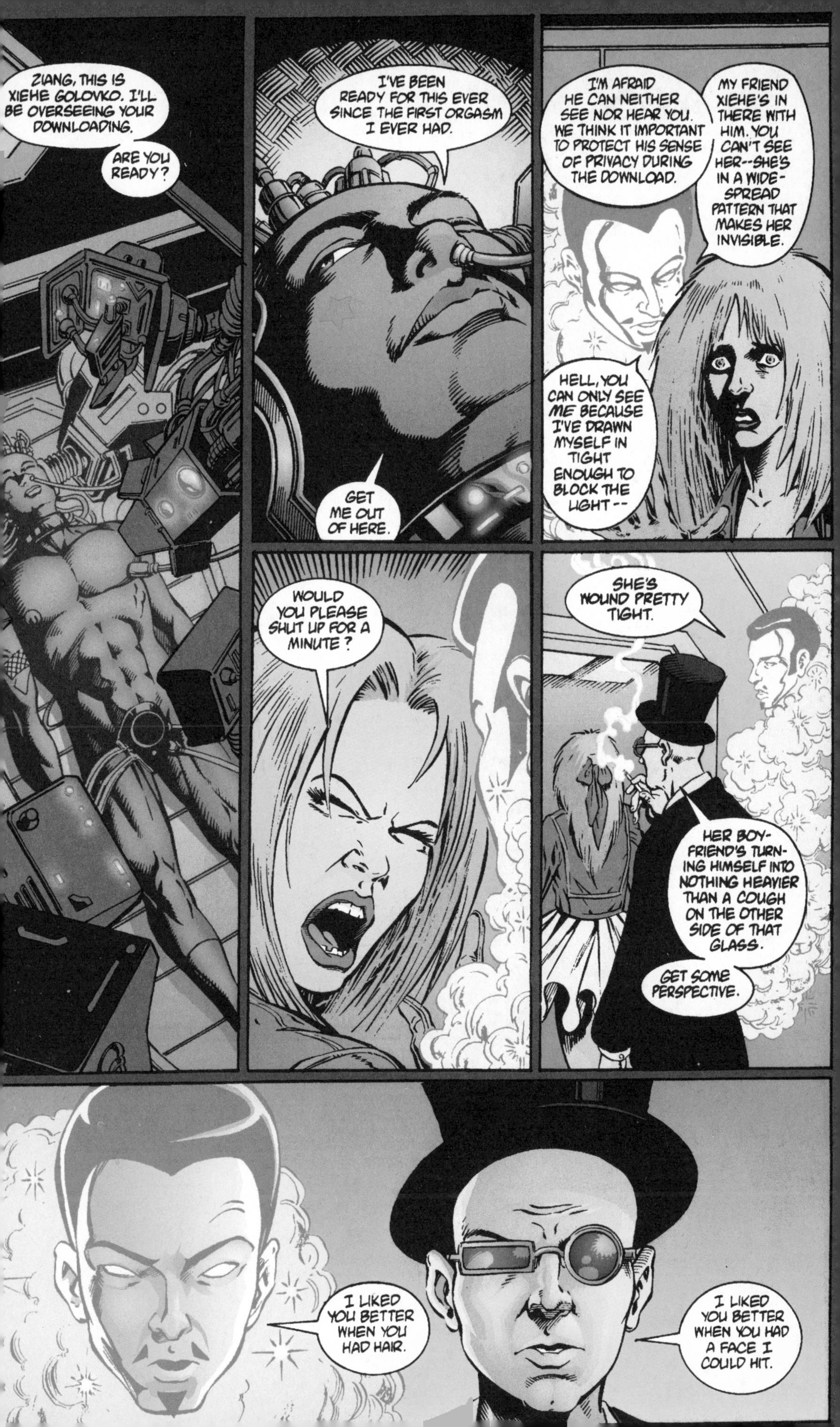

ZIANG, THIS IS XIEHE GOLOVKO. I'LL BE OVERSEEING YOUR DOWNLOADING.
ARE YOU READY?
I'VE BEEN READY FOR THIS EVER SINCE THE FIRST ORGASM I EVER HAD.
GET ME OUT OF HERE.
I'M AFRAID HE CAN NEITHER SEE NOR HEAR YOU. WE THINK IT IMPORTANT TO PROTECT HIS SENSE OF PRIVACY DURING THE DOWNLOAD.
MY FRIEND XIEHE'S IN THERE WITH HIM. YOU CAN'T SEE HER--SHE'S IN A WIDE-SPREAD PATTERN THAT MAKES HER INVISIBLE.
HELL, YOU CAN ONLY SEE ME BECAUSE I'VE DRAWN MYSELF IN TIGHT ENOUGH TO BLOCK THE LIGHT--
WOULD YOU PLEASE SHUT UP FOR A MINUTE?
SHE'S WOUND PRETTY TIGHT.
HER BOY-FRIEND'S TURNING HIMSELF INTO NOTHING HEAVIER THAN A COUGH ON THE OTHER SIDE OF THAT GLASS.
GET SOME PERSPECTIVE.
I LIKED YOU BETTER WHEN YOU HAD HAIR.
I LIKED YOU BETTER WHEN YOU HAD A FACE I COULD HIT.

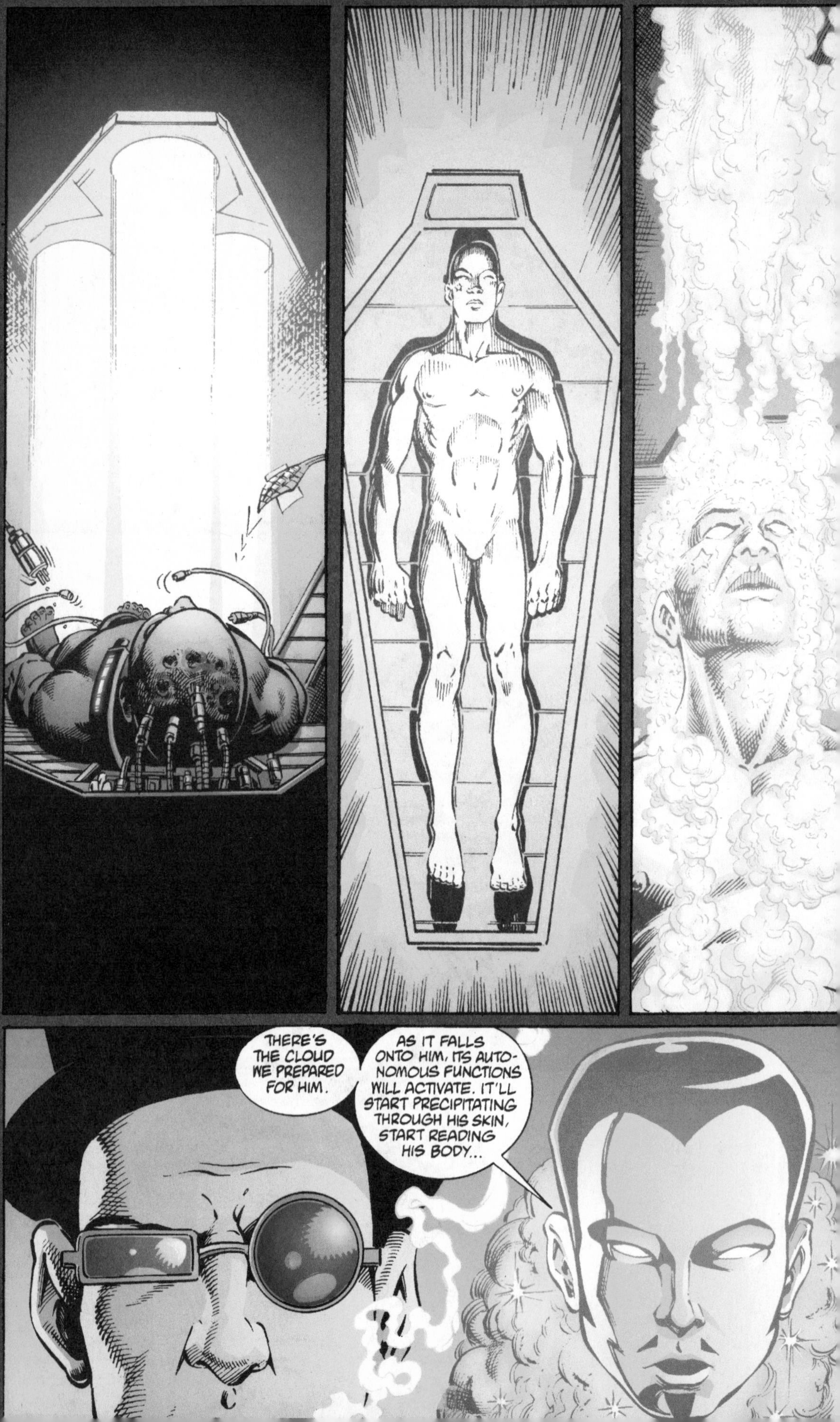

THERE'S THE CLOUD WE PREPARED FOR HIM.
AS IT FALLS ONTO HIM, ITS AUTO-NOMOUS FUNCTIONS WILL ACTIVATE. IT'LL START PRECIPITATING THROUGH HIS SKIN, START READING HIS BODY...

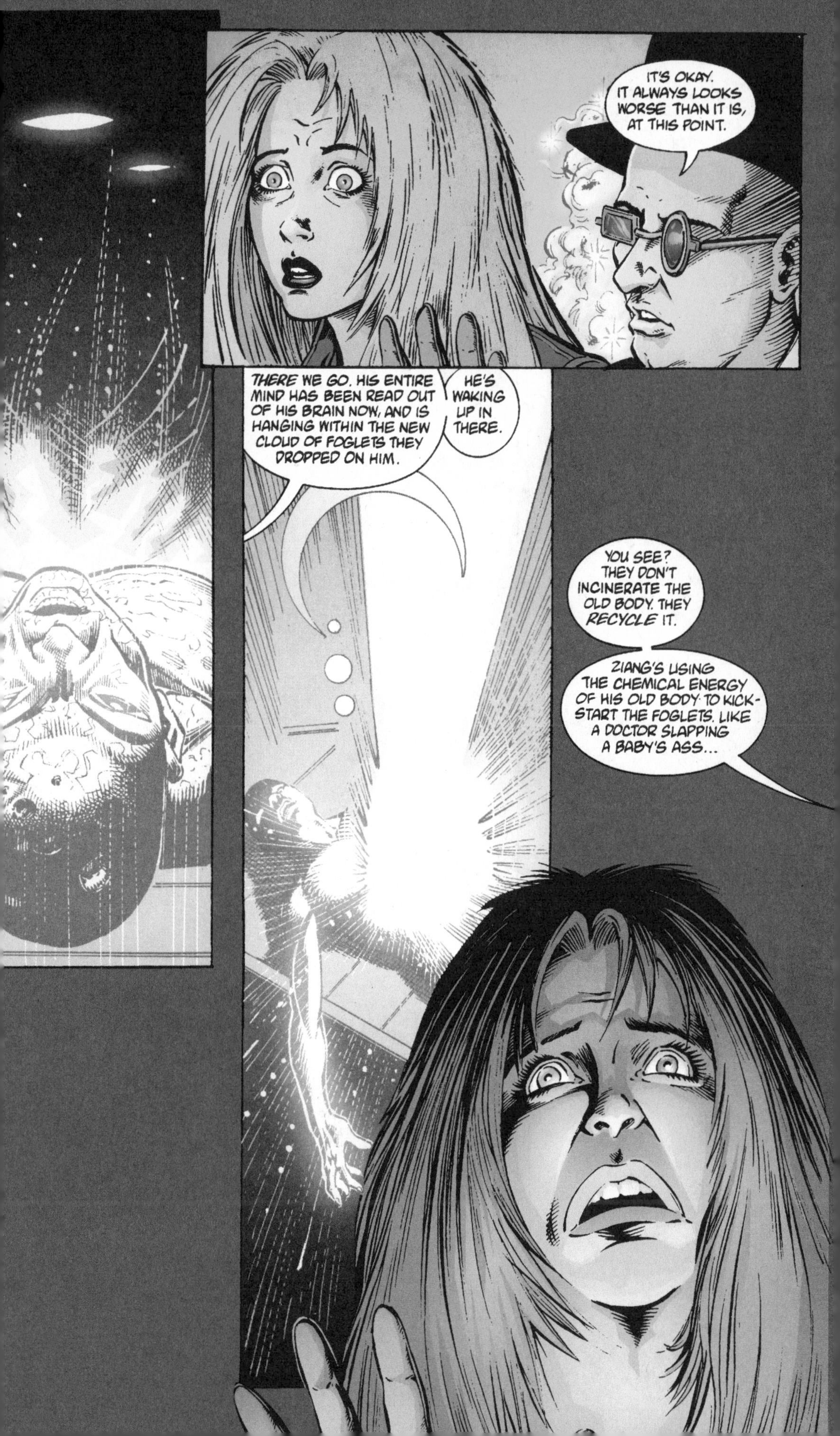
IT'S OKAY. IT ALWAYS LOOKS WORSE THAN IT IS, AT THIS POINT.
THERE WE GO. HIS ENTIRE MIND HAS BEEN READ OUT OF HIS BRAIN NOW, AND IS HANGING WITHIN THE NEW CLOUD OF FOGLETS THEY DROPPED ON HIM.
HE'S WAKING UP IN THERE.
YOU SEE? THEY DON'T INCINERATE THE OLD BODY. THEY RECYCLE IT.
ZIANG'S USING THE CHEMICAL ENERGY OF HIS OLD BODY TO KICK-START THE FOGLETS. LIKE A DOCTOR SLAPPING A BABY'S ASS...

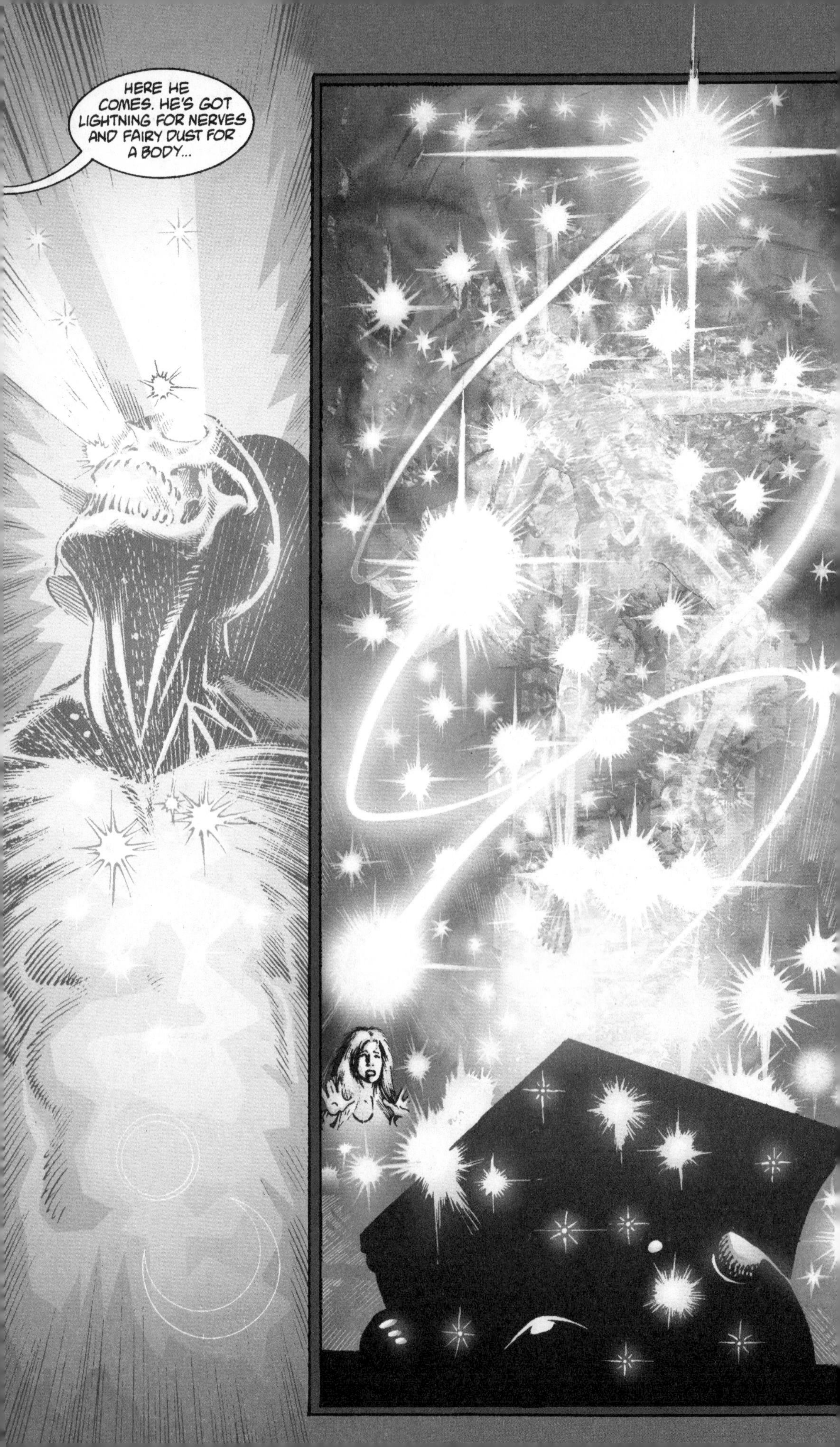
HERE HE COMES. HE'S GOT LIGHTNING FOR NERVES AND FAIRY DUST FOR A BODY...

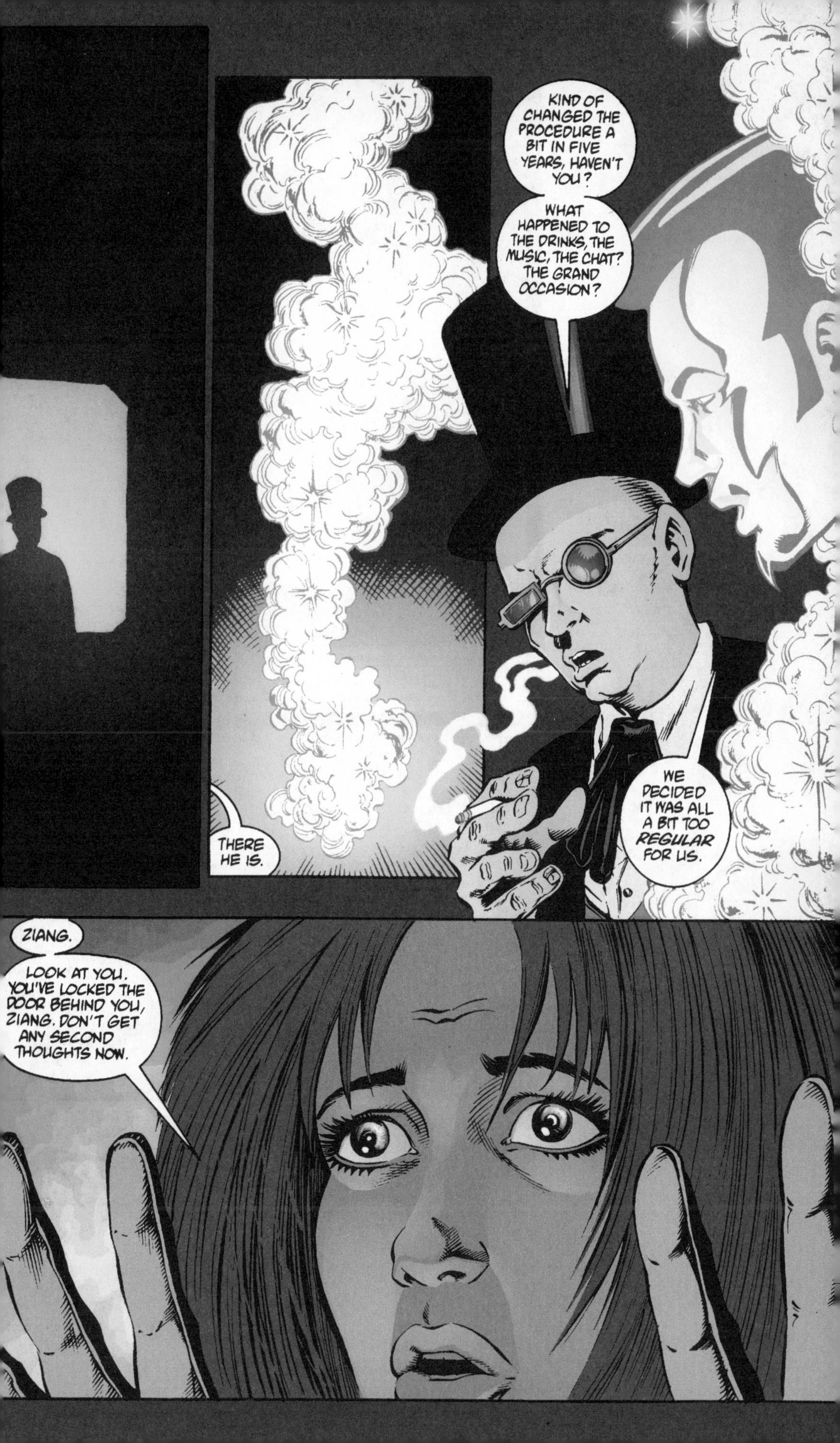
THERE HE IS.
KIND OF CHANGED THE PROCEDURE A BIT IN FIVE YEARS, HAVEN'T YOU?
WHAT HAPPENED TO THE DRINKS, THE MUSIC, THE CHAT? THE GRAND OCCASION?
WE DECIDED IT WAS ALL A BIT TOO *REGULAR* FOR US.
ZIANG.
LOOK AT YOU. YOU'VE LOCKED THE DOOR BEHIND YOU, ZIANG. DON'T GET ANY SECOND THOUGHTS NOW.

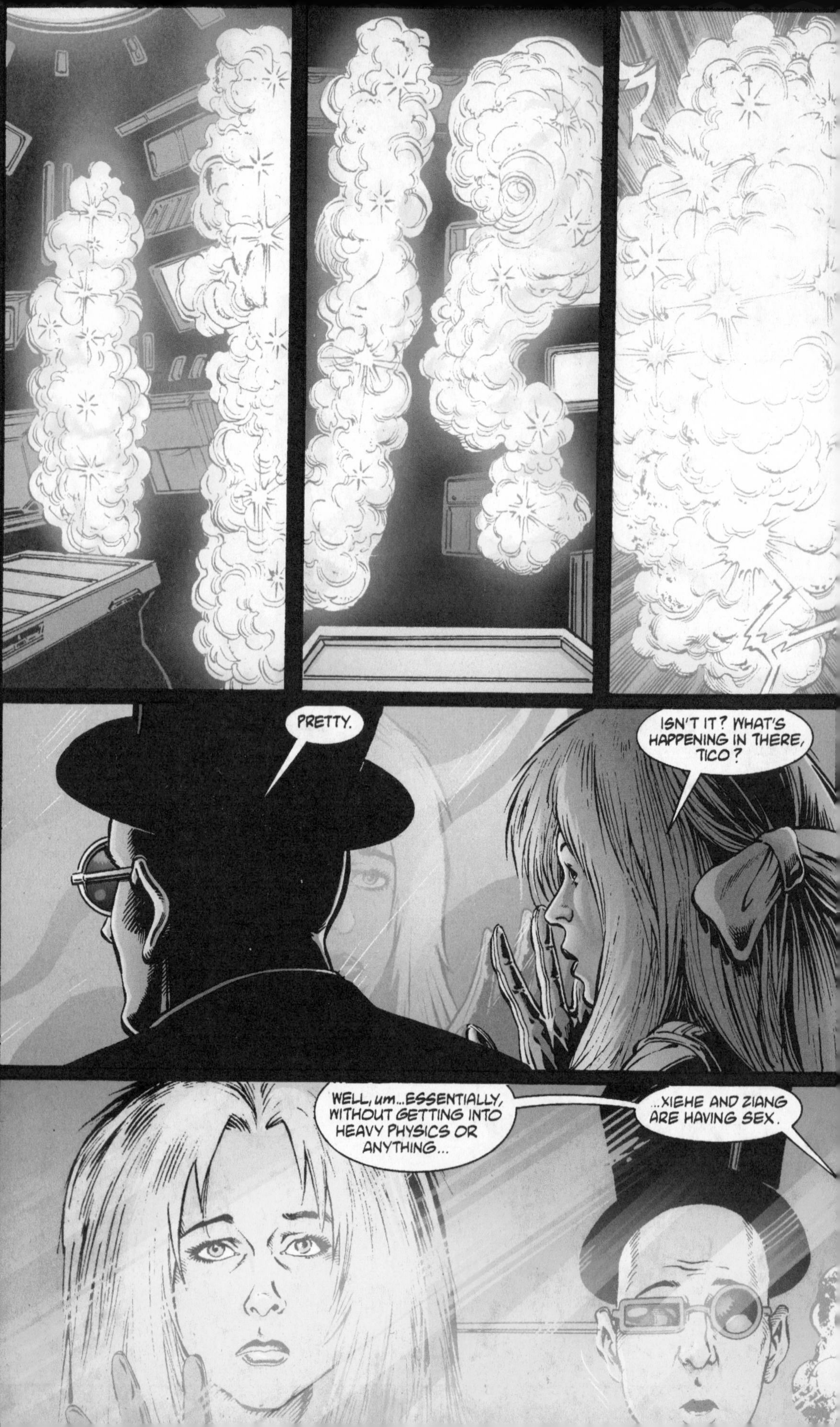
PRETTY.
ISN'T IT? WHAT'S HAPPENING IN THERE, TICO?
WELL, um...ESSENTIALLY, WITHOUT GETTING INTO HEAVY PHYSICS OR ANYTHING...
...XIEHE AND ZIANG ARE HAVING SEX.

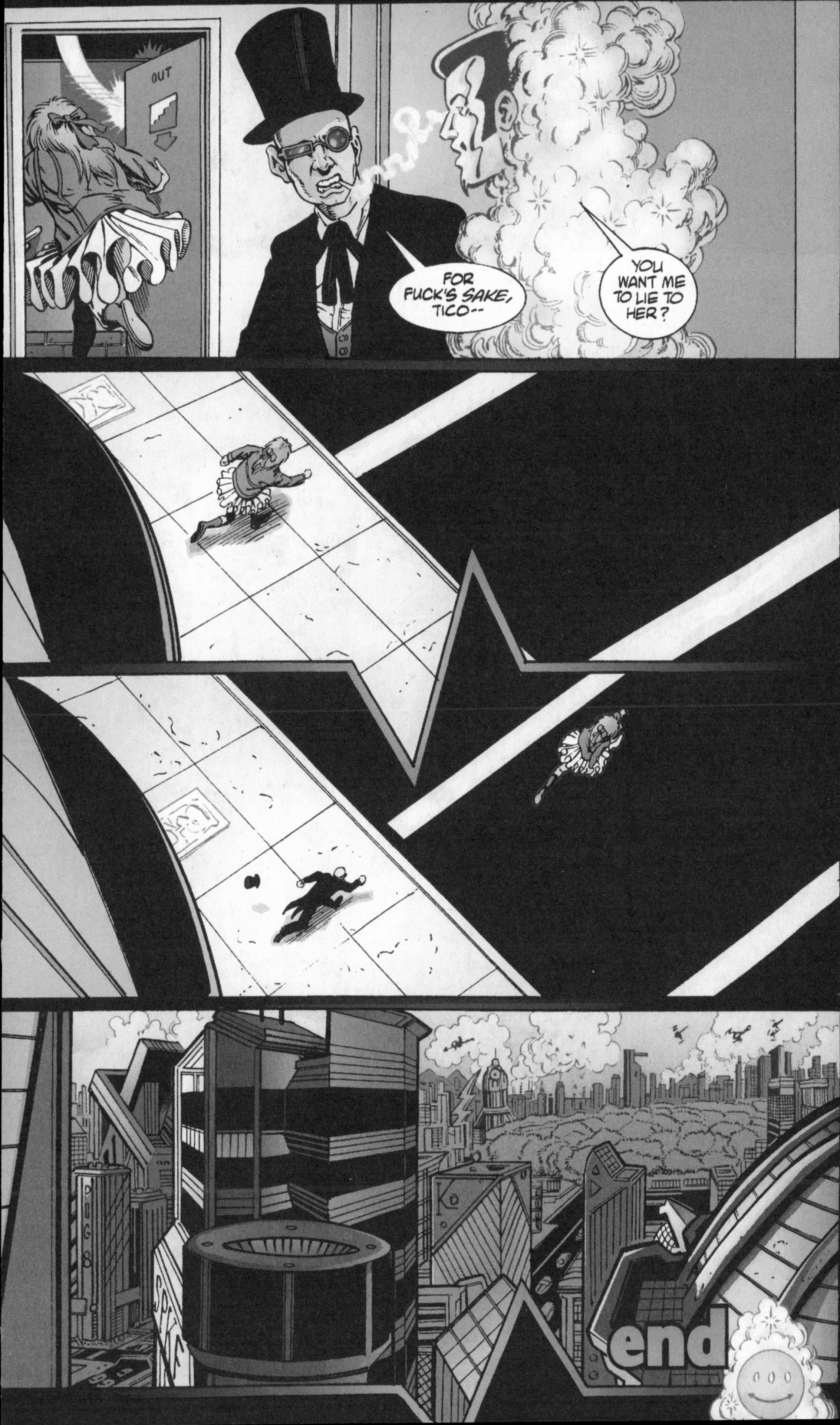
OUT
FOR FUCK'S SAKE, TICO--
YOU WANT ME TO LIE TO HER?
end

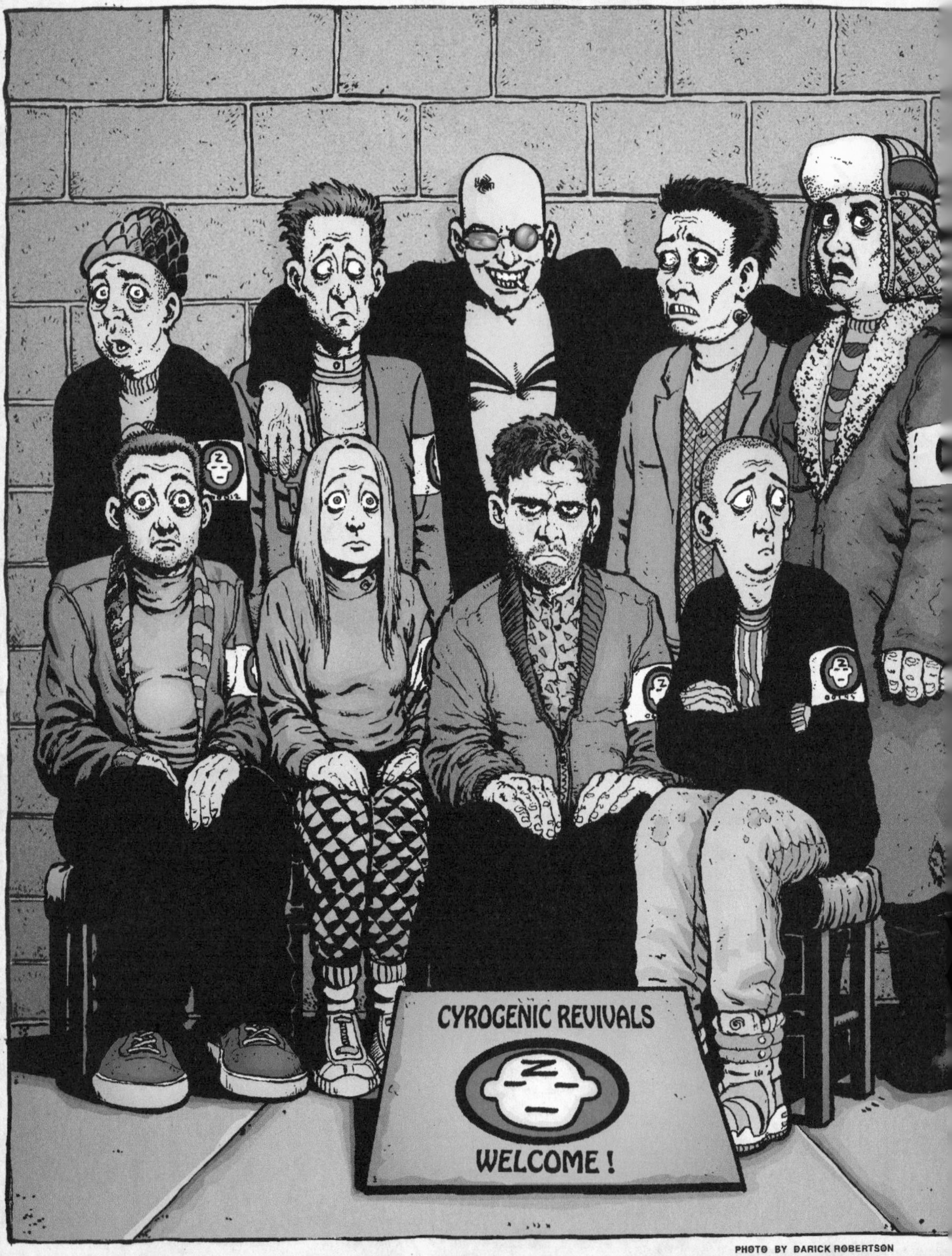
CYROGENIC REVIVALS
WELCOME !

PHOTO BY DARICK ROBERTSON

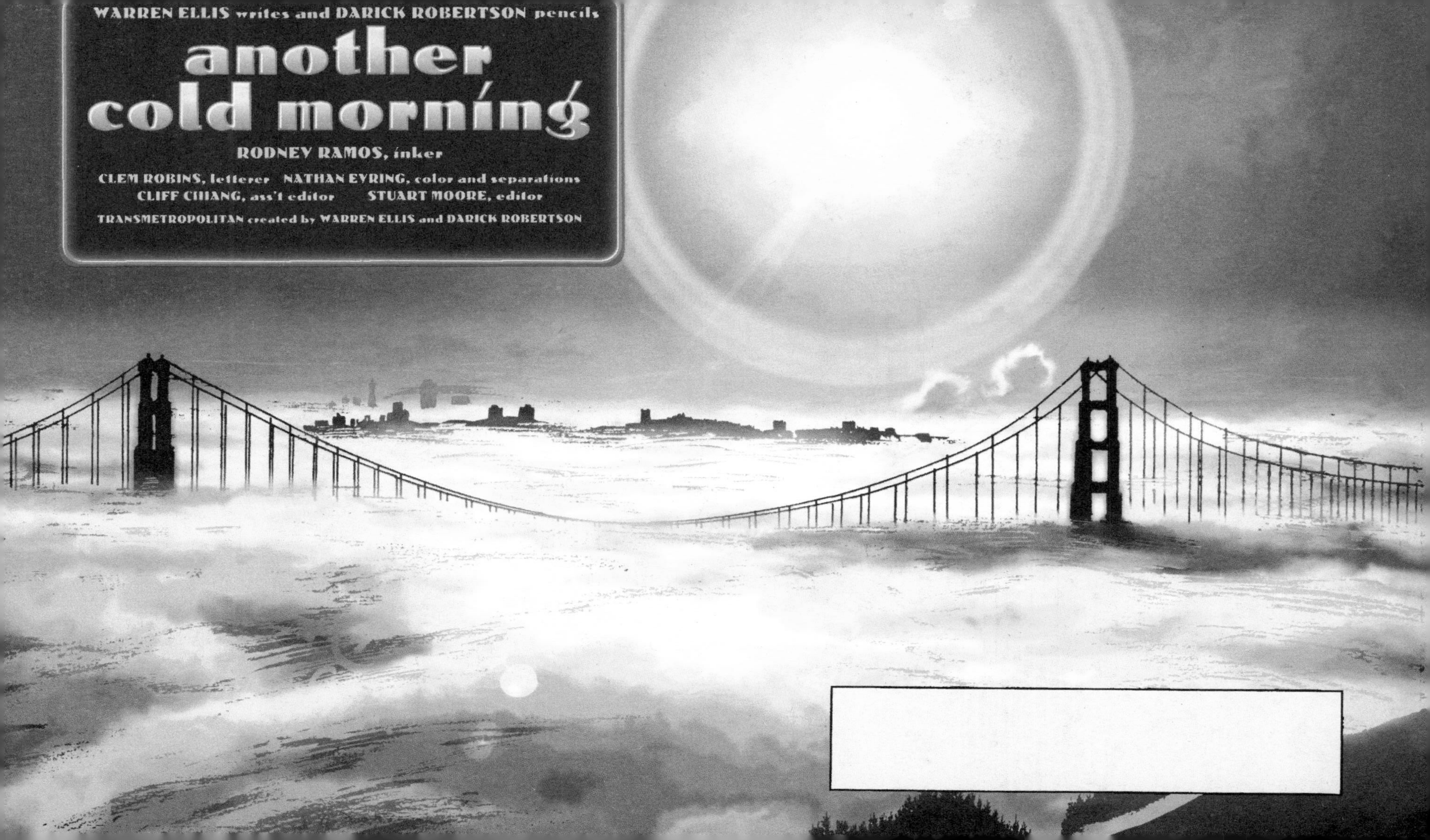

WARREN ELLIS writes and DARICK ROBERTSON pencils
another cold morning
RODNEY RAMOS, inker
CLEM ROBINS, letterer NATHAN EYRING, color and separations
CLIFF CHIANG, ass't editor STUART MOORE, editor
TRANSMETROPOLITAN created by WARREN ELLIS and DARICK ROBERTSON

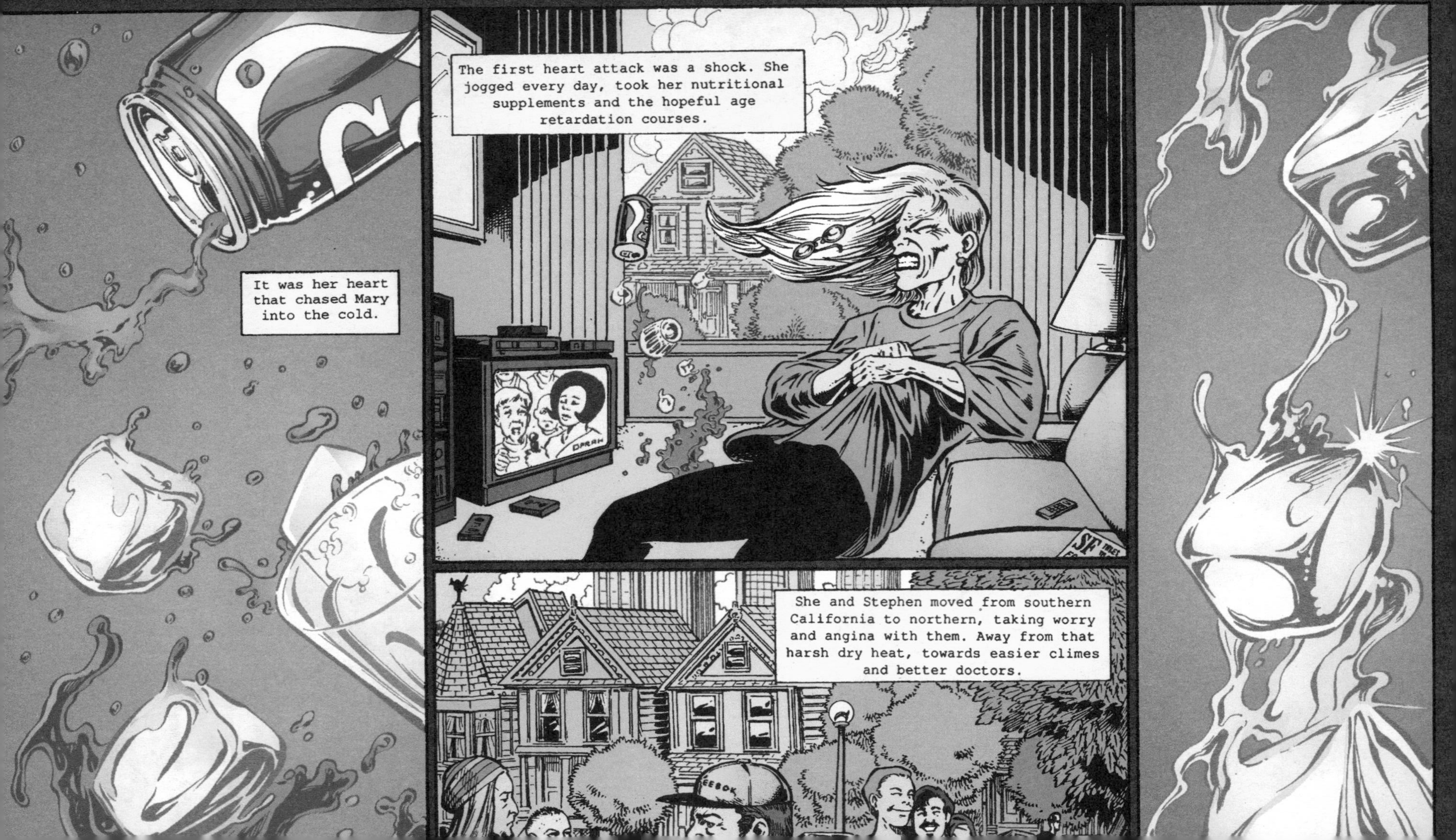
It was her heart that chased Mary into the cold.
The first heart attack was a shock. She jogged every day, took her nutritional supplements and the hopeful age retardation courses.
OPRAH
She and Stephen moved from southern California to northern, taking worry and angina with them. Away from that harsh dry heat, towards easier climes and better doctors.

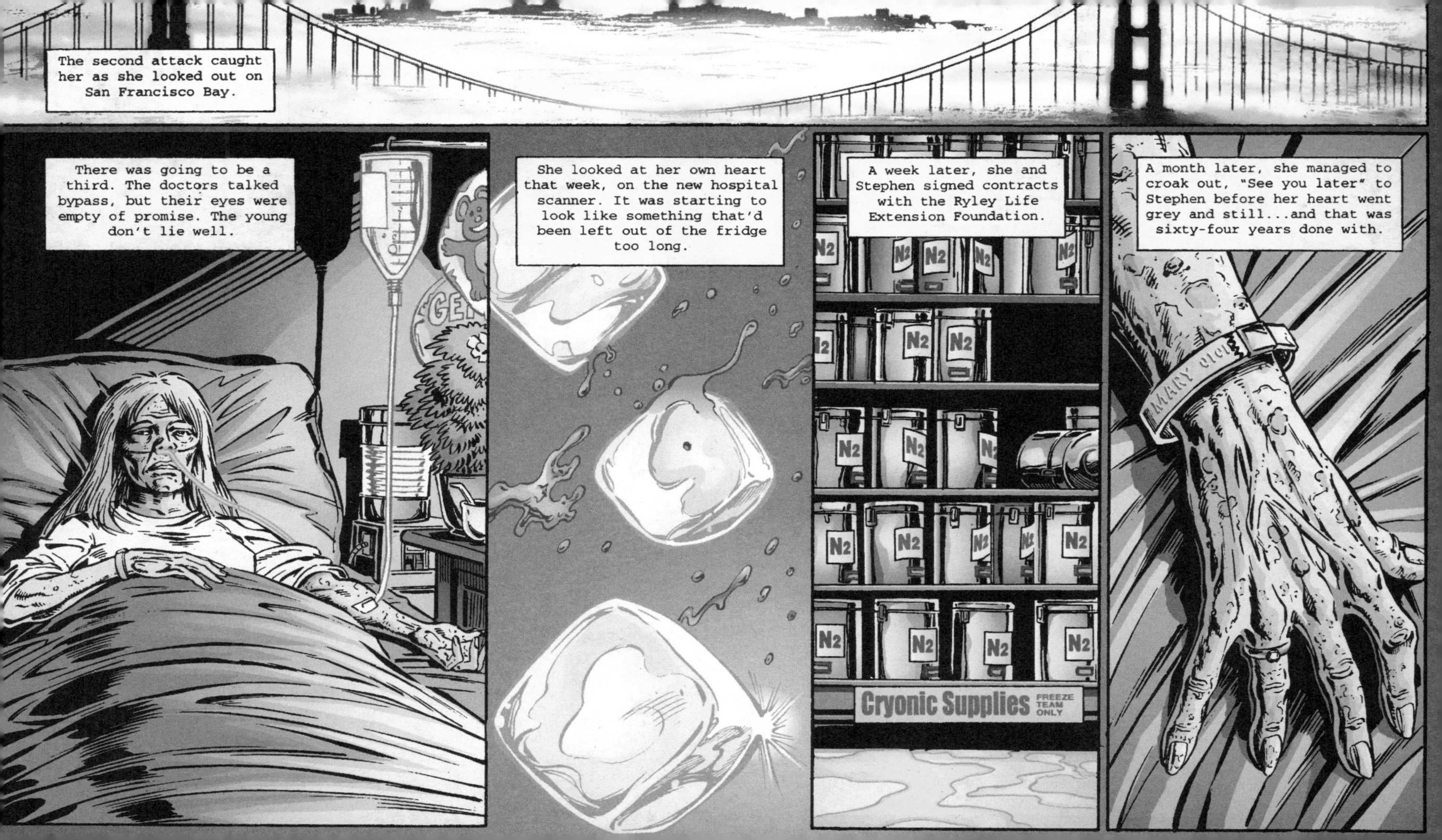

The second attack caught her as she looked out on San Francisco Bay.
There was going to be a third. The doctors talked bypass, but their eyes were empty of promise. The young don't lie well.
She looked at her own heart that week, on the new hospital scanner. It was starting to look like something that'd been left out of the fridge too long.
A week later, she and Stephen signed contracts with the Ryley Life Extension Foundation.
N2
Cryonic Supplies
FREEZE TEAM ONLY
A month later, she managed to croak out, "See you later" to Stephen before her heart went grey and still...and that was sixty-four years done with.

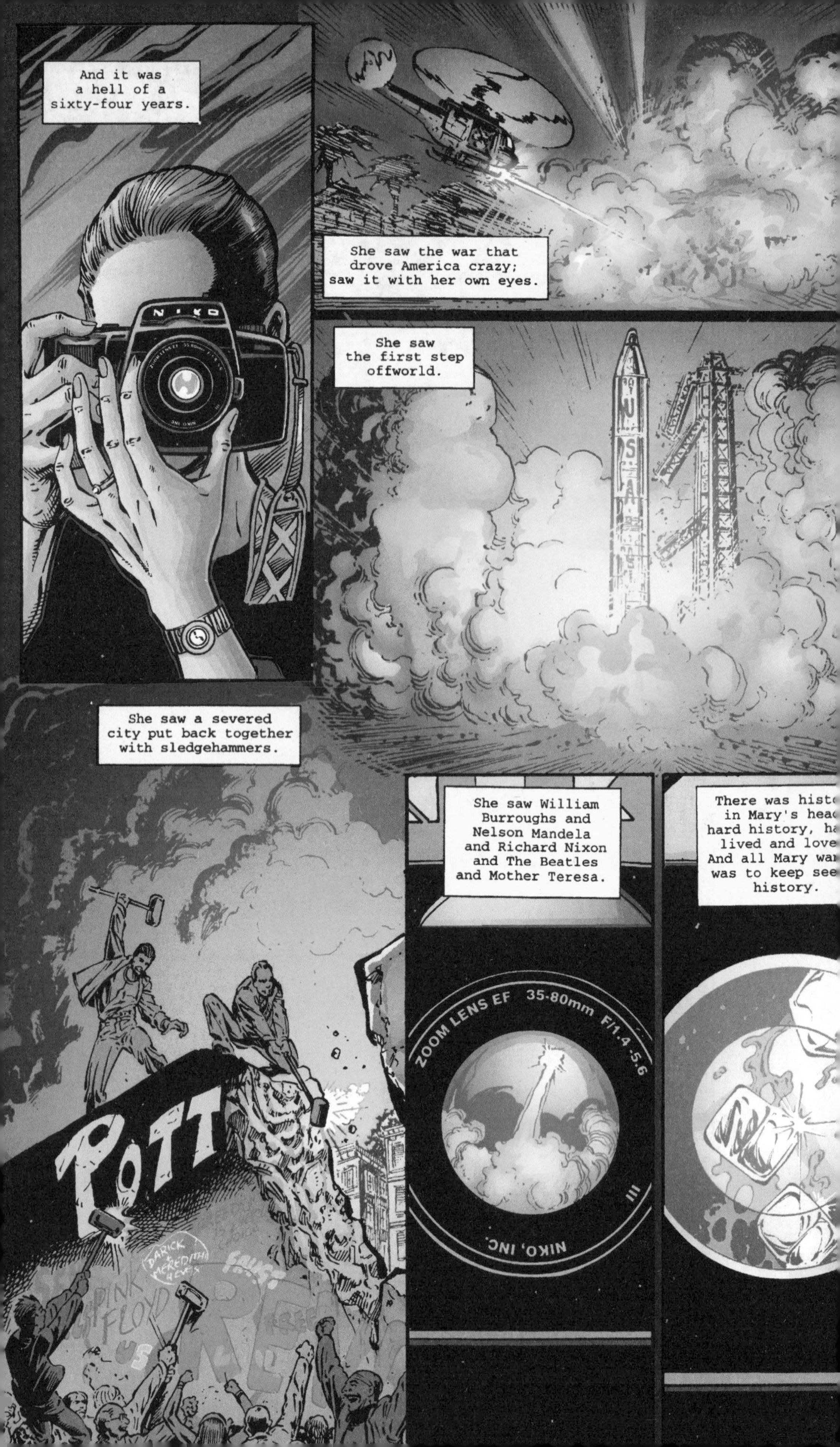
And it was a hell of a sixty-four years.
NIKO
She saw the war that drove America crazy; saw it with her own eyes.
She saw the first step offworld.
She saw a severed city put back together with sledgehammers.
POTT
PINK FLOYD
She saw William Burroughs and Nelson Mandela and Richard Nixon and The Beatles and Mother Teresa.
ZOOM LENS EF 35-80mm F/1.4 -5.6
NIKO, INC.
There was histo
in Mary's heac
hard history, ha
lived and love
And all Mary war
was to keep see
history.

her contract was for a neuro job. Neurological suspension.

N2

N2 N2

N2 N2

N2 N2 N2

N2 N2 N2

yonic Supplies FREEZE TEAM ONLY

The busy optimists at Ryley ever so gently hacked off Mary's head, wrapped it in fairly crude protective fabrics, and dropped it into a steel can full of liquid nitrogen, like throwing a coin into a wishing well.

Mary's head was frozen at -186°C, and racked up with everyone else they were tossing down into time.

CRYO-FREEZE
#239
DO NOT OPEN

-186°

Stephen died of some disgusting disease in ala Lumpur three years ter, way the hell too far from Ryley.

He died hard, fists clenched, eyes shining with anger. An endless future with his beautiful wife had been stolen from him, and he died with hate and a sadness too big for his mouth to capture.

Stephen's last words were, "If you people ever washed your fucking toilet seats--"

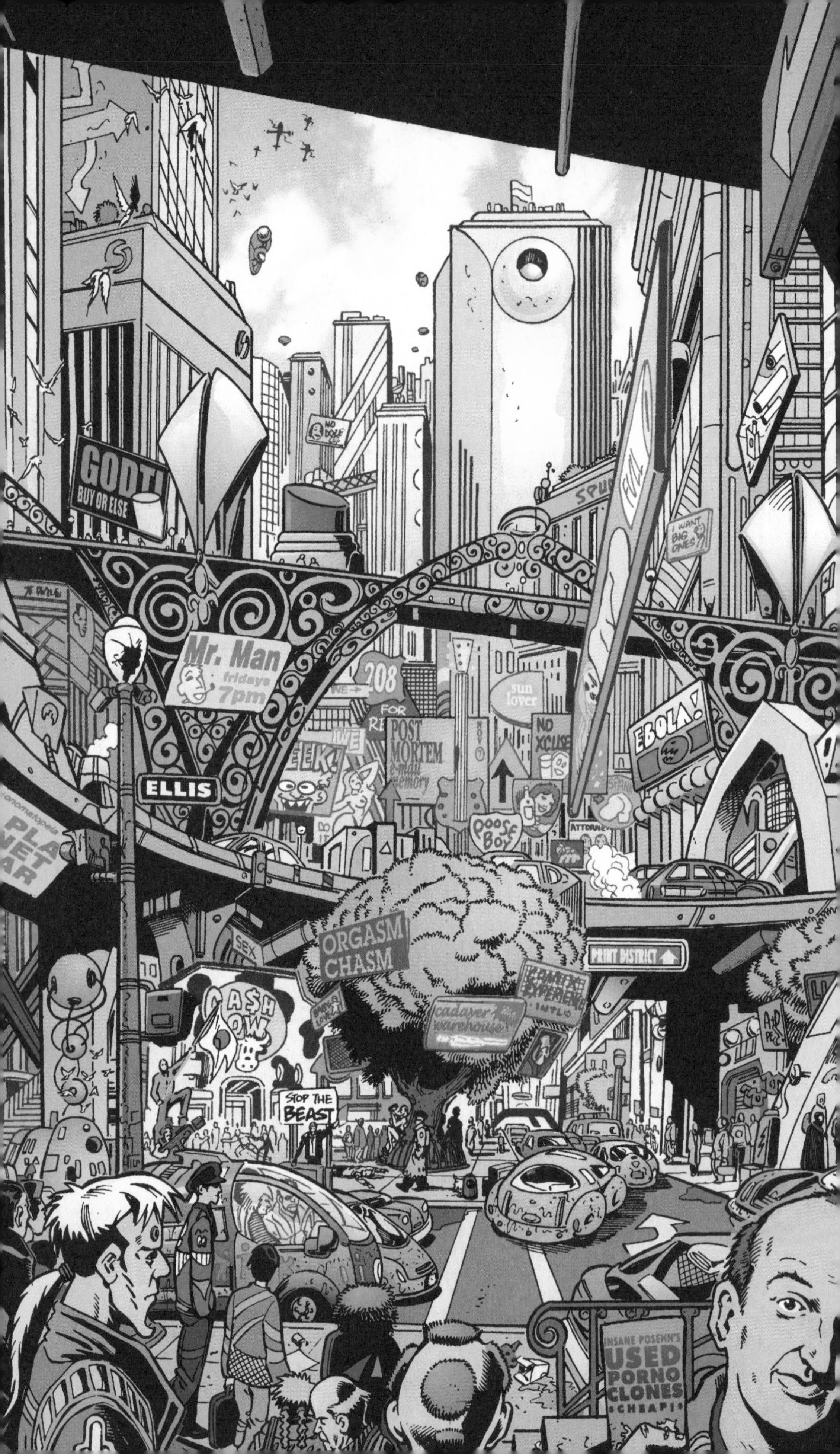

GODTI
BUY OR ELSE
Mr. Man
fridays
7pm
208
POST MORTEM
e-mail
memory
sun
lover
NO
XCUSE
EBOLA!
ELLIS
POOSE
Boy
ORGASM
CHASM
PRINT DISTRICT
cadaver
warehouse
SEX
CA$H
COW
STOP THE
BEAST
INSANE POSEHN'S
USED
PORNO
CLONES
CHEAP!

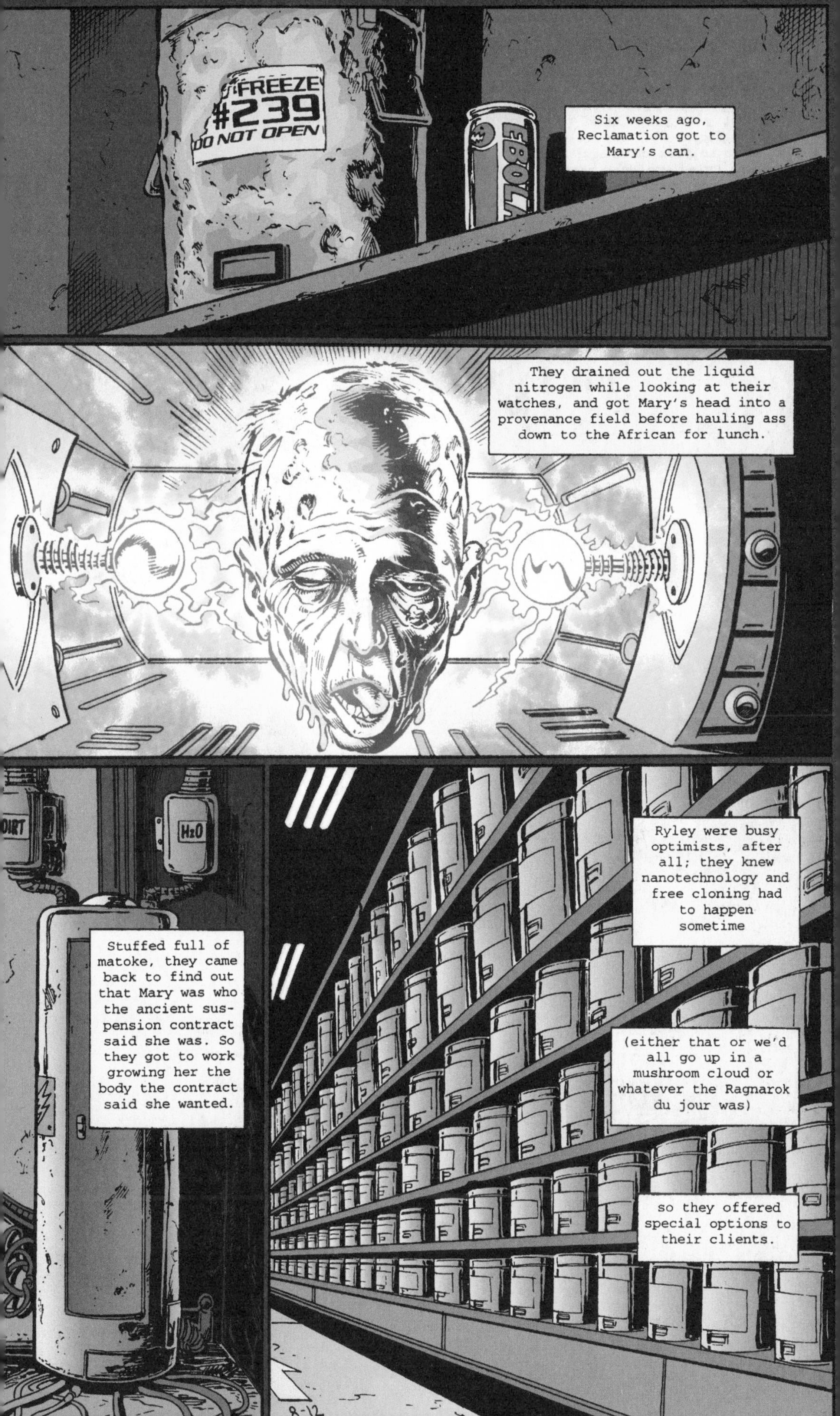

FREEZE #239 DO NOT OPEN
EBOLA
Six weeks ago, Reclamation got to Mary's can.
They drained out the liquid nitrogen while looking at their watches, and got Mary's head into a provenance field before hauling ass down to the African for lunch.
DIRT
H2O
Stuffed full of matoke, they came back to find out that Mary was who the ancient suspension contract said she was. So they got to work growing her the body the contract said she wanted.
Ryley were busy optimists, after all; they knew nanotechnology and free cloning had to happen sometime
(either that or we'd all go up in a mushroom cloud or whatever the Ragnarok du jour was)
so they offered special options to their clients.

8-12

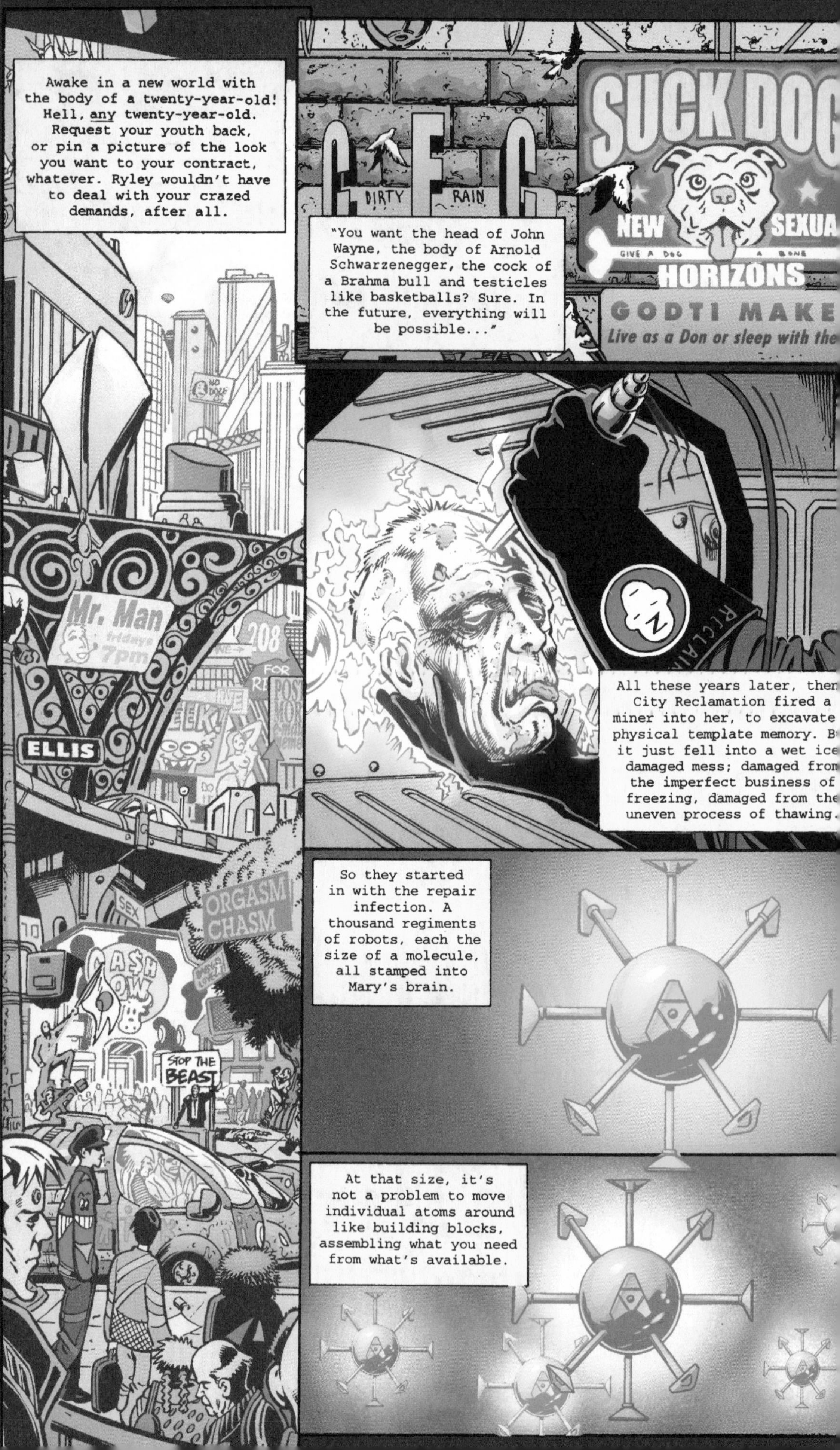
Awake in a new world with the body of a twenty-year-old! Hell, any twenty-year-old. Request your youth back, or pin a picture of the look you want to your contract, whatever. Ryley wouldn't have to deal with your crazed demands, after all.
DIRTY RAIN
SUCK DOG
NEW SEXUA
GIVE A DOG A BONE
HORIZONS
GODTI MAKE
Live as a Don or sleep with the
"You want the head of John Wayne, the body of Arnold Schwarzenegger, the cock of a Brahma bull and testicles like basketballs? Sure. In the future, everything will be possible..."
Mr. Man
fridays
7pm
208
ELLIS
SEX
ORGASM CHASM
STOP THE BEAST
All these years later, then City Reclamation fired a miner into her, to excavate physical template memory. B it just fell into a wet ice damaged mess; damaged from the imperfect business of freezing, damaged from the uneven process of thawing.
So they started in with the repair infection. A thousand regiments of robots, each the size of a molecule, all stamped into Mary's brain.
At that size, it's not a problem to move individual atoms around like building blocks, assembling what you need from what's available.

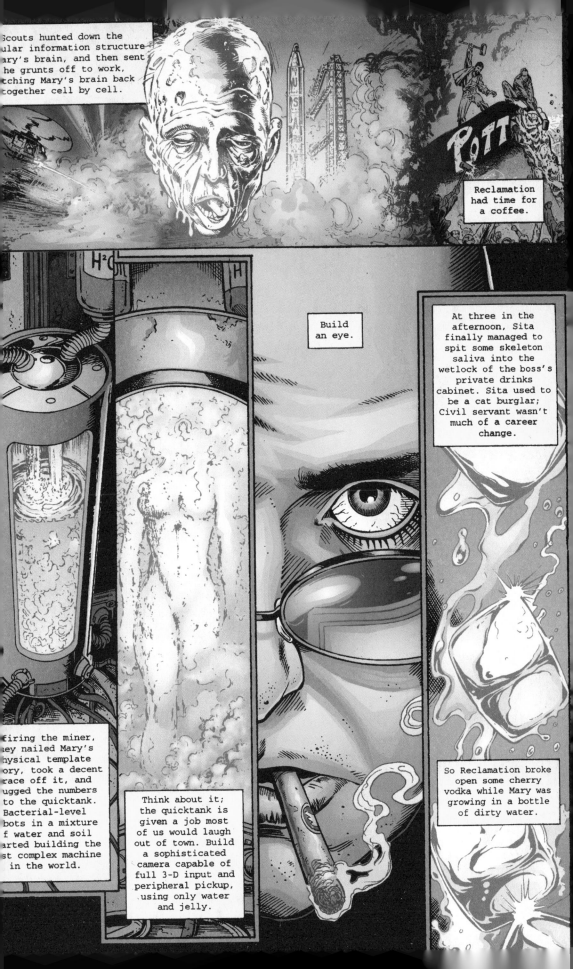

Scouts hunted down the [cell]ular information structure [in M]ary's brain, and then sent [t]he grunts off to work, [stit]ching Mary's brain back [together cell by cell.

Reclamation had time for a coffee.

Build an eye.

At three in the afternoon, Sita finally managed to spit some skeleton saliva into the wetlock of the boss's private drinks cabinet. Sita used to be a cat burglar; Civil servant wasn't much of a career change.

[Fi]ring the miner, [th]ey nailed Mary's [p]hysical template [m]ory, took a decent [t]race off it, and [pl]ugged the numbers [in]to the quicktank. Bacterial-level [r]obots in a mixture [o]f water and soil [st]arted building the [mo]st complex machine in the world.

Think about it; the quicktank is given a job most of us would laugh out of town. Build a sophisticated camera capable of full 3-D input and peripheral pickup, using only water and jelly.

So Reclamation broke open some cherry vodka while Mary was growing in a bottle of dirty water.

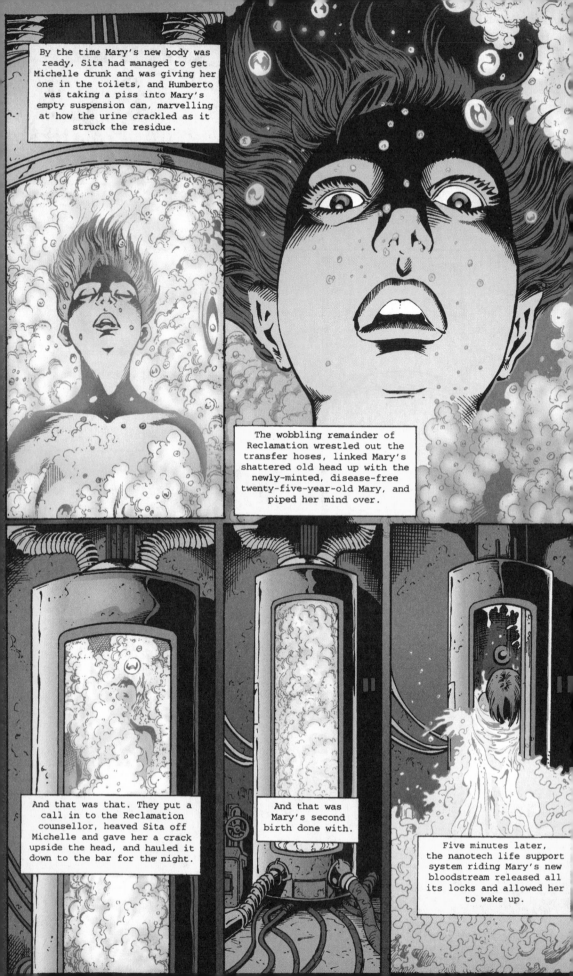

By the time Mary's new body was ready, Sita had managed to get Michelle drunk and was giving her one in the toilets, and Humberto was taking a piss into Mary's empty suspension can, marvelling at how the urine crackled as it struck the residue.

The wobbling remainder of Reclamation wrestled out the transfer hoses, linked Mary's shattered old head up with the newly-minted, disease-free twenty-five-year-old Mary, and piped her mind over.

And that was that. They put a call in to the Reclamation counsellor, heaved Sita off Michelle and gave her a crack upside the head, and hauled it down to the bar for the night.

And that was Mary's second birth done with.

Five minutes later, the nanotech life support system riding Mary's new bloodstream released all its locks and allowed her to wake up.

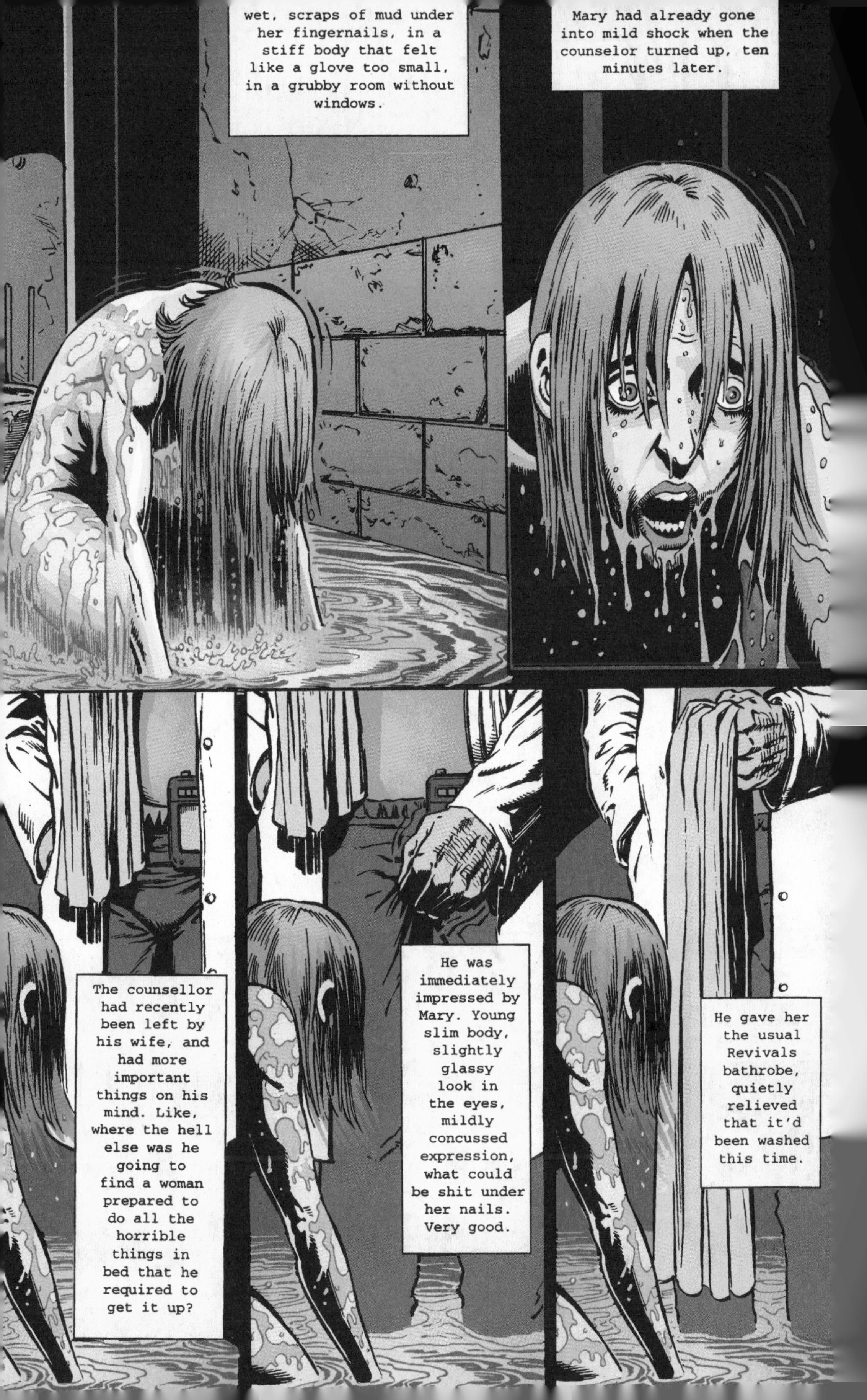
wet, scraps of mud under her fingernails, in a stiff body that felt like a glove too small, in a grubby room without windows.
Mary had already gone into mild shock when the counselor turned up, ten minutes later.
The counsellor had recently been left by his wife, and had more important things on his mind. Like, where the hell else was he going to find a woman prepared to do all the horrible things in bed that he required to get it up?
He was immediately impressed by Mary. Young slim body, slightly glassy look in the eyes, mildly concussed expression, what could be shit under her nails. Very good.
He gave her the usual Revivals bathrobe, quietly relieved that it'd been washed this time.

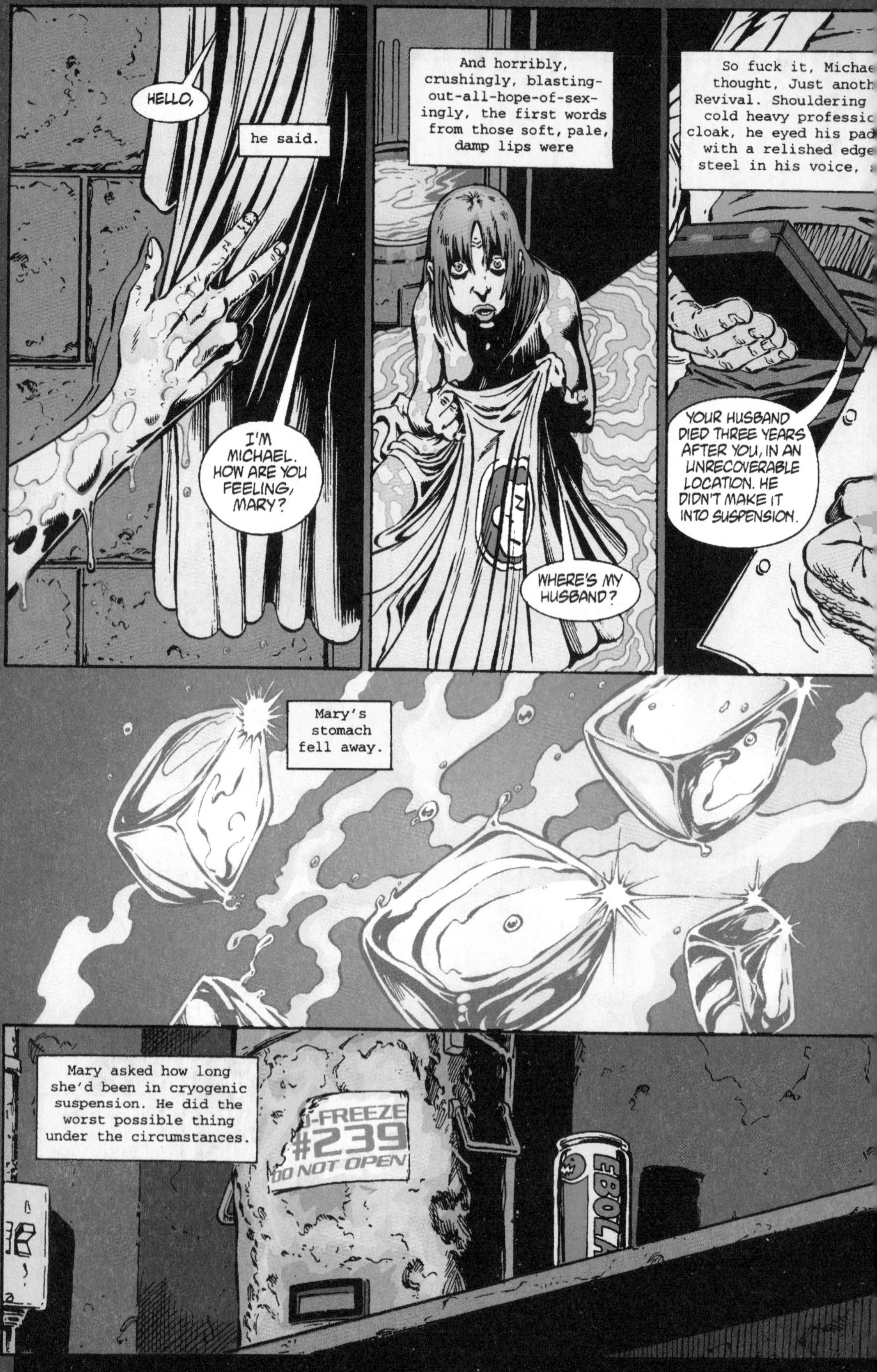
HELLO,
he said.
I'M MICHAEL. HOW ARE YOU FEELING, MARY?
And horribly, crushingly, blasting-out-all-hope-of-sex-ingly, the first words from those soft, pale, damp lips were
WHERE'S MY HUSBAND?
So fuck it, Michae thought, Just anoth Revival. Shouldering cold heavy professic cloak, he eyed his pad with a relished edge steel in his voice,
YOUR HUSBAND DIED THREE YEARS AFTER YOU, IN AN UNRECOVERABLE LOCATION. HE DIDN'T MAKE IT INTO SUSPENSION.
Mary's stomach fell away.
Mary asked how long she'd been in cryogenic suspension. He did the worst possible thing under the circumstances.
-FREEZE #239 DO NOT OPEN
EBOLA

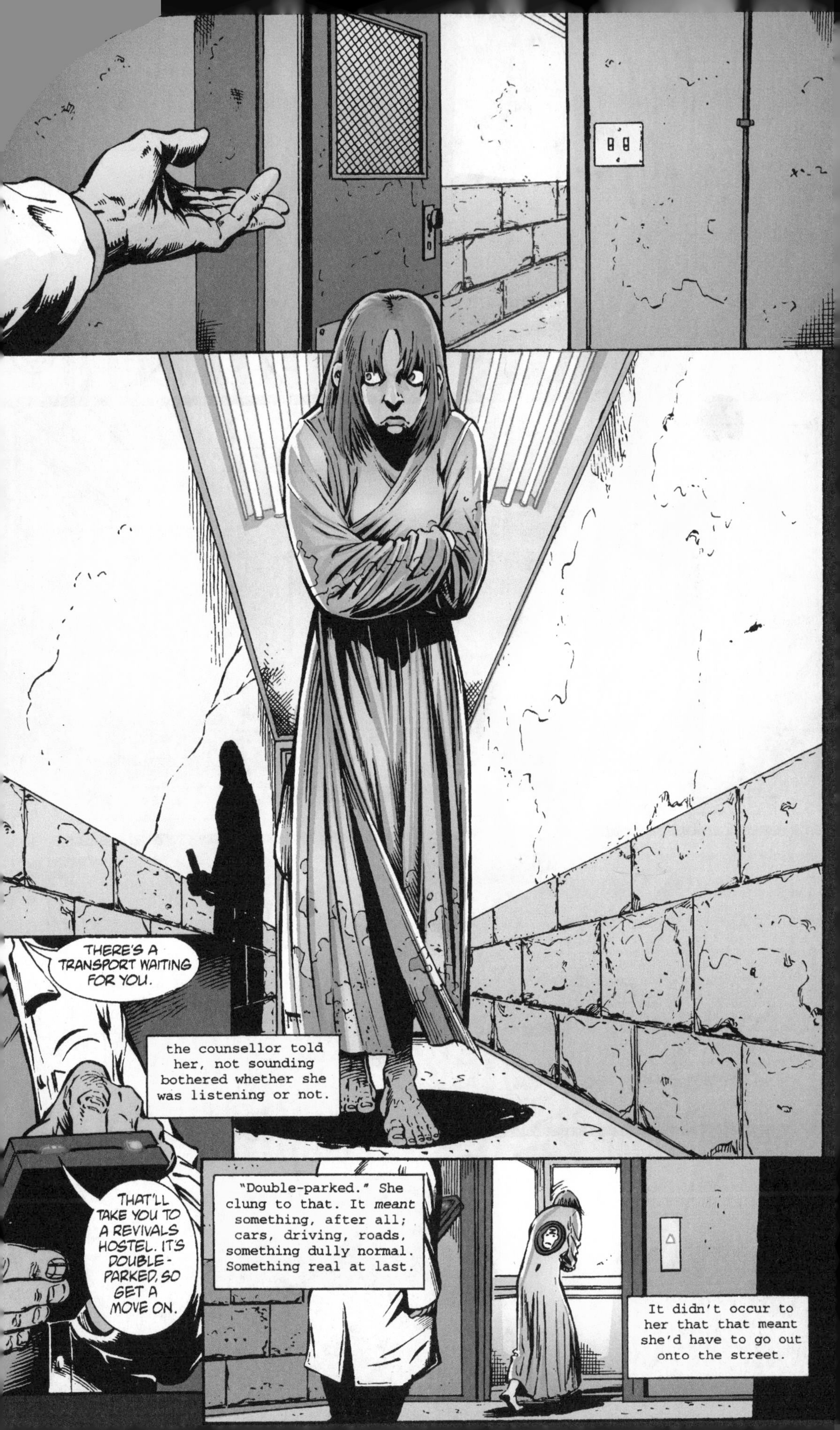

THERE'S A TRANSPORT WAITING FOR YOU.
the counsellor told her, not sounding bothered whether she was listening or not.
THAT'LL TAKE YOU TO A REVIVALS HOSTEL. IT'S DOUBLE-PARKED, SO GET A MOVE ON.
"Double-parked." She clung to that. It *meant* something, after all; cars, driving, roads, something dully normal. Something real at last.
It didn't occur to her that that meant she'd have to go out onto the street.

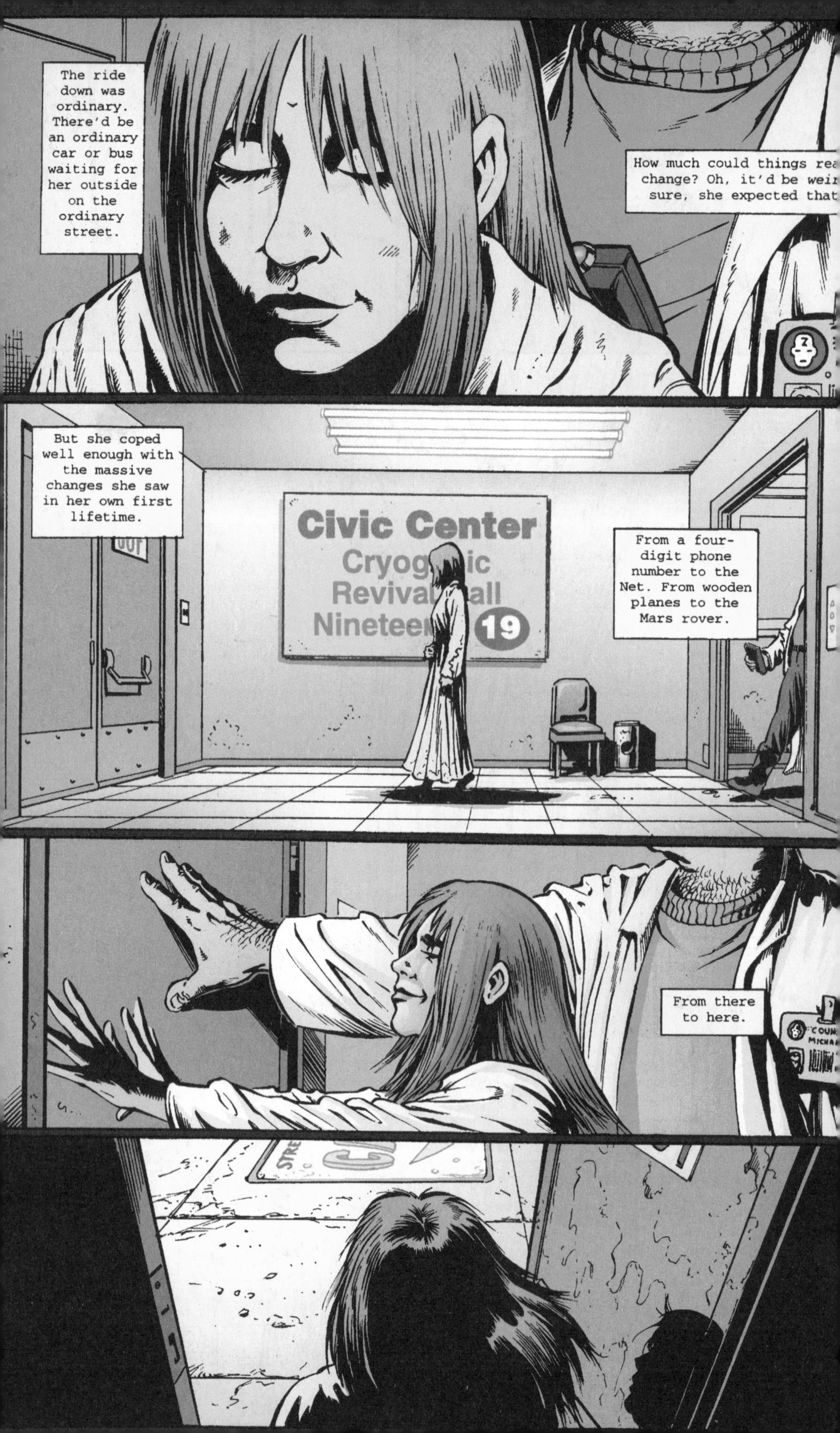
The ride down was ordinary. There'd be an ordinary car or bus waiting for her outside on the ordinary street.
How much could things rea change? Oh, it'd be weir sure, she expected that
But she coped well enough with the massive changes she saw in her own first lifetime.
Civic Center
Cryog ic
Revival all
Ninetee
19
OUT
From a four-digit phone number to the Net. From wooden planes to the Mars rover.
From there to here.
STRE

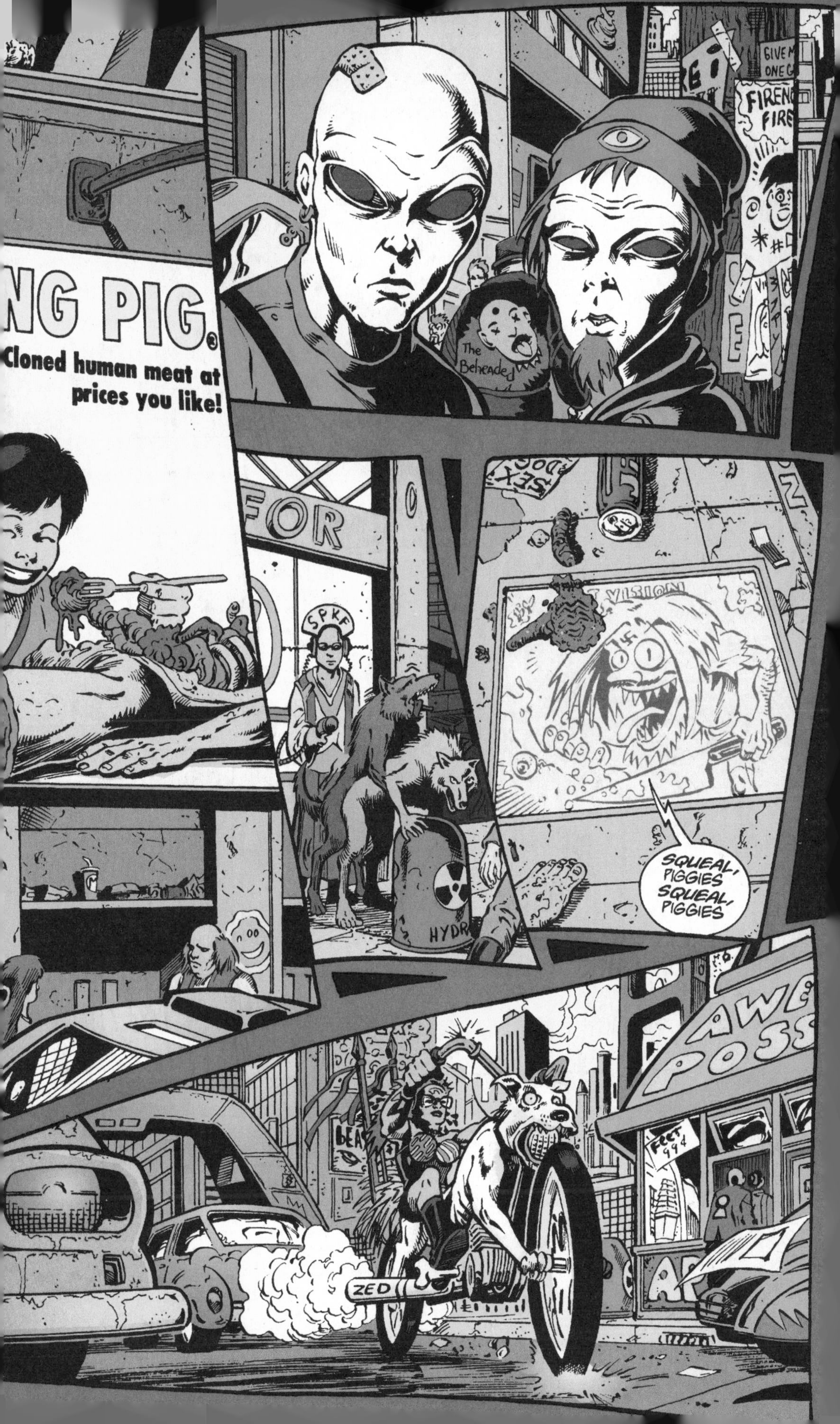
NG PIG®
Cloned human meat at prices you like!
The Beheaded
FOR
SPKF
SEX
HYDR
SQUEAL, PIGGIES SQUEAL, PIGGIES
ZED

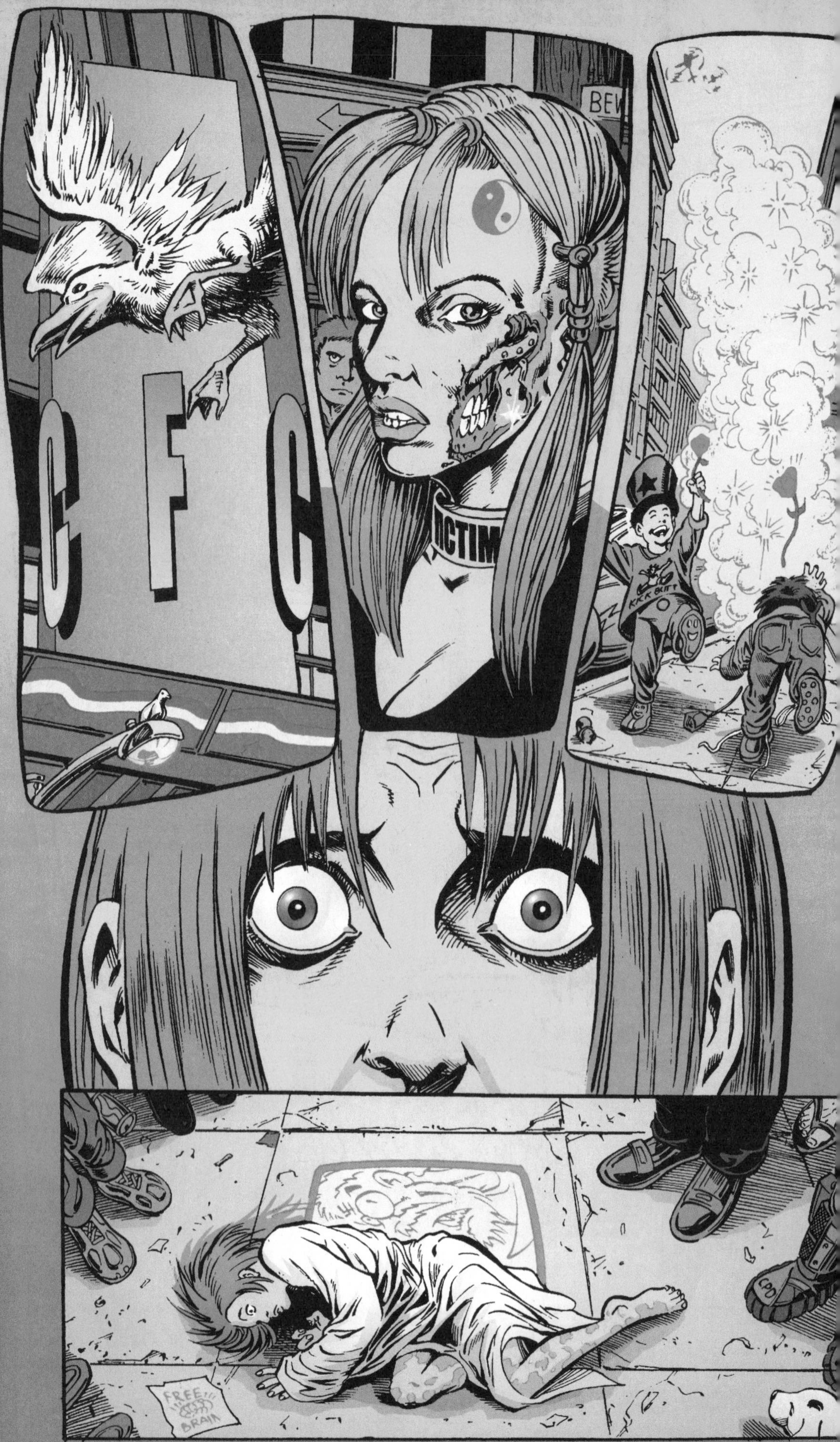
C F C
FREE
BRAIN

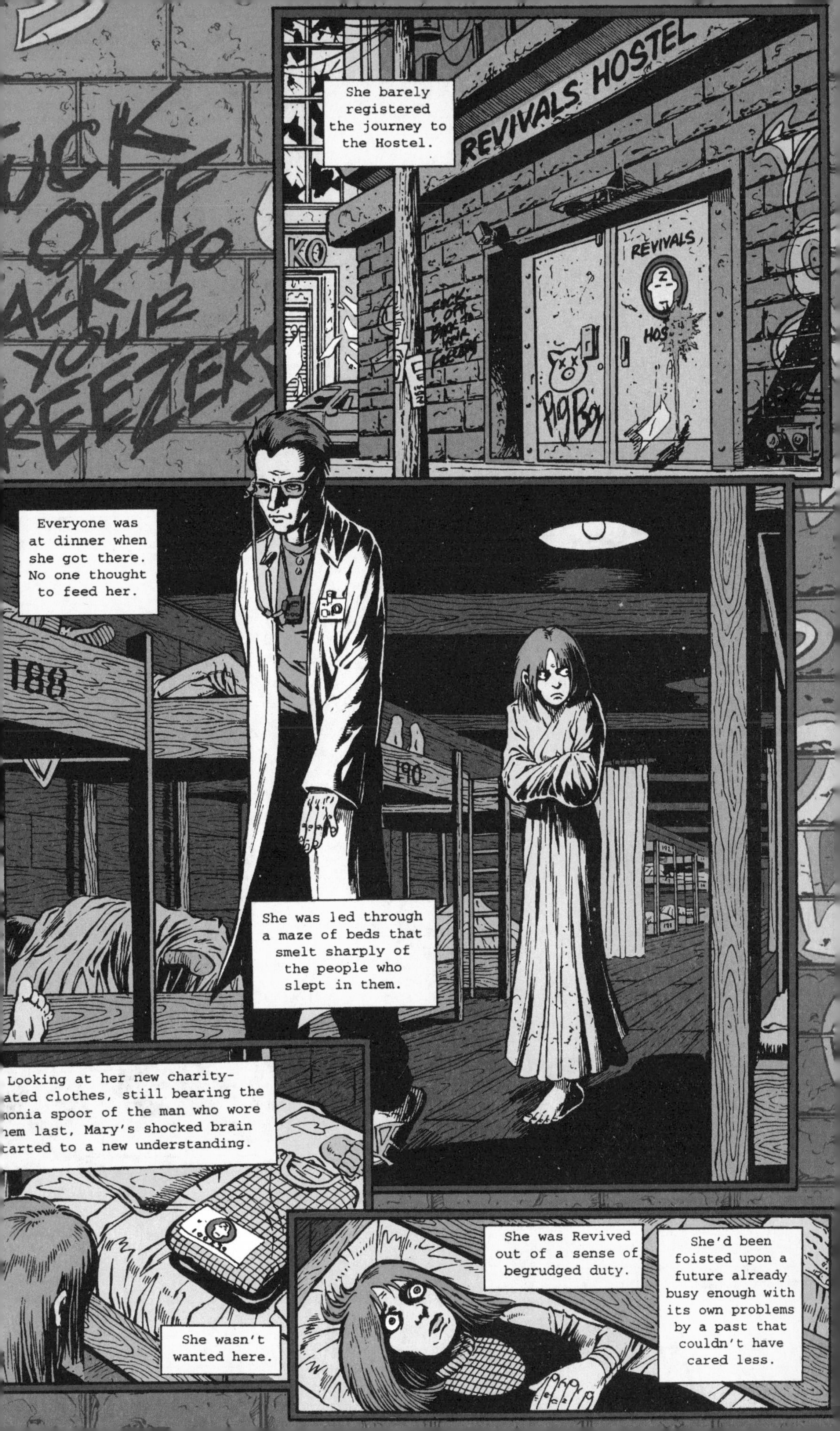
REVIVALS HOSTEL
She barely registered the journey to the Hostel.
REVIVALS
HOS
Pig Boy
Everyone was at dinner when she got there. No one thought to feed her.
188
190
She was led through a maze of beds that smelt sharply of the people who slept in them.
Looking at her new charity-
ated clothes, still bearing the
nonia spoor of the man who wore
nem last, Mary's shocked brain
tarted to a new understanding.
She wasn't wanted here.
She was Revived out of a sense of begrudged duty.
She'd been foisted upon a future already busy enough with its own problems by a past that couldn't have cared less.

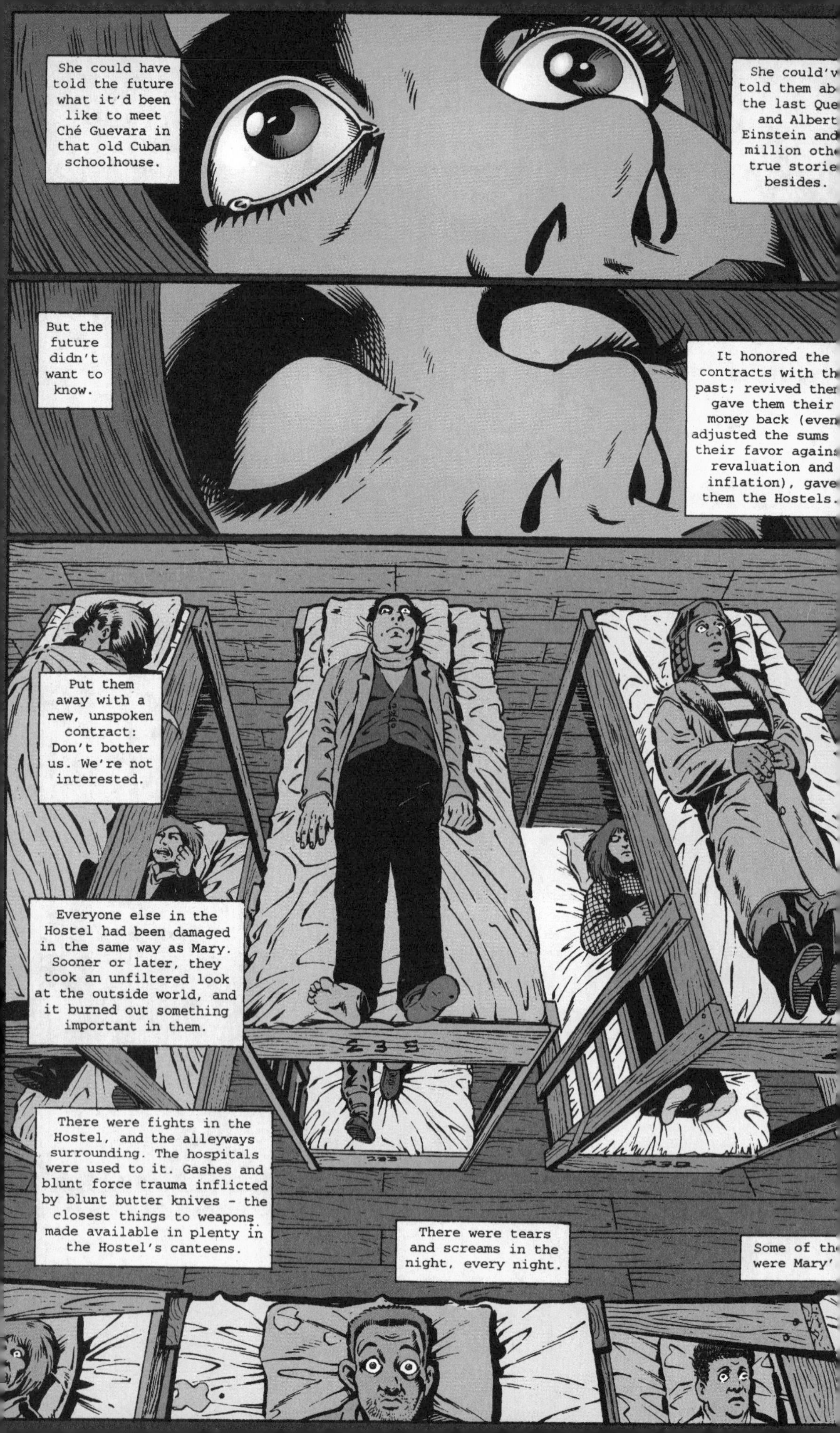
She could have told the future what it'd been like to meet Ché Guevara in that old Cuban schoolhouse.
She could'v told them ab the last Que and Albert Einstein and million othe true storie besides.
But the future didn't want to know.
It honored the contracts with th past; revived ther gave them their money back (even adjusted the sums their favor agains revaluation and inflation), gave them the Hostels.
Put them away with a new, unspoken contract: Don't bother us. We're not interested.
Everyone else in the Hostel had been damaged in the same way as Mary. Sooner or later, they took an unfiltered look at the outside world, and it burned out something important in them.
There were fights in the Hostel, and the alleyways surrounding. The hospitals were used to it. Gashes and blunt force trauma inflicted by blunt butter knives - the closest things to weapons made available in plenty in the Hostel's canteens.
There were tears and screams in the night, every night.
Some of th were Mary'

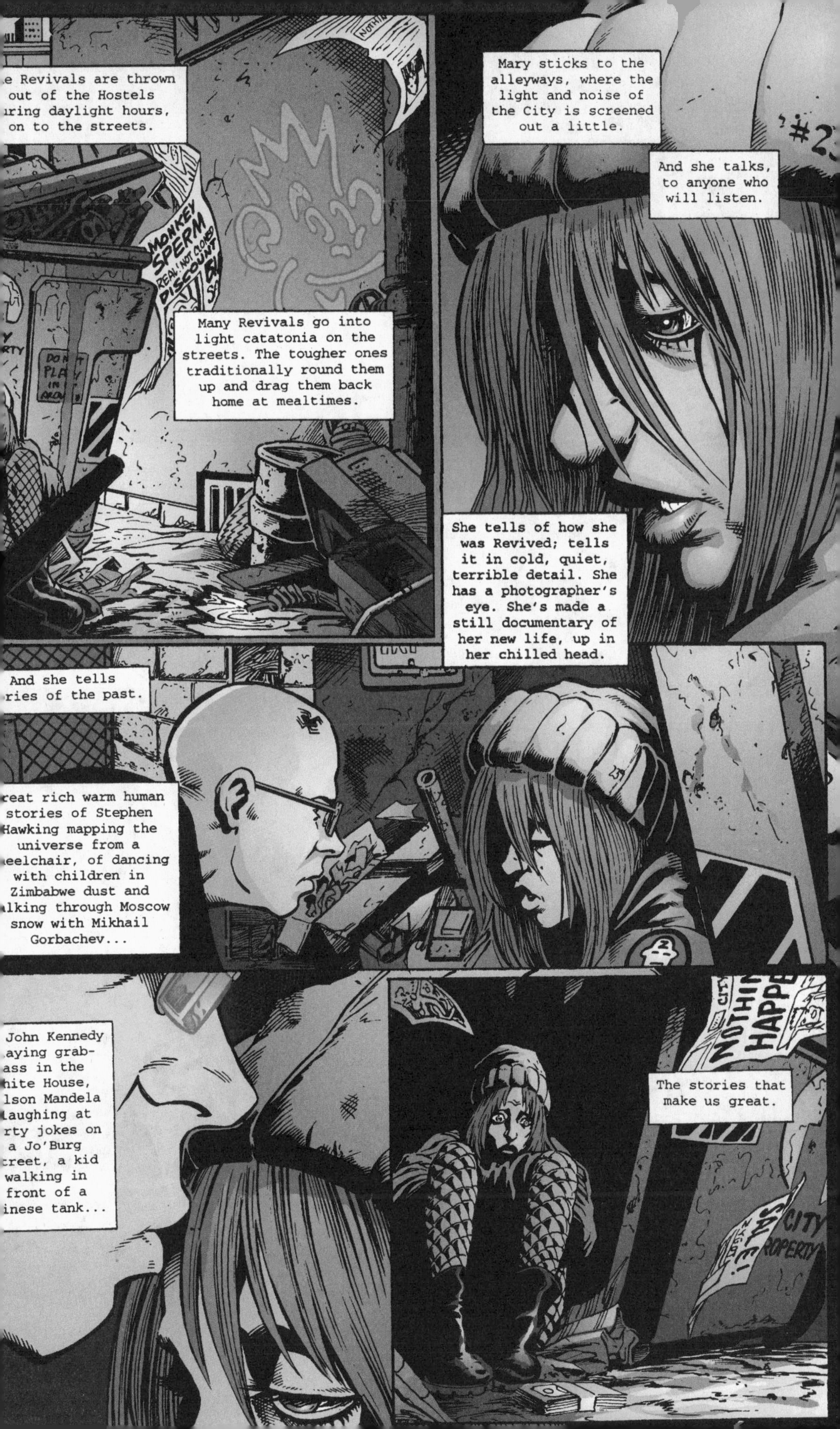
e Revivals are thrown out of the Hostels uring daylight hours, on to the streets.
MONKEY SPERM
REAL! NOT CLONED!
DISCOUNT
Many Revivals go into light catatonia on the streets. The tougher ones traditionally round them up and drag them back home at mealtimes.
Mary sticks to the alleyways, where the light and noise of the City is screened out a little.
And she talks, to anyone who will listen.
She tells of how she was Revived; tells it in cold, quiet, terrible detail. She has a photographer's eye. She's made a still documentary of her new life, up in her chilled head.
And she tells ries of the past.
reat rich warm human stories of Stephen Hawking mapping the universe from a eelchair, of dancing with children in Zimbabwe dust and lking through Moscow snow with Mikhail Gorbachev...
John Kennedy aying grab-ass in the hite House, lson Mandela laughing at rty jokes on a Jo'Burg reet, a kid walking in front of a inese tank...
The stories that make us great.

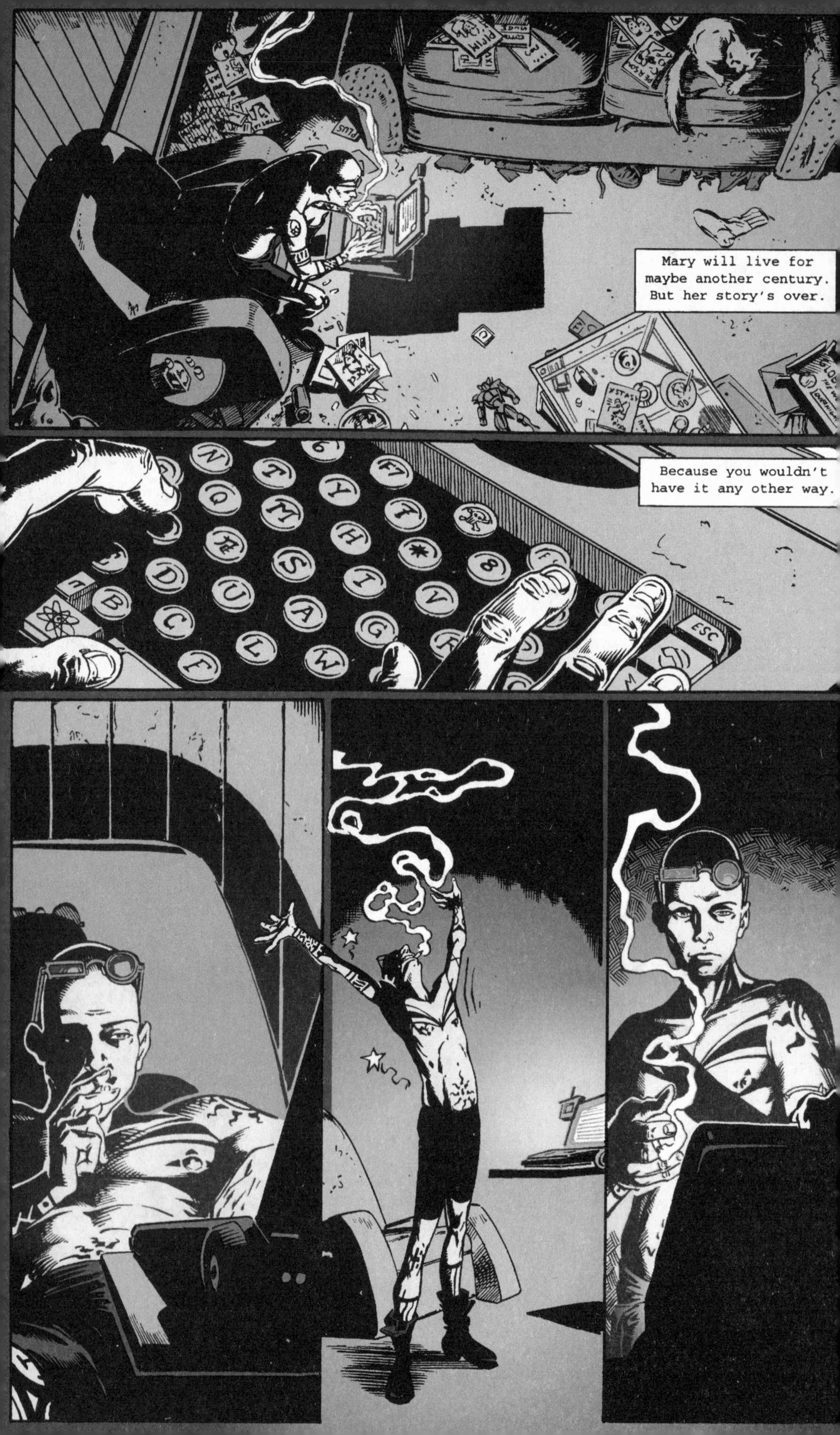
Mary will live for maybe another century. But her story's over.
Because you wouldn't have it any other way.

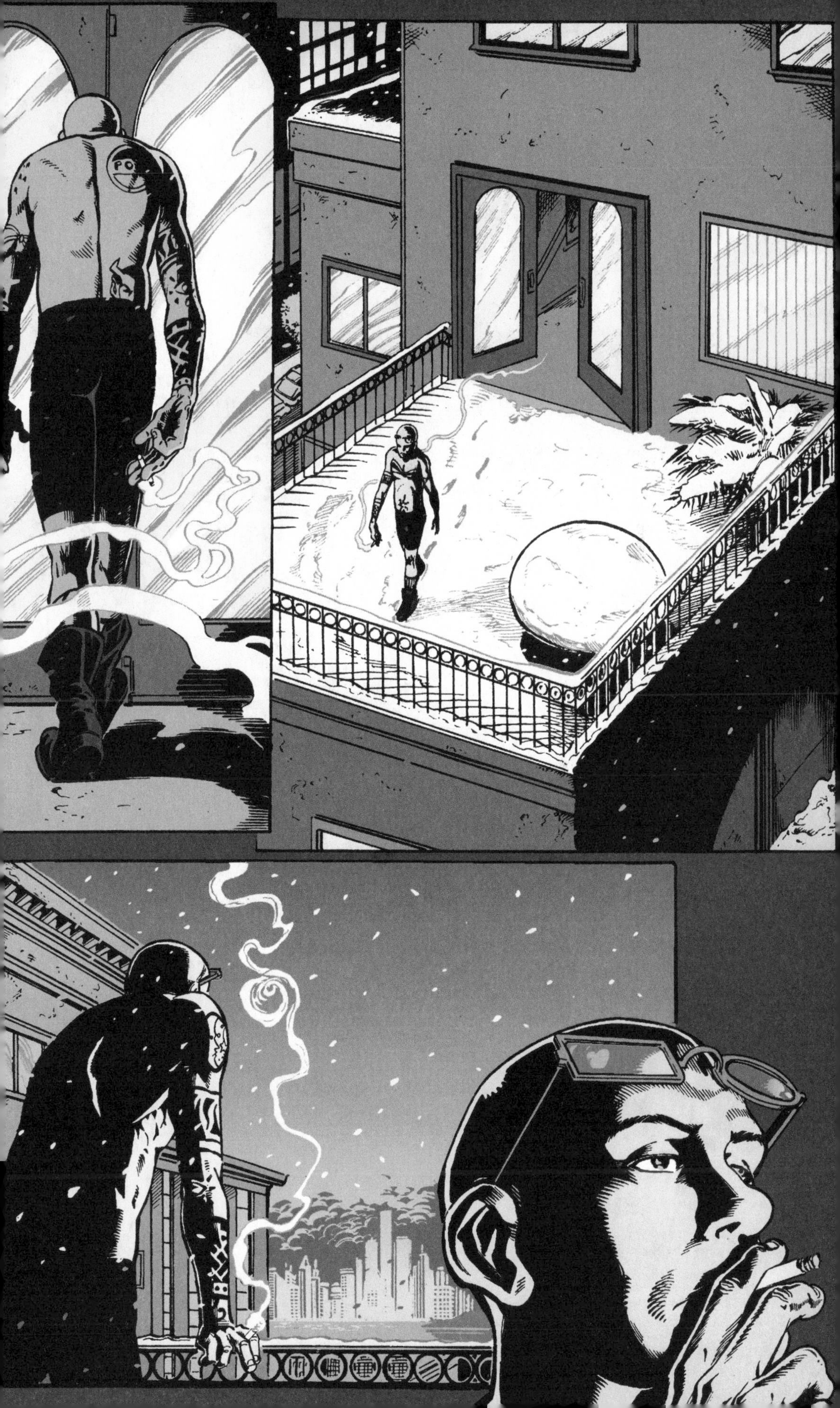

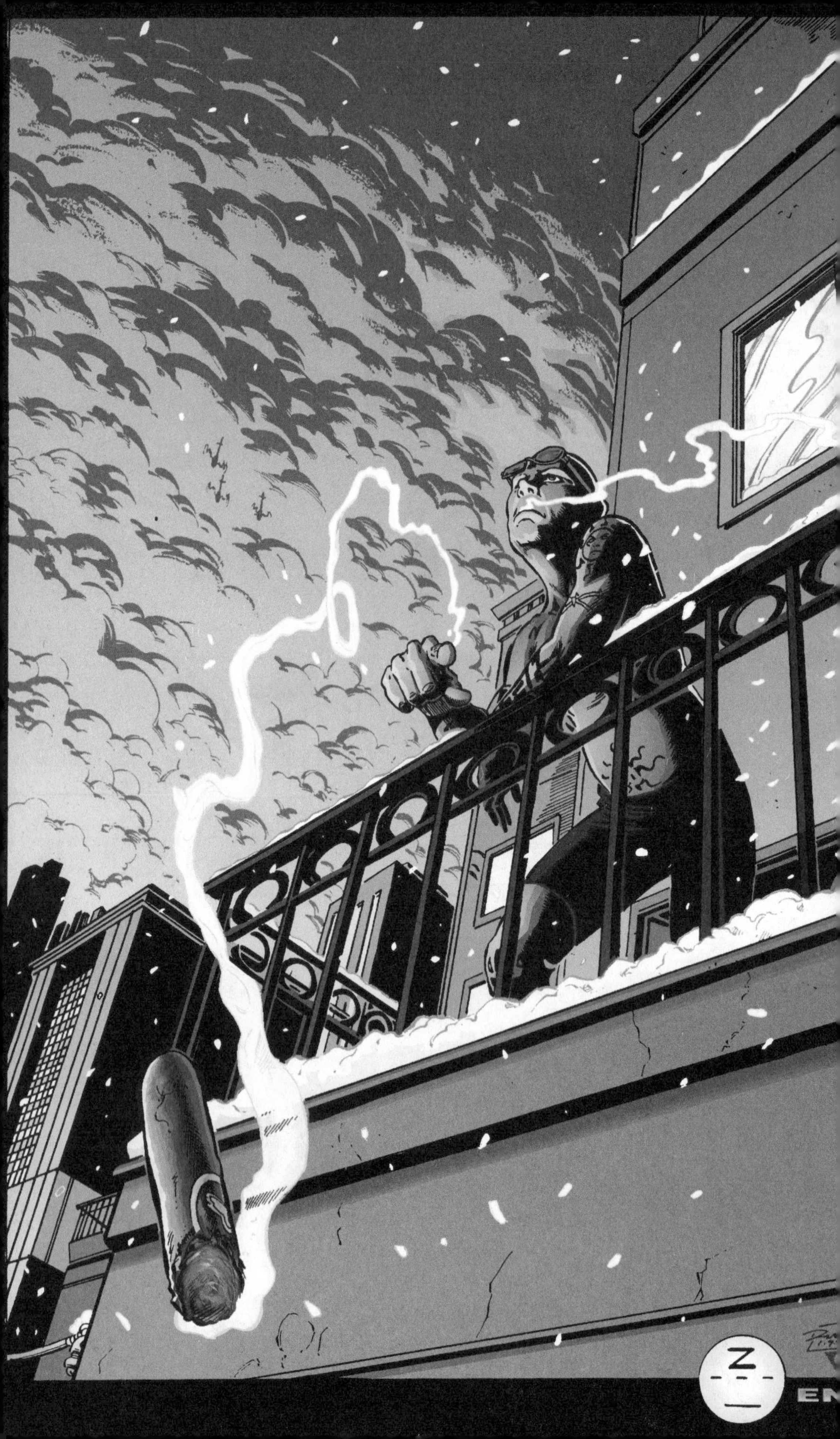
EN

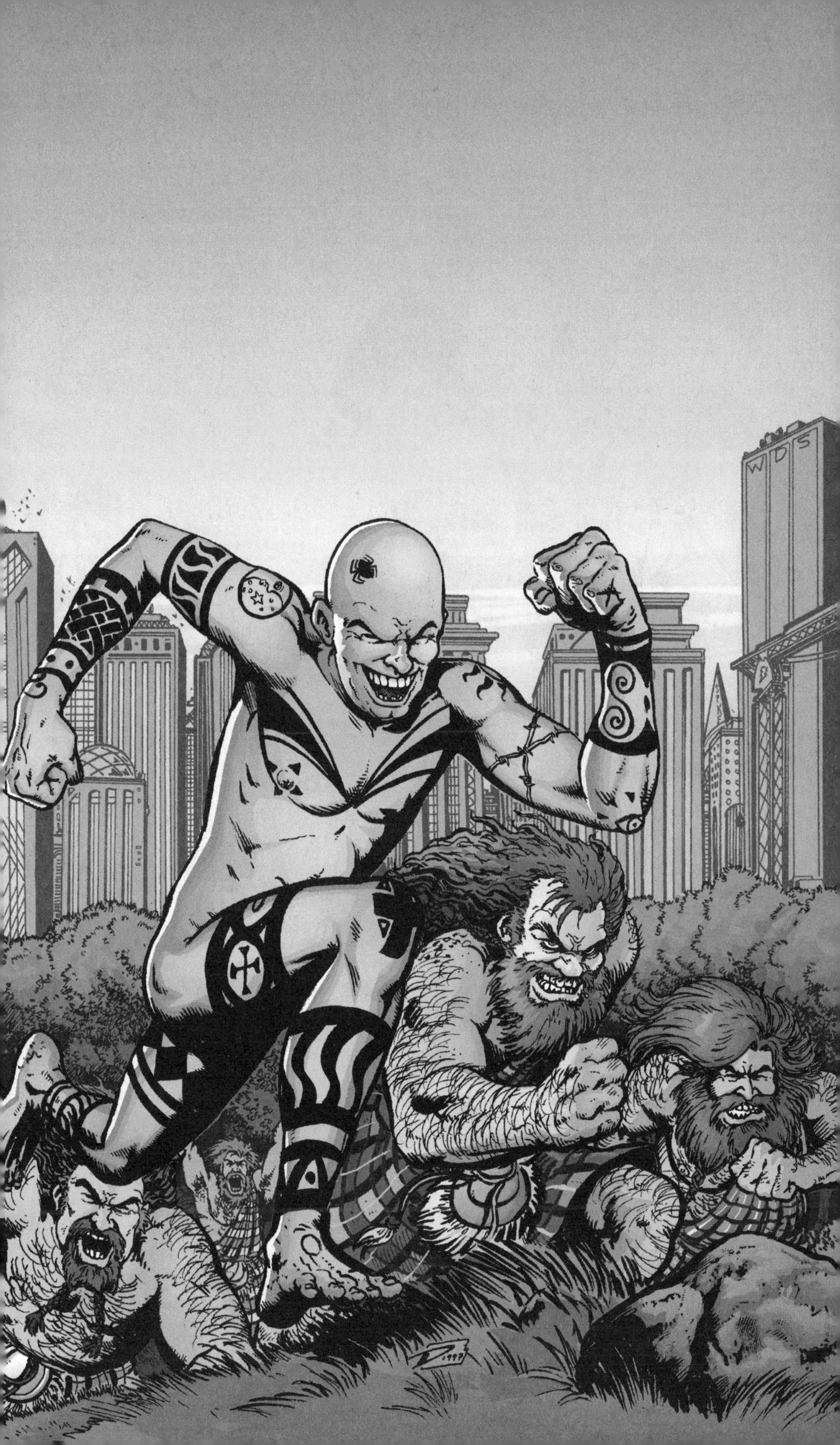
WDS

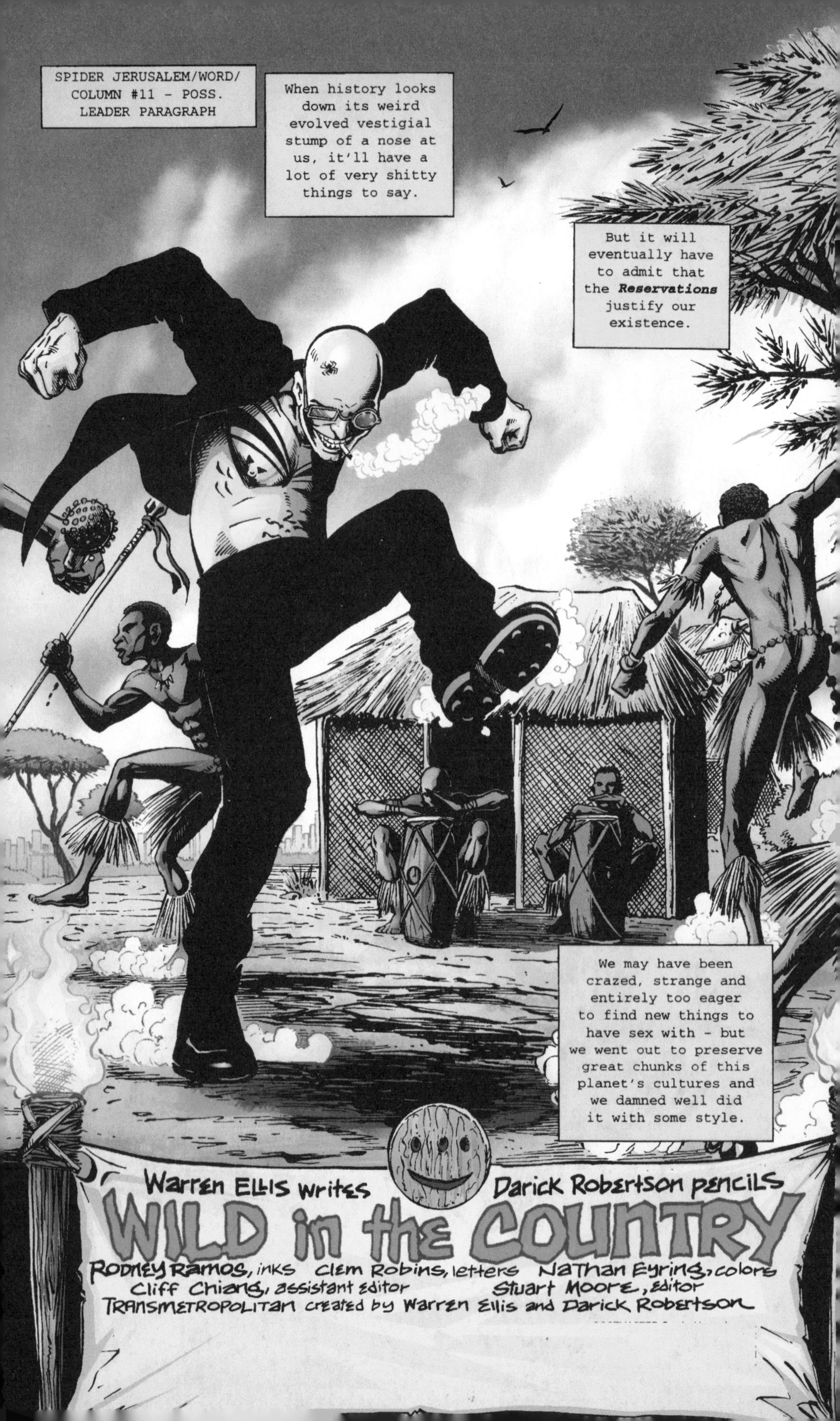
SPIDER JERUSALEM/WORD/ COLUMN #11 - POSS. LEADER PARAGRAPH
When history looks down its weird evolved vestigial stump of a nose at us, it'll have a lot of very shitty things to say.
But it will eventually have to admit that the ***Reservations*** justify our existence.
We may have been crazed, strange and entirely too eager to find new things to have sex with - but we went out to preserve great chunks of this planet's cultures and we damned well did it with some style.
Warren Ellis writes
Darick Robertson pencils
WILD in the COUNTRY
Rodney Ramos, inks
Clem Robins, letters
Nathan Eyring, colors
Cliff Chiang, assistant editor
Stuart Moore, Editor
TRANSMETROPOLITAN created by Warren Ellis and Darick Robertson

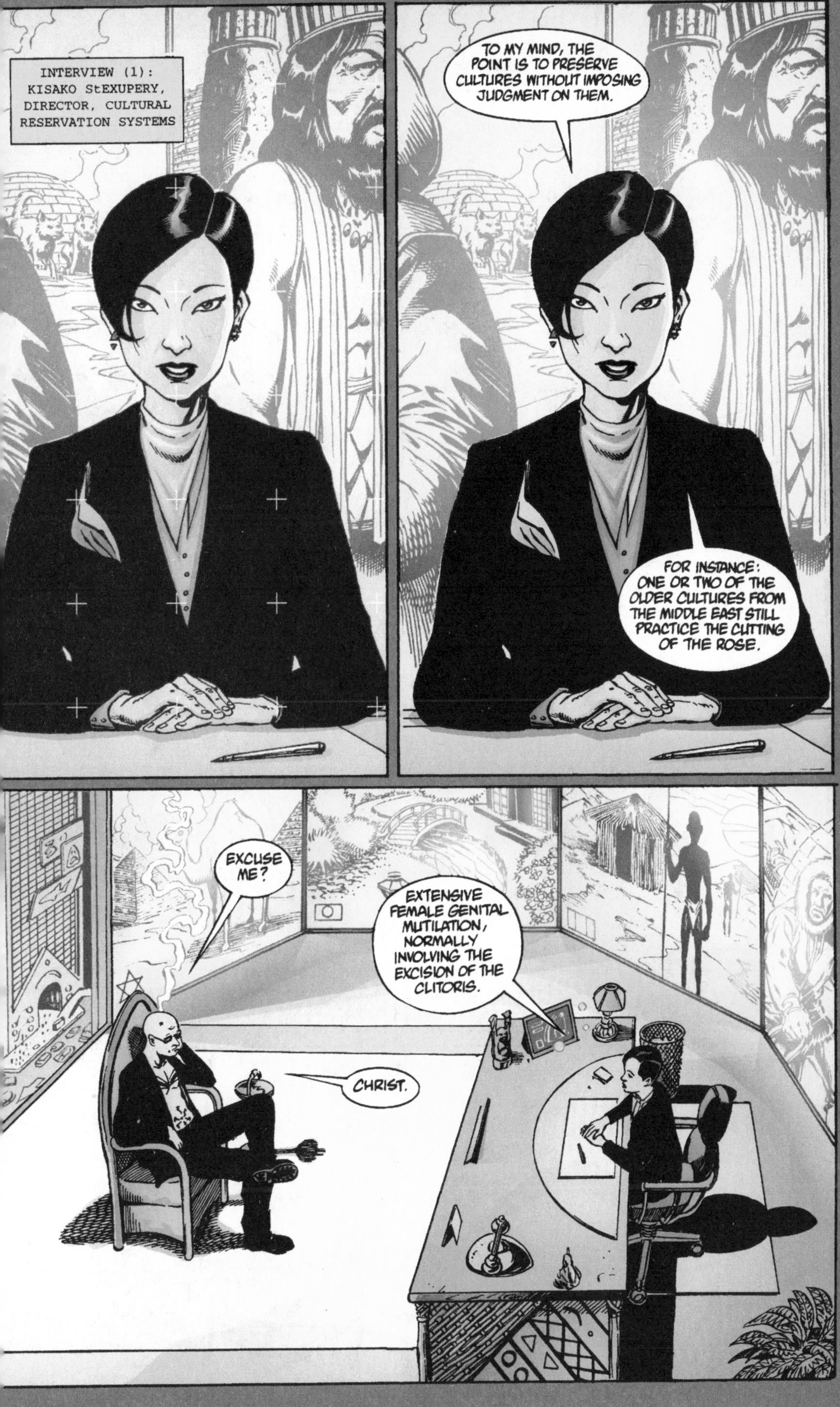
INTERVIEW (1):
KISAKO StEXUPERY,
DIRECTOR, CULTURAL
RESERVATION SYSTEMS
TO MY MIND, THE POINT IS TO PRESERVE CULTURES WITHOUT IMPOSING JUDGMENT ON THEM.
FOR INSTANCE: ONE OR TWO OF THE OLDER CULTURES FROM THE MIDDLE EAST STILL PRACTICE THE CUTTING OF THE ROSE.
EXCUSE ME?
EXTENSIVE FEMALE GENITAL MUTILATION, NORMALLY INVOLVING THE EXCISION OF THE CLITORIS.
CHRIST.

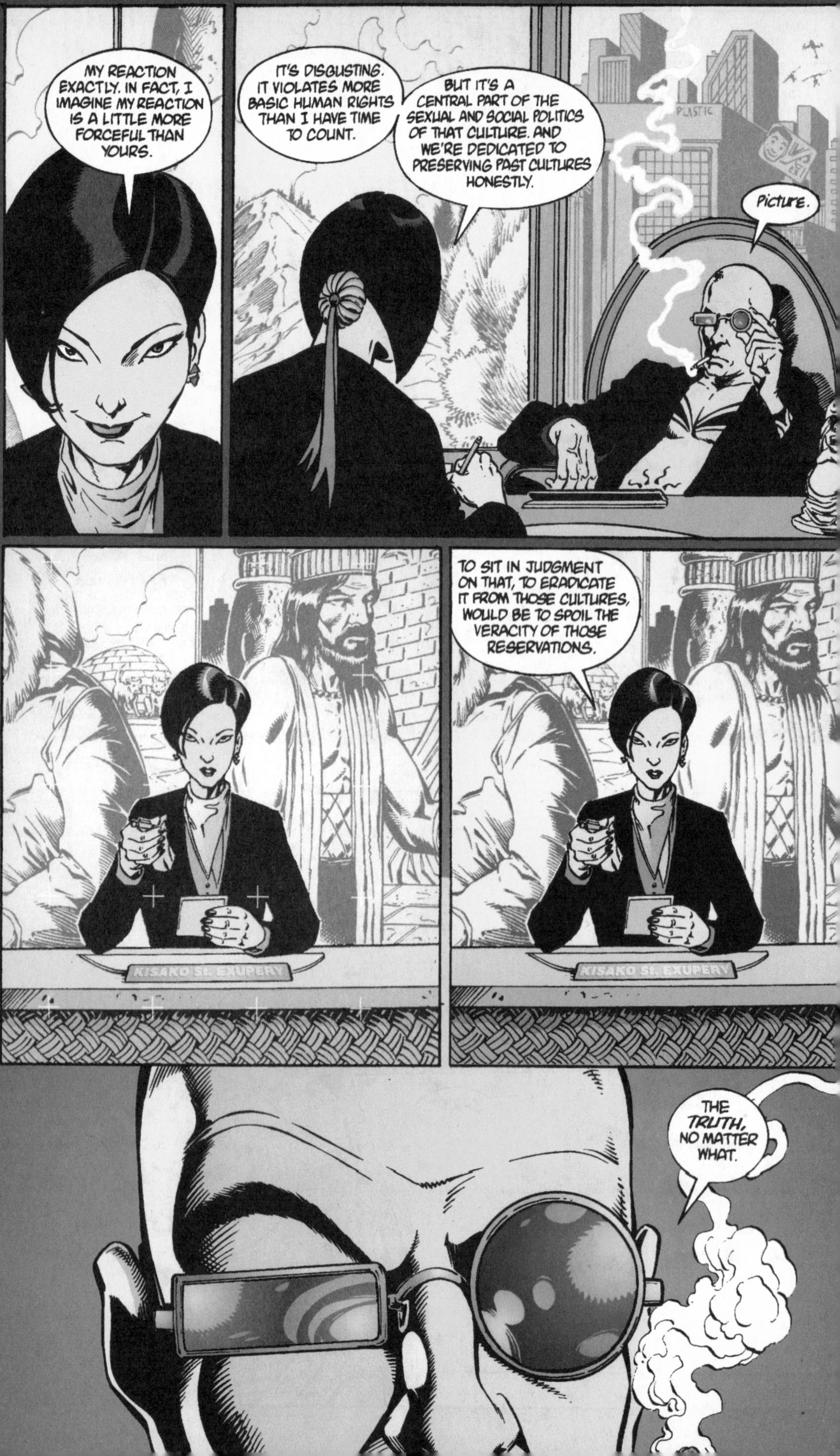
MY REACTION EXACTLY. IN FACT, I IMAGINE MY REACTION IS A LITTLE MORE FORCEFUL THAN YOURS.
IT'S DISGUSTING. IT VIOLATES MORE BASIC HUMAN RIGHTS THAN I HAVE TIME TO COUNT.
BUT IT'S A CENTRAL PART OF THE SEXUAL AND SOCIAL POLITICS OF THAT CULTURE. AND WE'RE DEDICATED TO PRESERVING PAST CULTURES HONESTLY.
PLASTIC
Picture.
KISAKO St. EXUPERY
TO SIT IN JUDGMENT ON THAT, TO ERADICATE IT FROM THOSE CULTURES, WOULD BE TO SPOIL THE VERACITY OF THOSE RESERVATIONS.
KISAKO St. EXUPERY
THE TRUTH, NO MATTER WHAT.

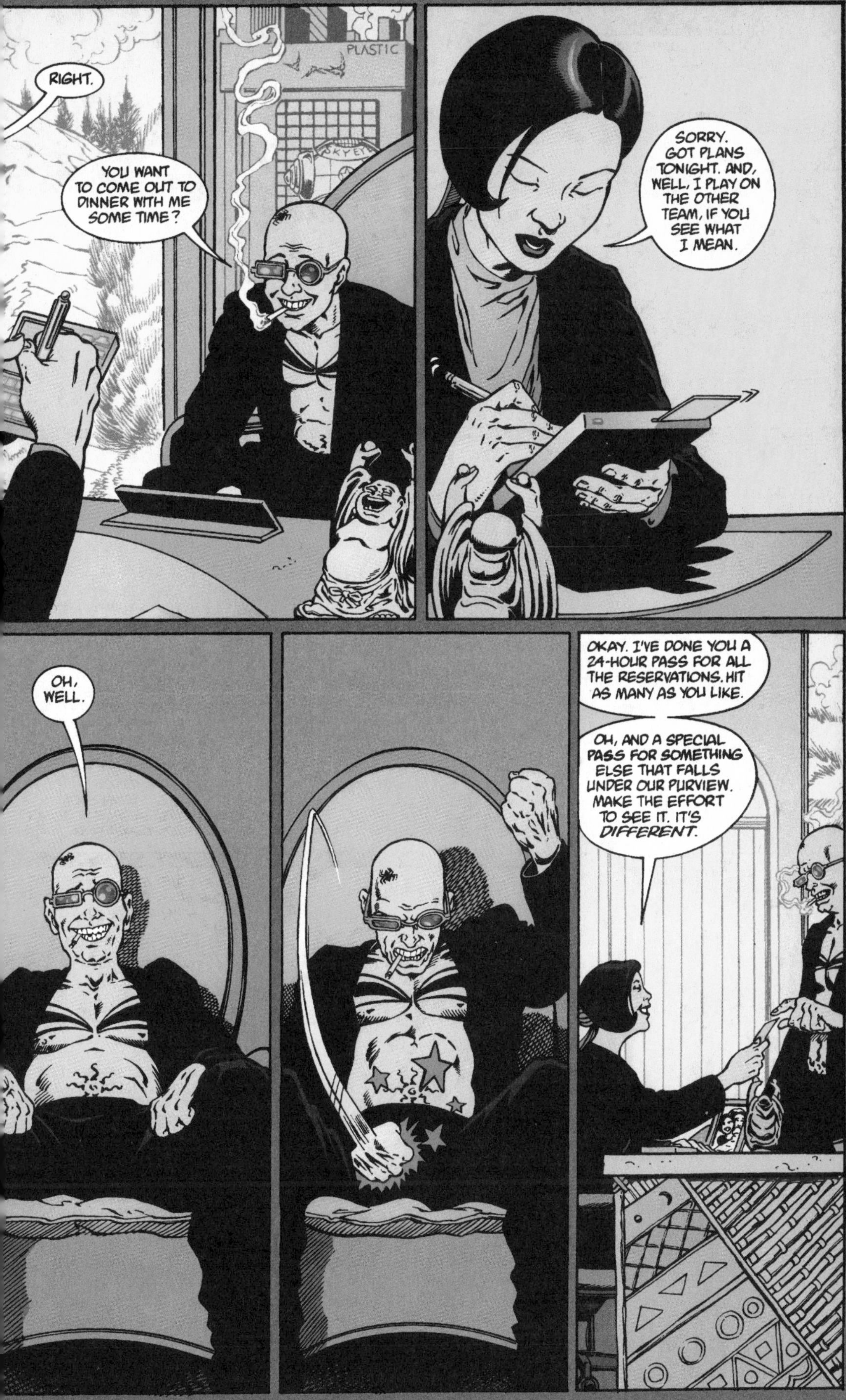
RIGHT.
YOU WANT TO COME OUT TO DINNER WITH ME SOME TIME?
PLASTIC
SORRY. GOT PLANS TONIGHT. AND, WELL, I PLAY ON THE OTHER TEAM, IF YOU SEE WHAT I MEAN.
OH, WELL.
OKAY. I'VE DONE YOU A 24-HOUR PASS FOR ALL THE RESERVATIONS. HIT AS MANY AS YOU LIKE.
OH, AND A SPECIAL PASS FOR SOMETHING ELSE THAT FALLS UNDER OUR PURVIEW. MAKE THE EFFORT TO SEE IT. IT'S *DIFFERENT*.

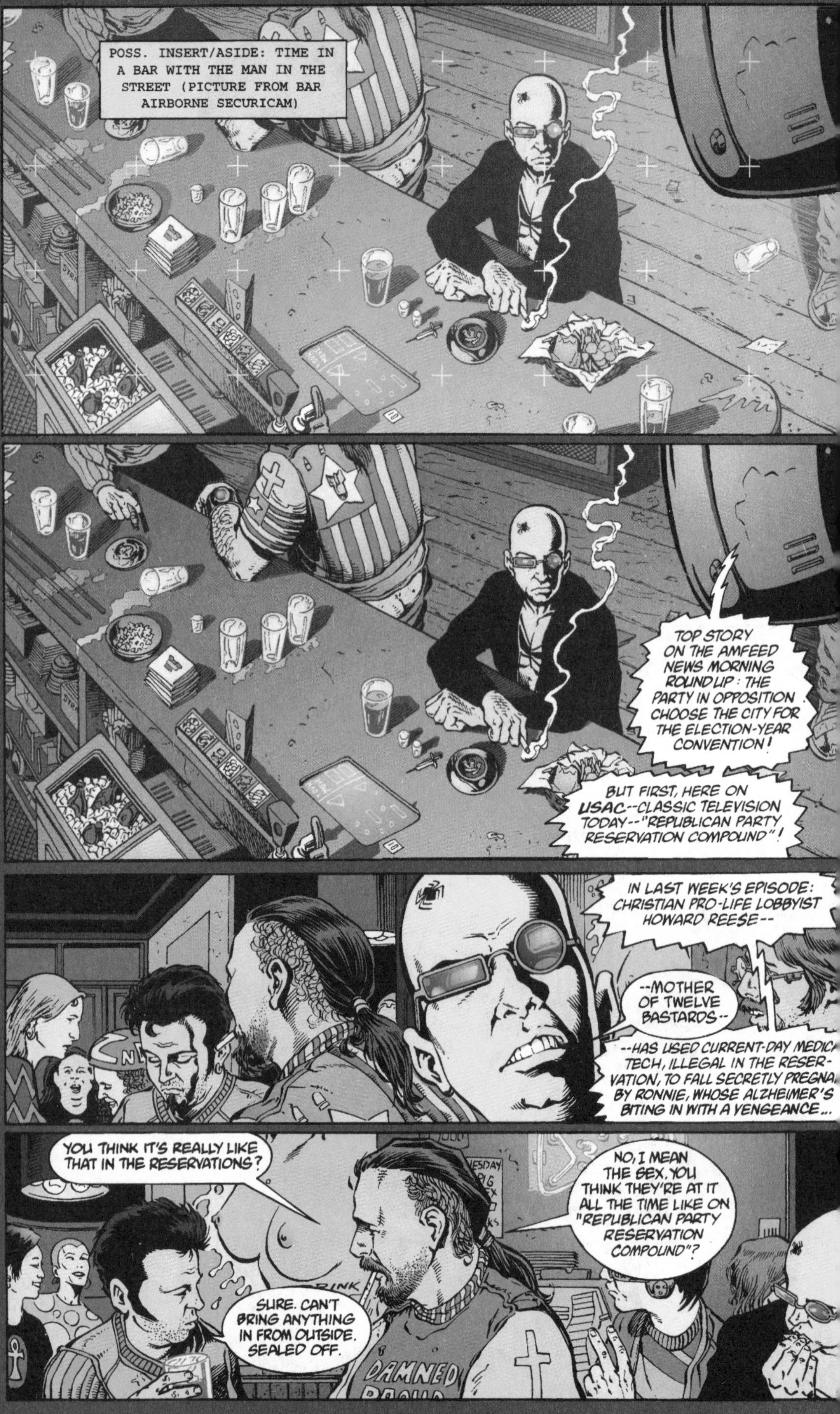
POSS. INSERT/ASIDE: TIME IN A BAR WITH THE MAN IN THE STREET (PICTURE FROM BAR AIRBORNE SECURICAM)
TOP STORY ON THE AMFEED NEWS MORNING ROUNDUP: THE PARTY IN OPPOSITION CHOOSE THE CITY FOR THE ELECTION-YEAR CONVENTION!
BUT FIRST, HERE ON USAC--CLASSIC TELEVISION TODAY--"REPUBLICAN PARTY RESERVATION COMPOUND"!
IN LAST WEEK'S EPISODE: CHRISTIAN PRO-LIFE LOBBYIST HOWARD REESE--
--MOTHER OF TWELVE BASTARDS--
--HAS USED CURRENT-DAY MEDIC TECH, ILLEGAL IN THE RESERVATION, TO FALL SECRETLY PREGNA BY RONNIE, WHOSE ALZHEIMER'S BITING IN WITH A VENGEANCE...
YOU THINK IT'S REALLY LIKE THAT IN THE RESERVATIONS?
SURE. CAN'T BRING ANYTHING IN FROM OUTSIDE. SEALED OFF.
NO, I MEAN THE SEX. YOU THINK THEY'RE AT IT ALL THE TIME LIKE ON "REPUBLICAN PARTY RESERVATION COMPOUND"?
DAMNED

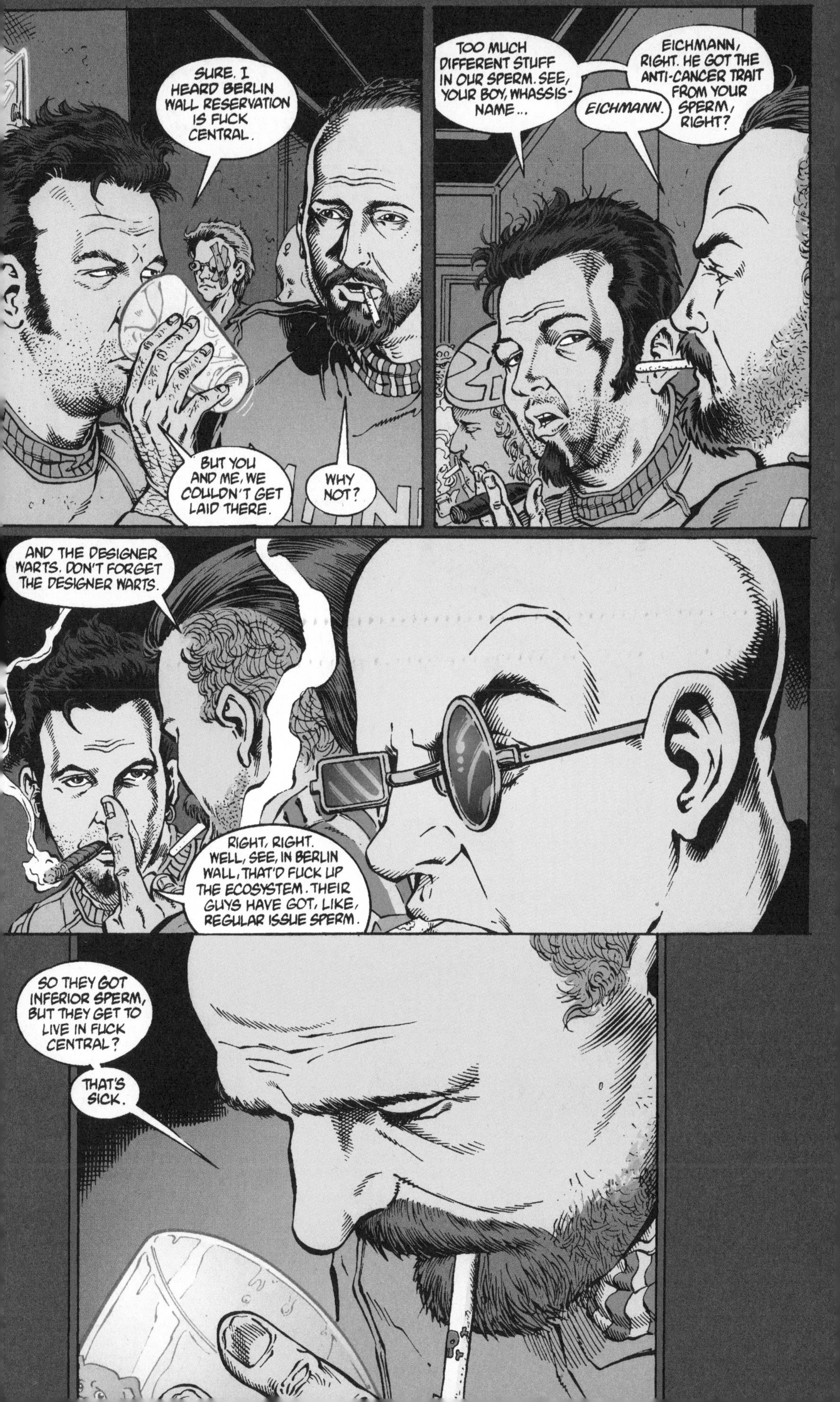
SURE. I HEARD BERLIN WALL RESERVATION IS FUCK CENTRAL.
BUT YOU AND ME, WE COULDN'T GET LAID THERE.
WHY NOT?
TOO MUCH DIFFERENT STUFF IN OUR SPERM. SEE, YOUR BOY, WHASSIS-NAME...
EICHMANN.
EICHMANN, RIGHT. HE GOT THE ANTI-CANCER TRAIT FROM YOUR SPERM, RIGHT?
AND THE DESIGNER WARTS. DON'T FORGET THE DESIGNER WARTS.
RIGHT, RIGHT. WELL, SEE, IN BERLIN WALL, THAT'D FUCK UP THE ECOSYSTEM. THEIR GUYS HAVE GOT, LIKE, REGULAR ISSUE SPERM.
SO THEY GOT INFERIOR SPERM, BUT THEY GET TO LIVE IN FUCK CENTRAL?
THAT'S SICK.

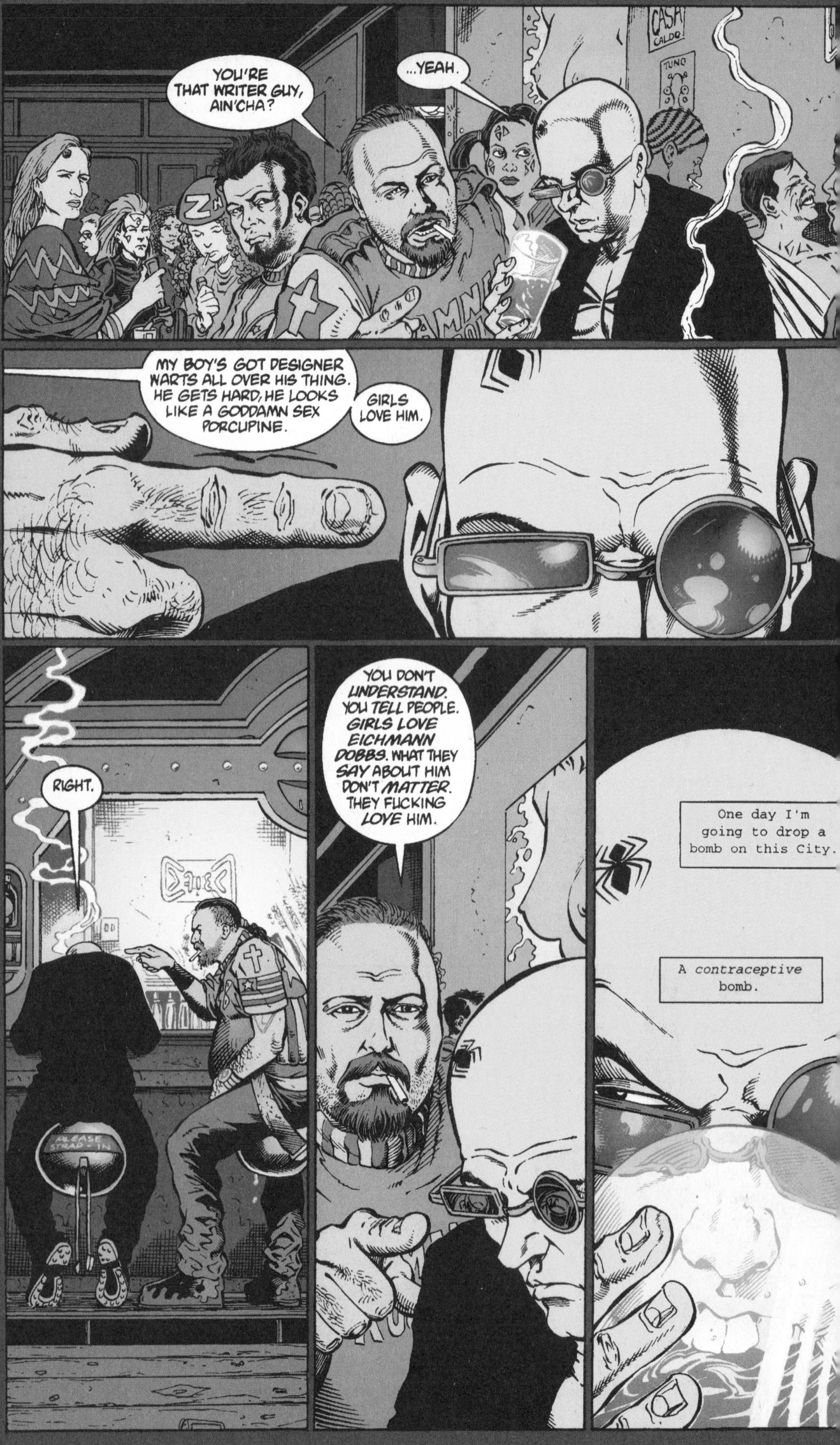
YOU'RE THAT WRITER GUY, AIN'CHA?
...YEAH.
MY BOY'S GOT DESIGNER WARTS ALL OVER HIS THING. HE GETS HARD, HE LOOKS LIKE A GODDAMN SEX PORCUPINE.
GIRLS LOVE HIM.
RIGHT.
PLEASE STRAP-IN
YOU DON'T UNDERSTAND. YOU TELL PEOPLE. GIRLS LOVE EICHMANN DOBBS. WHAT THEY SAY ABOUT HIM DON'T MATTER. THEY FUCKING LOVE HIM.
One day I'm going to drop a bomb on this City.
A contraceptive bomb.

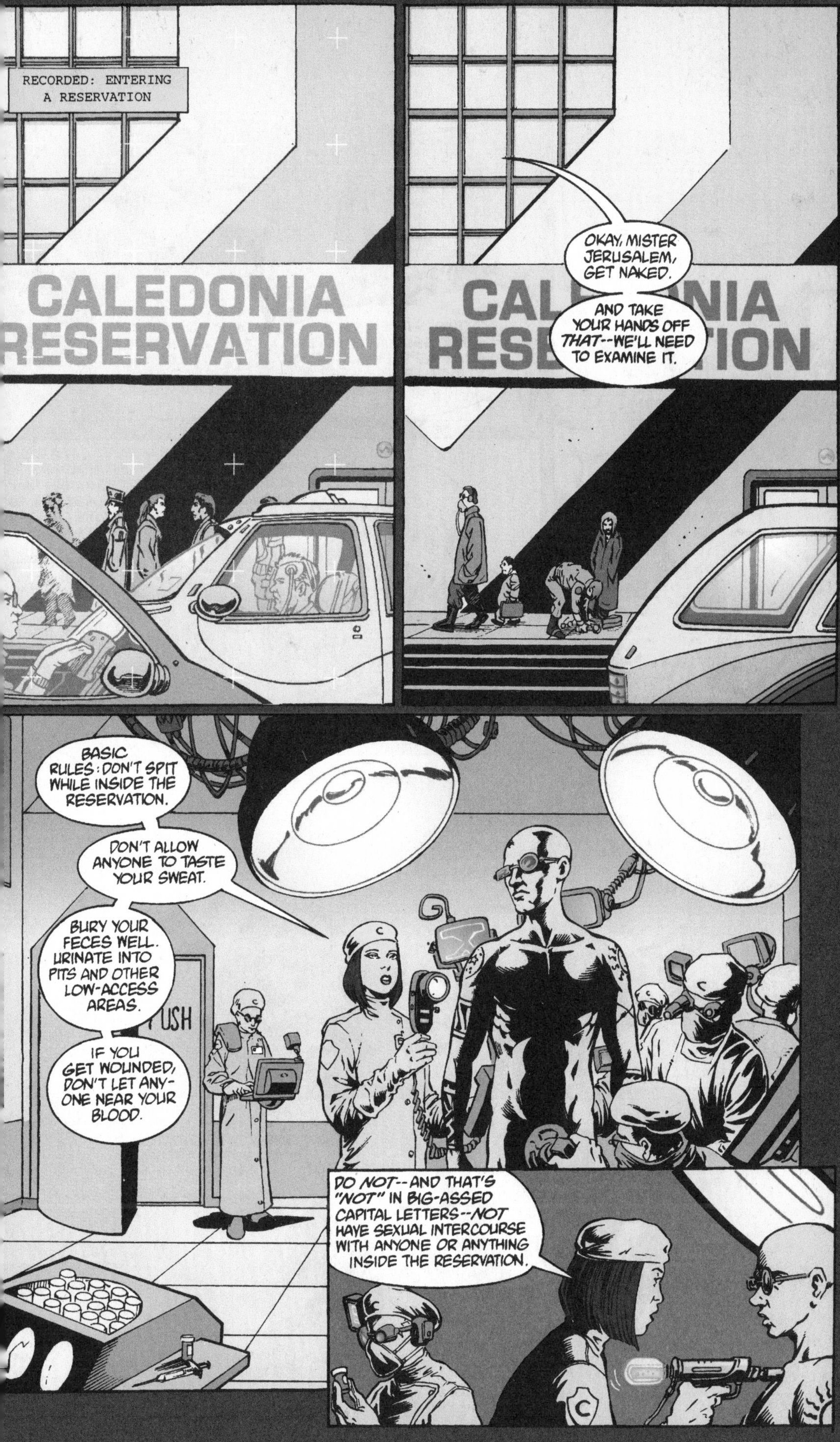
RECORDED: ENTERING A RESERVATION
CALEDONIA RESERVATION
CALEDONIA RESERVATION
OKAY, MISTER JERUSALEM, GET NAKED.
AND TAKE YOUR HANDS OFF *THAT*--WE'LL NEED TO EXAMINE IT.
BASIC RULES: DON'T SPIT WHILE INSIDE THE RESERVATION.
DON'T ALLOW ANYONE TO TASTE YOUR SWEAT.
BURY YOUR FECES WELL. URINATE INTO PITS AND OTHER LOW-ACCESS AREAS.
IF YOU GET WOUNDED, DON'T LET ANY-ONE NEAR YOUR BLOOD.
PUSH
DO NOT--AND THAT'S *"NOT"* IN BIG-ASSED CAPITAL LETTERS--*NOT* HAVE SEXUAL INTERCOURSE WITH ANYONE OR ANYTHING INSIDE THE RESERVATION.

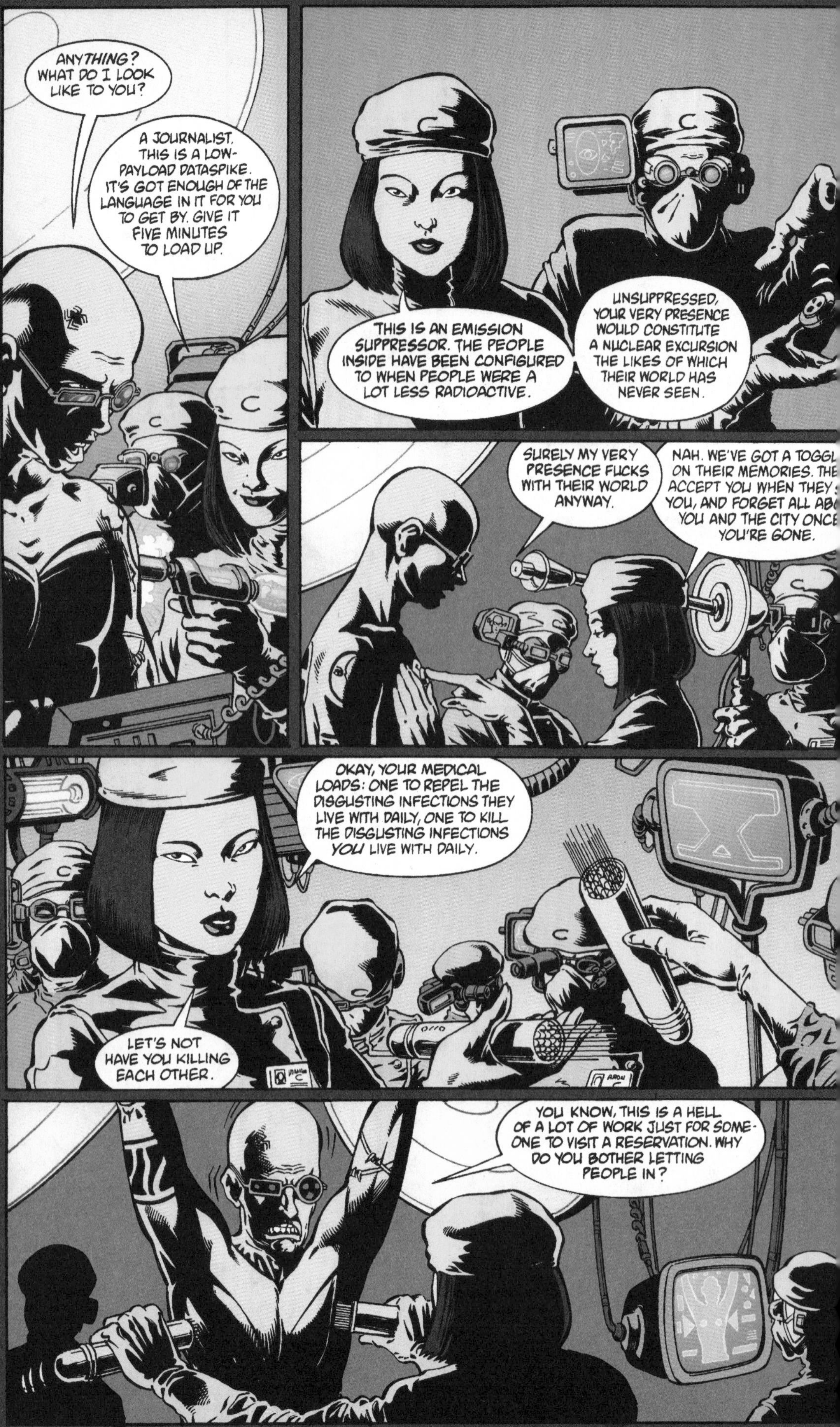
ANYTHING? WHAT DO I LOOK LIKE TO YOU?
A JOURNALIST. THIS IS A LOW-PAYLOAD DATASPIKE. IT'S GOT ENOUGH OF THE LANGUAGE IN IT FOR YOU TO GET BY. GIVE IT FIVE MINUTES TO LOAD UP.
THIS IS AN EMISSION SUPPRESSOR. THE PEOPLE INSIDE HAVE BEEN CONFIGURED TO WHEN PEOPLE WERE A LOT LESS RADIOACTIVE.
UNSUPPRESSED, YOUR VERY PRESENCE WOULD CONSTITUTE A NUCLEAR EXCURSION THE LIKES OF WHICH THEIR WORLD HAS NEVER SEEN.
SURELY MY VERY PRESENCE FUCKS WITH THEIR WORLD ANYWAY.
NAH. WE'VE GOT A TOGG ON THEIR MEMORIES. THE ACCEPT YOU WHEN THEY YOU, AND FORGET ALL AB YOU AND THE CITY ONCE YOU'RE GONE.
OKAY, YOUR MEDICAL LOADS: ONE TO REPEL THE DISGUSTING INFECTIONS THEY LIVE WITH DAILY, ONE TO KILL THE DISGUSTING INFECTIONS YOU LIVE WITH DAILY.
LET'S NOT HAVE YOU KILLING EACH OTHER.
YOU KNOW, THIS IS A HELL OF A LOT OF WORK JUST FOR SOME-ONE TO VISIT A RESERVATION. WHY DO YOU BOTHER LETTING PEOPLE IN?

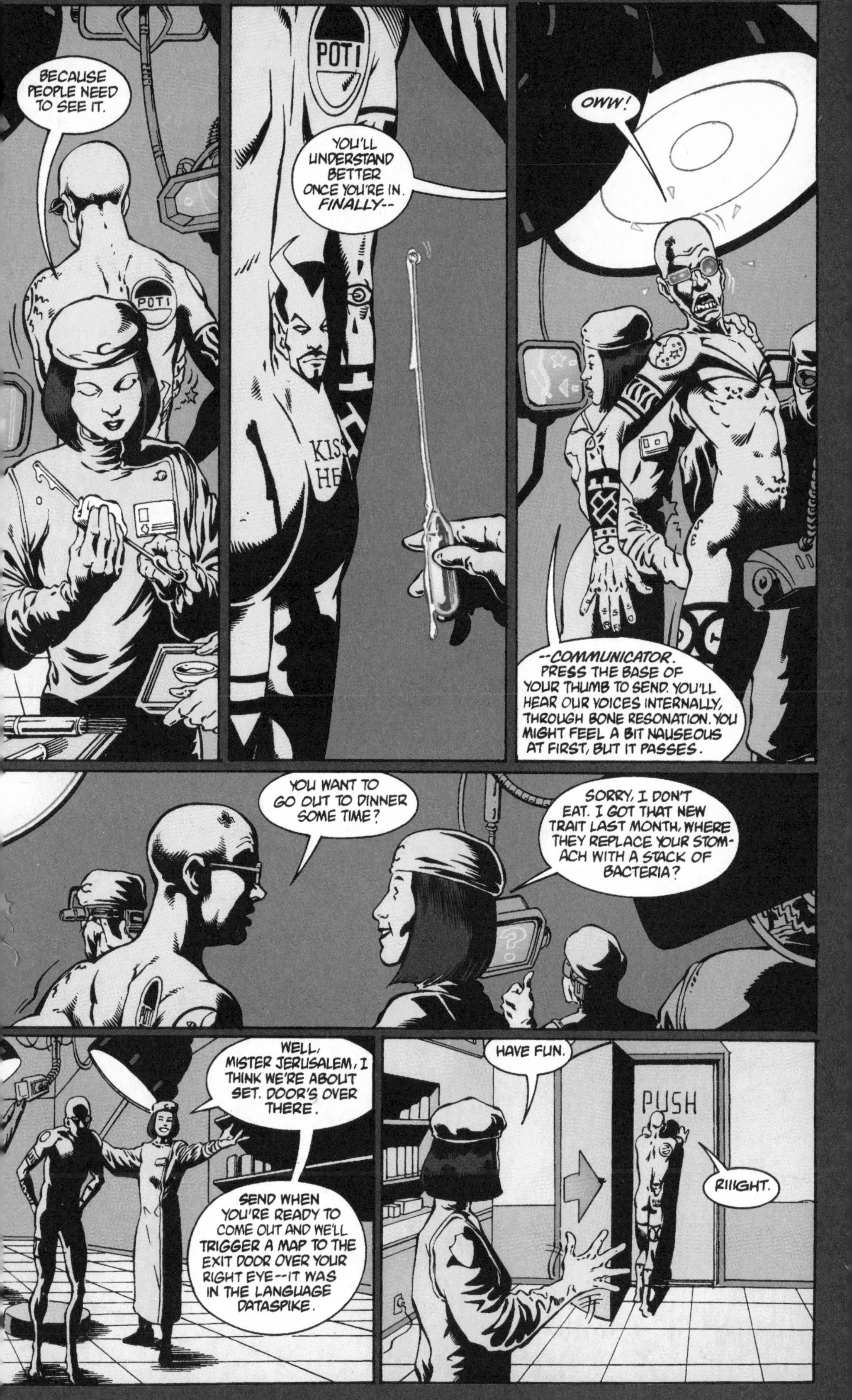
BECAUSE PEOPLE NEED TO SEE IT.
POTI
POTI
YOU'LL UNDERSTAND BETTER ONCE YOU'RE IN. FINALLY--
KISS HE
OWW!
--COMMUNICATOR. PRESS THE BASE OF YOUR THUMB TO SEND. YOU'LL HEAR OUR VOICES INTERNALLY, THROUGH BONE RESONATION. YOU MIGHT FEEL A BIT NAUSEOUS AT FIRST, BUT IT PASSES.
YOU WANT TO GO OUT TO DINNER SOME TIME?
SORRY, I DON'T EAT. I GOT THAT NEW TRAIT LAST MONTH, WHERE THEY REPLACE YOUR STOMACH WITH A STACK OF BACTERIA?
WELL, MISTER JERUSALEM, I THINK WE'RE ABOUT SET. DOOR'S OVER THERE.
SEND WHEN YOU'RE READY TO COME OUT AND WE'LL TRIGGER A MAP TO THE EXIT DOOR OVER YOUR RIGHT EYE--IT WAS IN THE LANGUAGE DATASPIKE.
HAVE FUN.
PUSH
RIIIGHT.

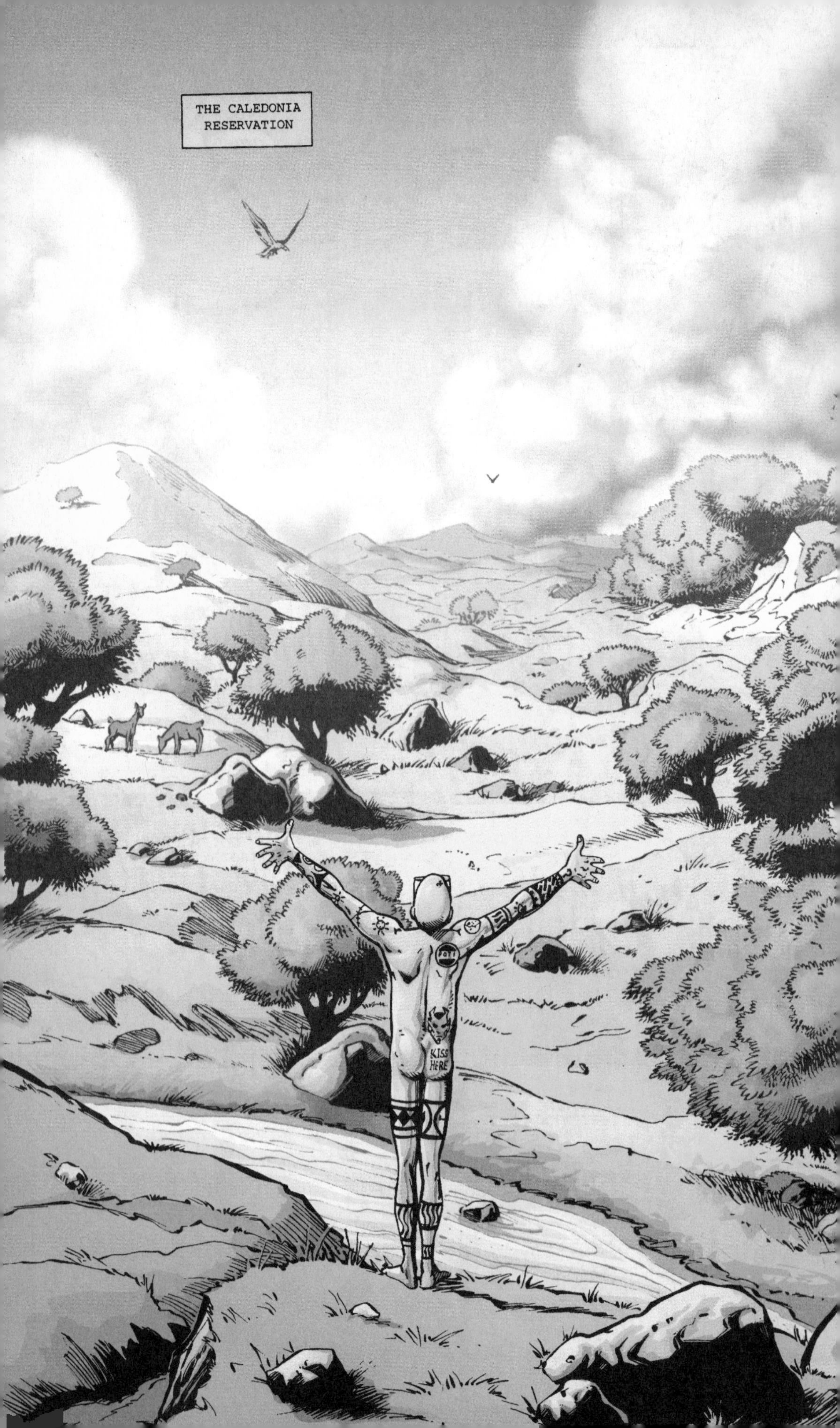
THE CALEDONIA RESERVATION
KISS HERE

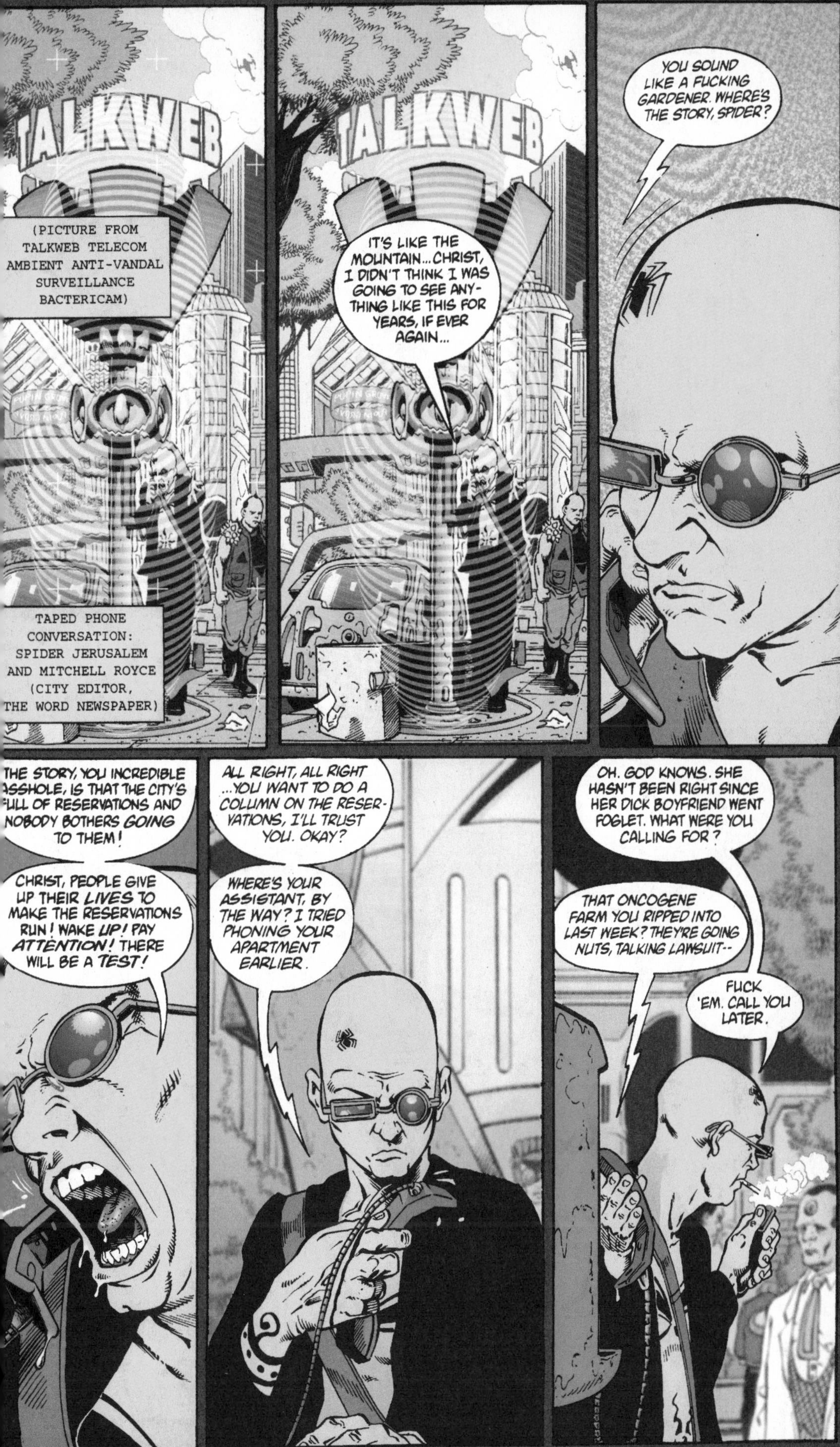
(PICTURE FROM TALKWEB TELECOM AMBIENT ANTI-VANDAL SURVEILLANCE BACTERICAM)
TAPED PHONE CONVERSATION: SPIDER JERUSALEM AND MITCHELL ROYCE (CITY EDITOR, THE WORD NEWSPAPER)
IT'S LIKE THE MOUNTAIN... CHRIST, I DIDN'T THINK I WAS GOING TO SEE ANYTHING LIKE THIS FOR YEARS, IF EVER AGAIN...
YOU SOUND LIKE A FUCKING GARDENER. WHERE'S THE STORY, SPIDER?
THE STORY, YOU INCREDIBLE ASSHOLE, IS THAT THE CITY'S FULL OF RESERVATIONS AND NOBODY BOTHERS GOING TO THEM!
CHRIST, PEOPLE GIVE UP THEIR LIVES TO MAKE THE RESERVATIONS RUN! WAKE UP! PAY ATTENTION! THERE WILL BE A TEST!
ALL RIGHT, ALL RIGHT ...YOU WANT TO DO A COLUMN ON THE RESERVATIONS, I'LL TRUST YOU. OKAY?
WHERE'S YOUR ASSISTANT, BY THE WAY? I TRIED PHONING YOUR APARTMENT EARLIER.
OH. GOD KNOWS. SHE HASN'T BEEN RIGHT SINCE HER DICK BOYFRIEND WENT FOGLET. WHAT WERE YOU CALLING FOR?
THAT ONCOGENE FARM YOU RIPPED INTO LAST WEEK? THEY'RE GOING NUTS, TALKING LAWSUIT--
FUCK 'EM. CALL YOU LATER.

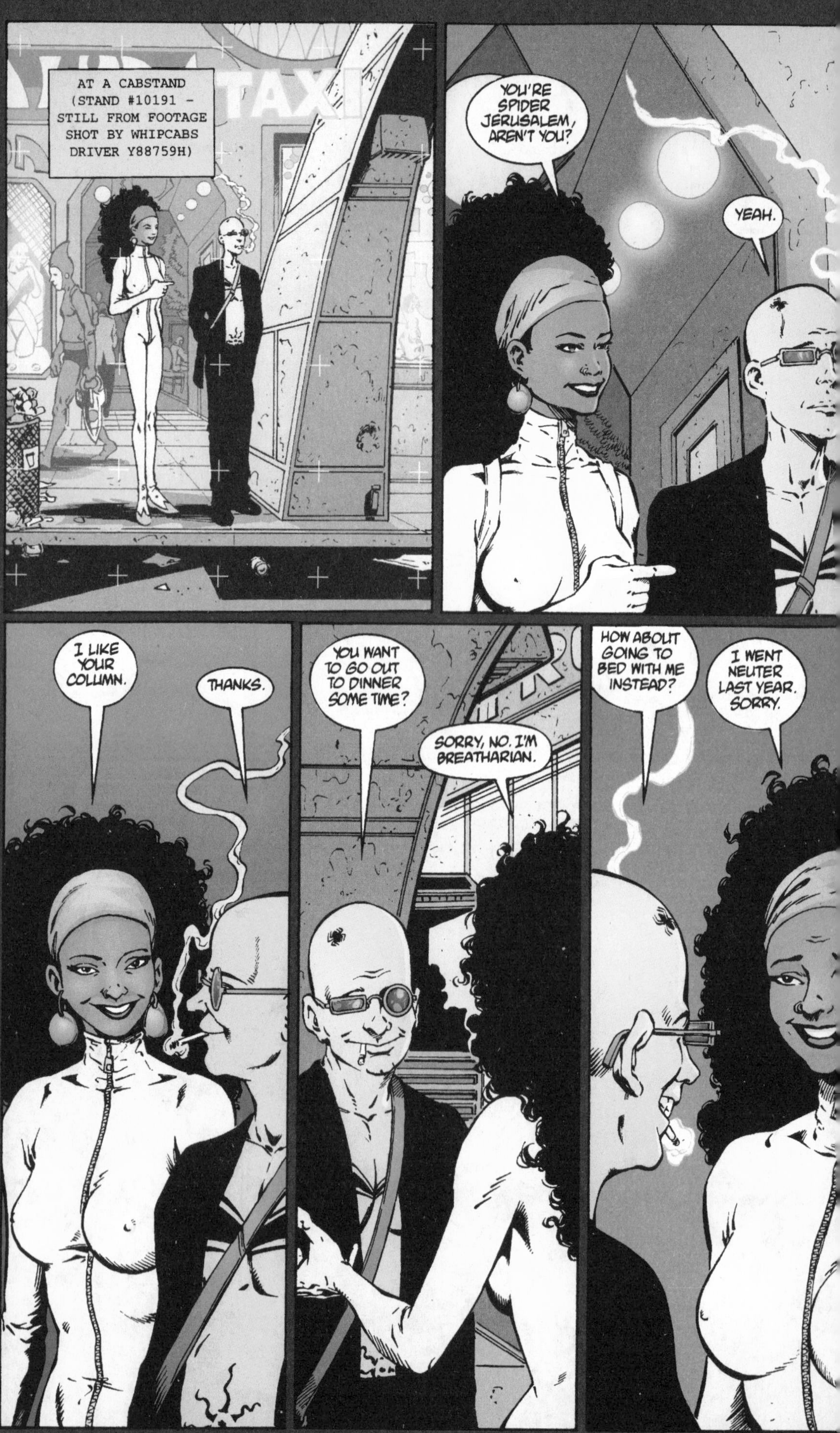
AT A CABSTAND (STAND #10191 - STILL FROM FOOTAGE SHOT BY WHIPCABS DRIVER Y88759H)
TAXI
YOU'RE SPIDER JERUSALEM, AREN'T YOU?
YEAH.
I LIKE YOUR COLUMN.
THANKS.
YOU WANT TO GO OUT TO DINNER SOME TIME?
SORRY, NO. I'M BREATHARIAN.
HOW ABOUT GOING TO BED WITH ME INSTEAD?
I WENT NEUTER LAST YEAR. SORRY.

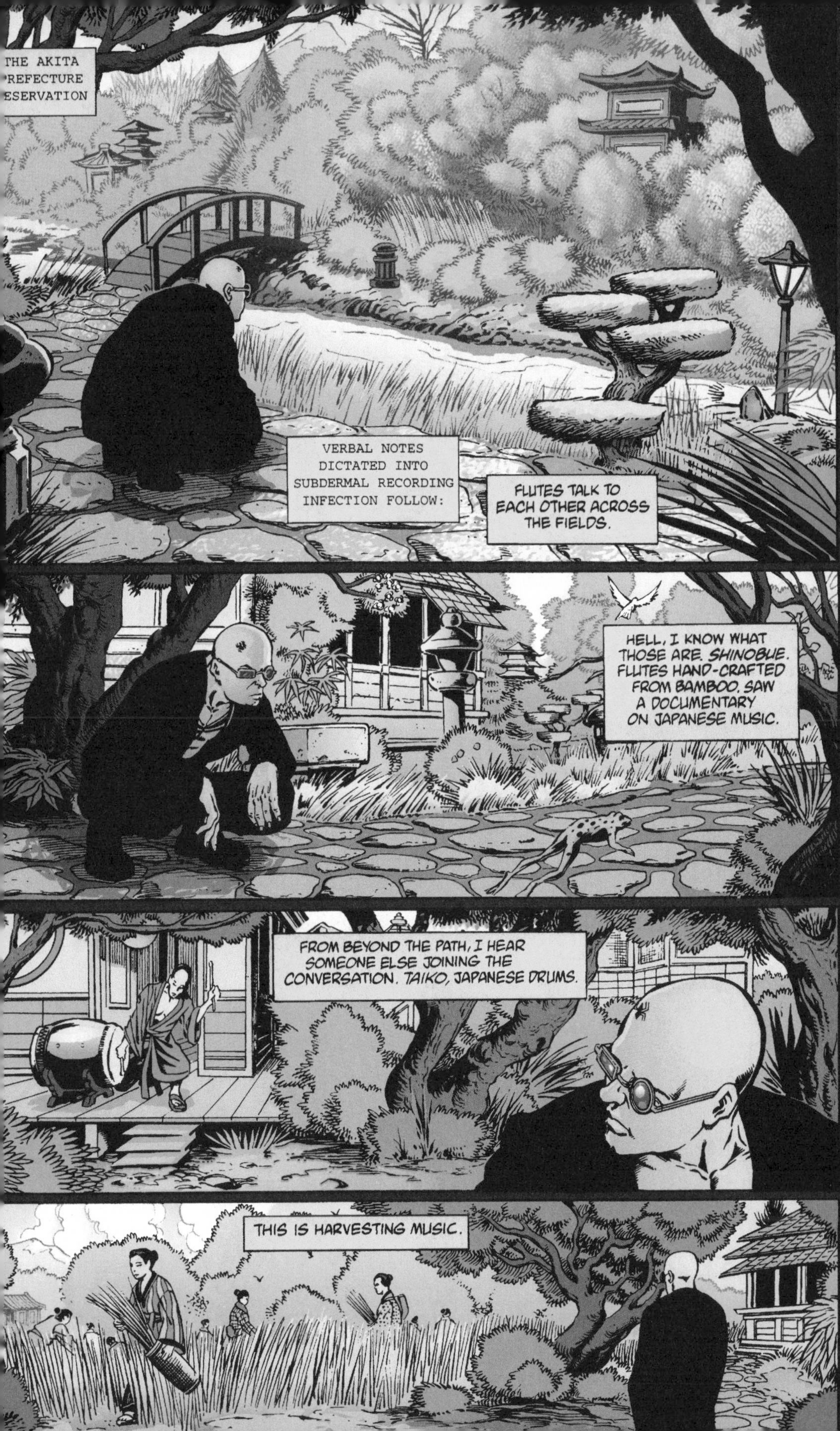
THE AKITA
REFECTURE
ESERVATION
VERBAL NOTES DICTATED INTO SUBDERMAL RECORDING INFECTION FOLLOW:
FLUTES TALK TO EACH OTHER ACROSS THE FIELDS.
HELL, I KNOW WHAT THOSE ARE. SHINOBUE. FLUTES HAND-CRAFTED FROM BAMBOO. SAW A DOCUMENTARY ON JAPANESE MUSIC.
FROM BEYOND THE PATH, I HEAR SOMEONE ELSE JOINING THE CONVERSATION. TAIKO, JAPANESE DRUMS.
THIS IS HARVESTING MUSIC.

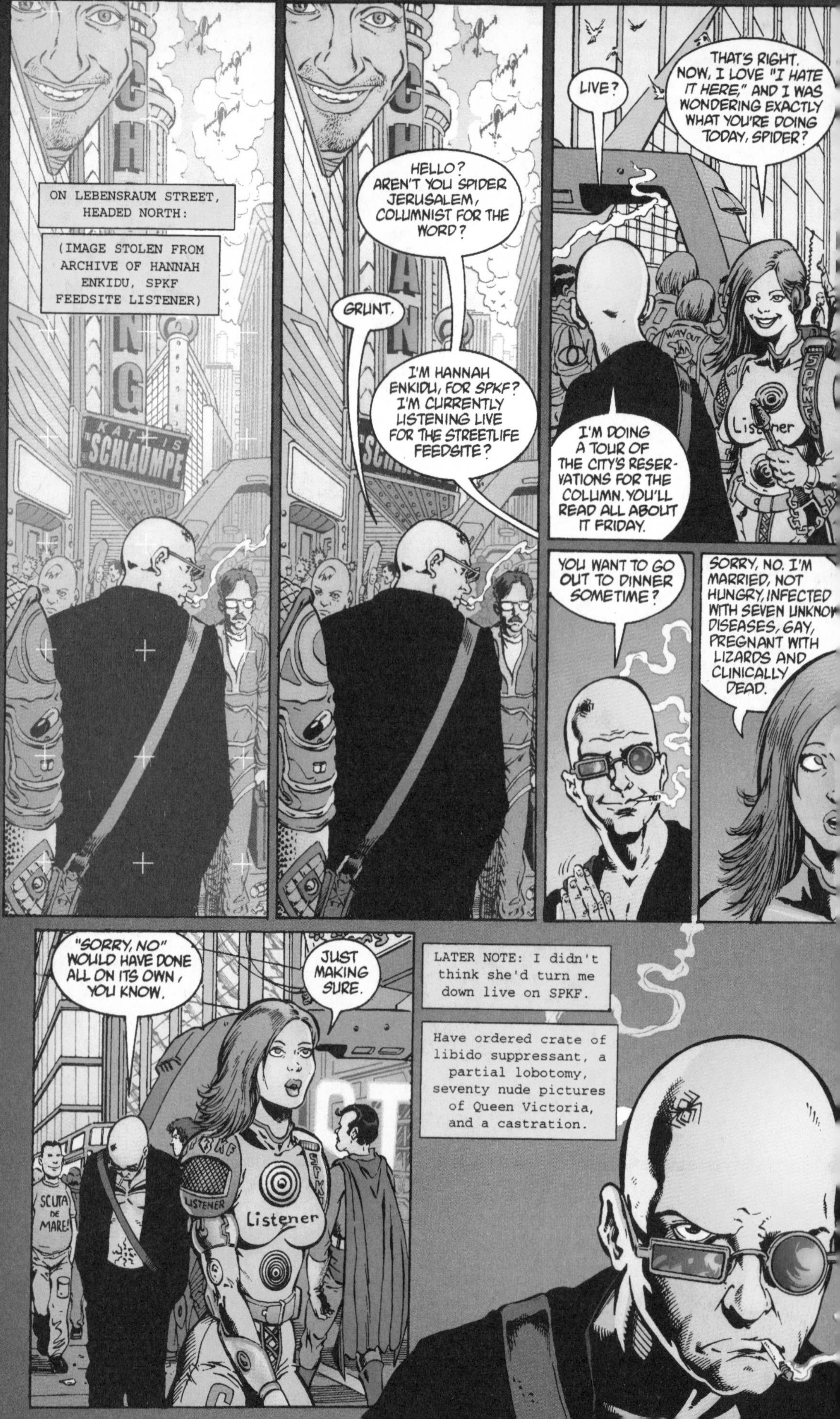
ON LEBENSRAUM STREET, HEADED NORTH:
(IMAGE STOLEN FROM ARCHIVE OF HANNAH ENKIDU, SPKF FEEDSITE LISTENER)
SCHLAUMPE
HELLO? AREN'T YOU SPIDER JERUSALEM, COLUMNIST FOR THE WORD?
GRUNT.
I'M HANNAH ENKIDU, FOR SPKF? I'M CURRENTLY LISTENING LIVE FOR THE STREETLIFE FEEDSITE?
LIVE?
THAT'S RIGHT. NOW, I LOVE "I HATE IT HERE," AND I WAS WONDERING EXACTLY WHAT YOU'RE DOING TODAY, SPIDER?
I'M DOING A TOUR OF THE CITY'S RESERVATIONS FOR THE COLUMN. YOU'LL READ ALL ABOUT IT FRIDAY.
Listener
YOU WANT TO GO OUT TO DINNER SOMETIME?
SORRY, NO. I'M MARRIED, NOT HUNGRY, INFECTED WITH SEVEN UNKNOW DISEASES, GAY, PREGNANT WITH LIZARDS AND CLINICALLY DEAD.
"SORRY, NO" WOULD HAVE DONE ALL ON ITS OWN, YOU KNOW.
JUST MAKING SURE.
LATER NOTE: I didn't think she'd turn me down live on SPKF.
Have ordered crate of libido suppressant, a partial lobotomy, seventy nude pictures of Queen Victoria, and a castration.
SCUTA DE MARE!
LISTENER
Listener

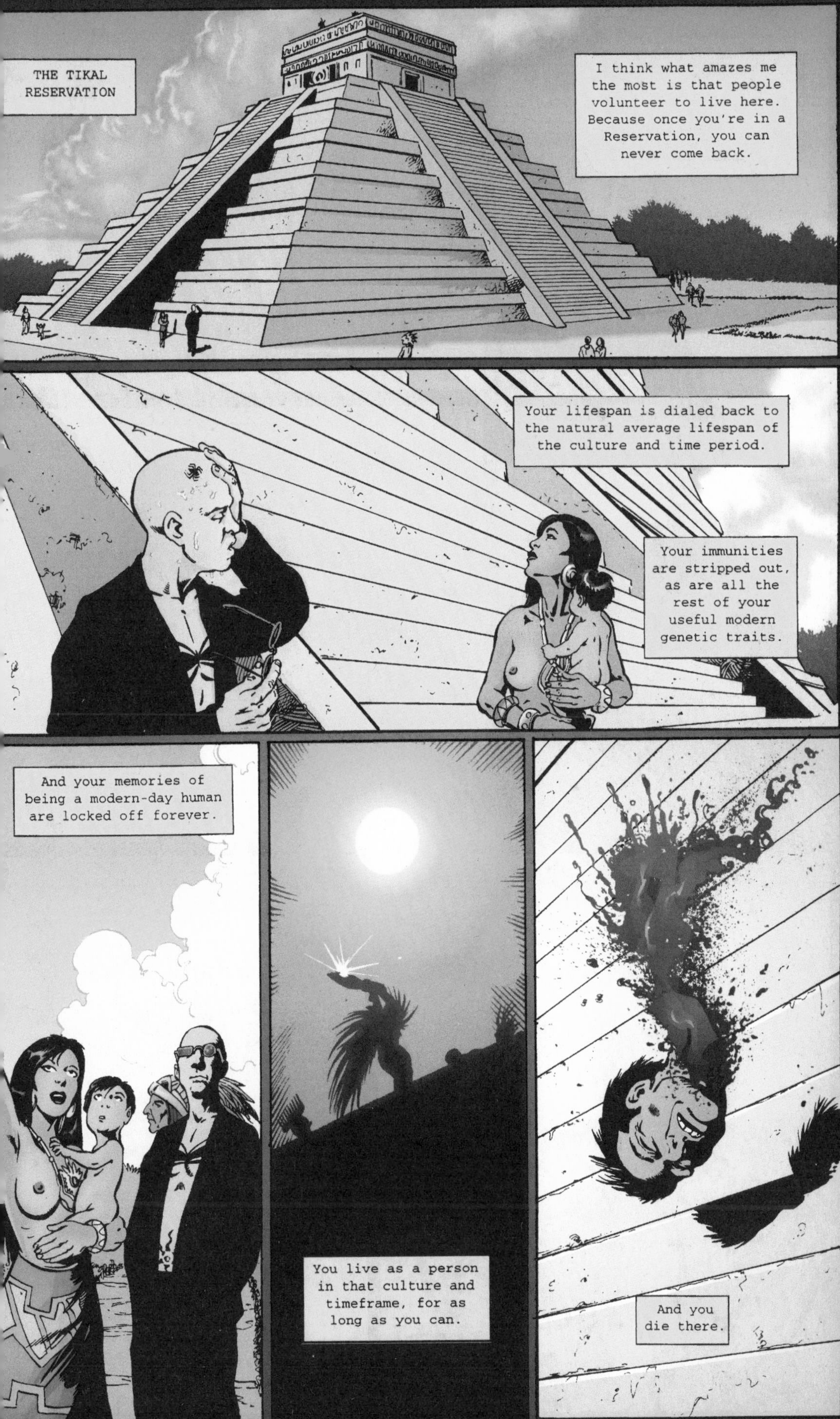
THE TIKAL RESERVATION
I think what amazes me the most is that people volunteer to live here. Because once you're in a Reservation, you can never come back.
Your lifespan is dialed back to the natural average lifespan of the culture and time period.
Your immunities are stripped out, as are all the rest of your useful modern genetic traits.
And your memories of being a modern-day human are locked off forever.
You live as a person in that culture and timeframe, for as long as you can.
And you die there.

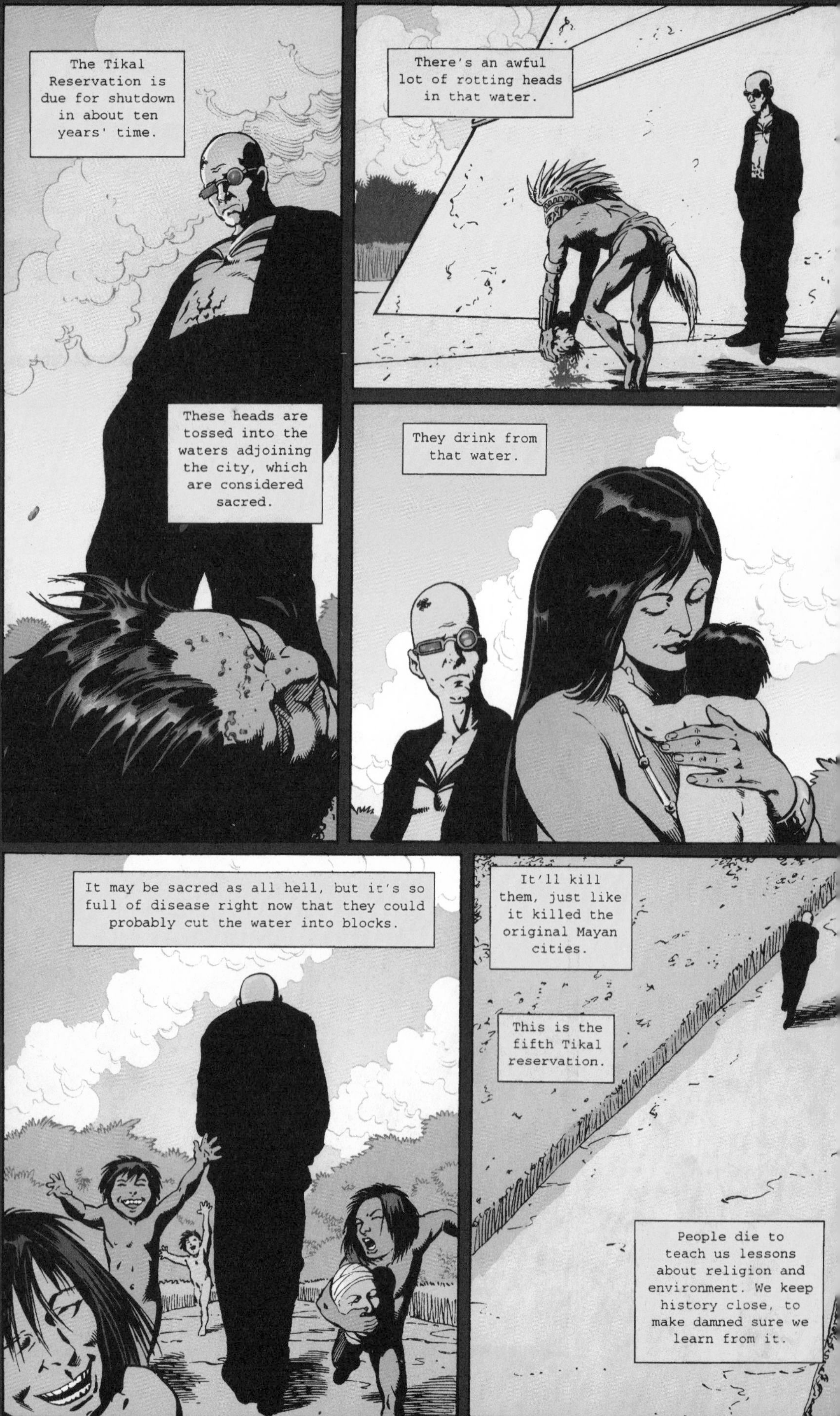
The Tikal Reservation is due for shutdown in about ten years' time.
These heads are tossed into the waters adjoining the city, which are considered sacred.
There's an awful lot of rotting heads in that water.
They drink from that water.
It may be sacred as all hell, but it's so full of disease right now that they could probably cut the water into blocks.
It'll kill them, just like it killed the original Mayan cities.
This is the fifth Tikal reservation.
People die to teach us lessons about religion and environment. We keep history close, to make damned sure we learn from it.

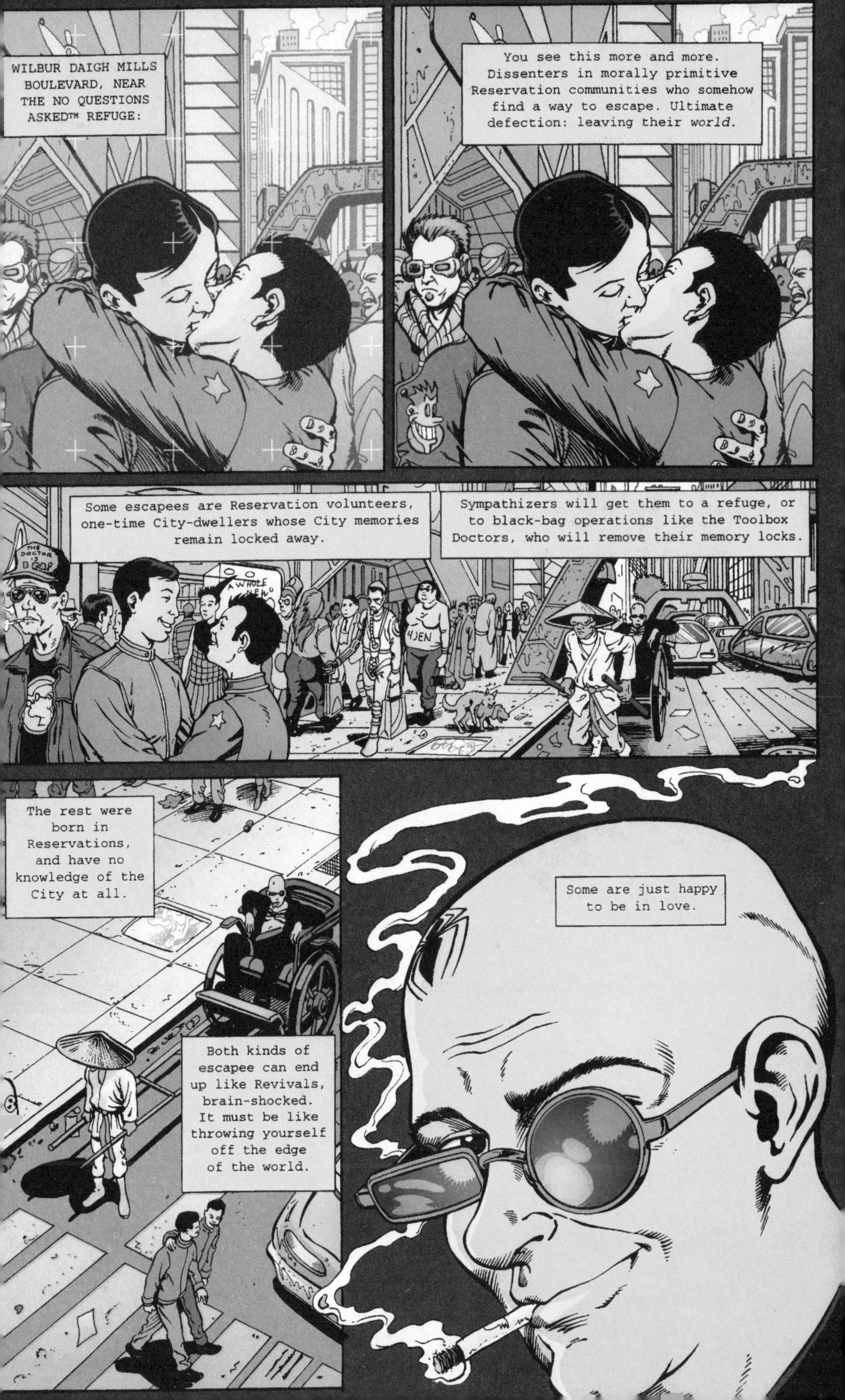

WILBUR DAIGH MILLS BOULEVARD, NEAR THE NO QUESTIONS ASKED™ REFUGE:
You see this more and more. Dissenters in morally primitive Reservation communities who somehow find a way to escape. Ultimate defection: leaving their *world*.
Some escapees are Reservation volunteers, one-time City-dwellers whose City memories remain locked away.
Sympathizers will get them to a refuge, or to black-bag operations like the Toolbox Doctors, who will remove their memory locks.
The rest were born in Reservations, and have no knowledge of the City at all.
Both kinds of escapee can end up like Revivals, brain-shocked. It must be like throwing yourself off the edge of the world.
Some are just happy to be in love.

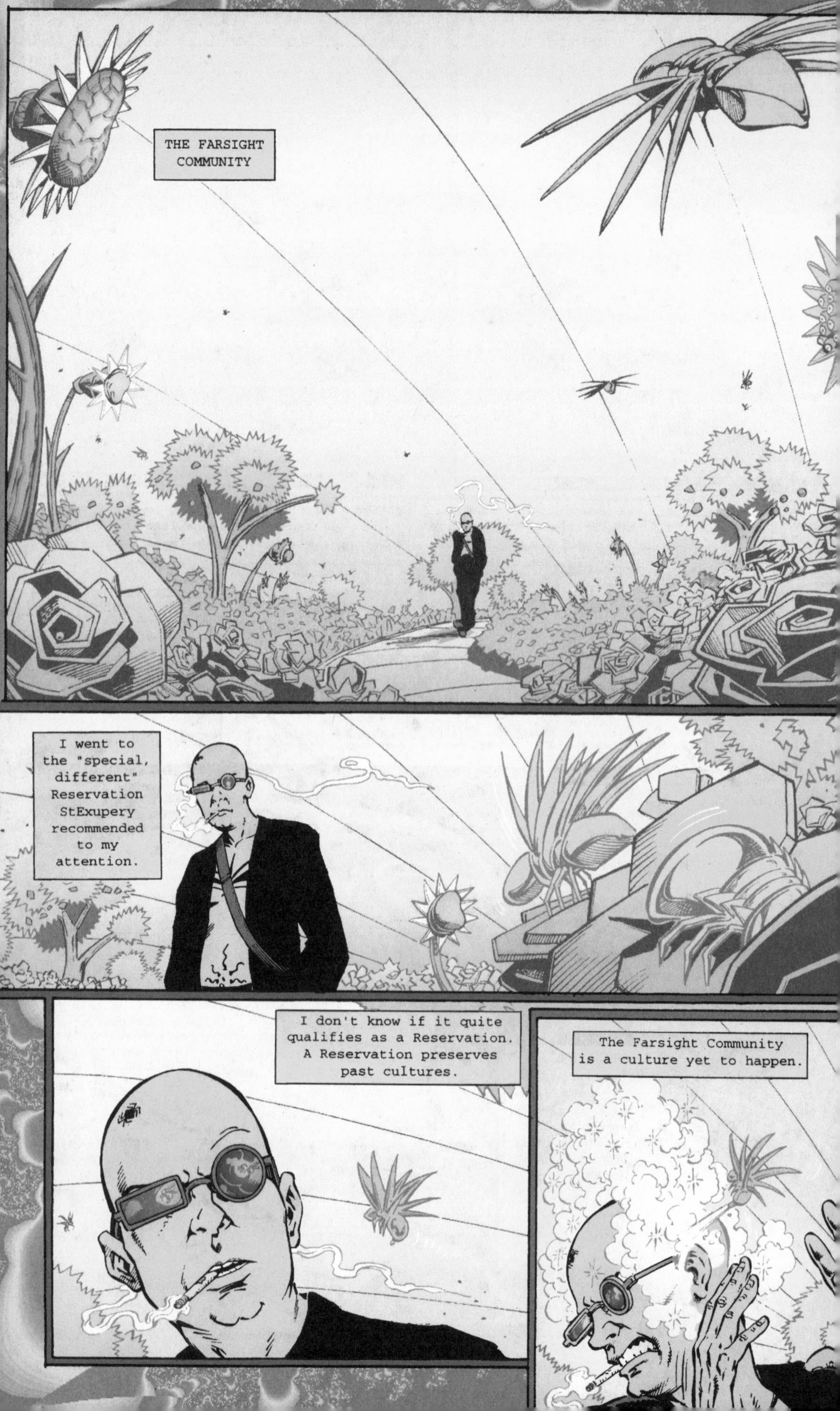
THE FARSIGHT COMMUNITY
I went to the "special, different" Reservation StExupery recommended to my attention.
I don't know if it quite qualifies as a Reservation. A Reservation preserves past cultures.
The Farsight Community is a culture yet to happen.

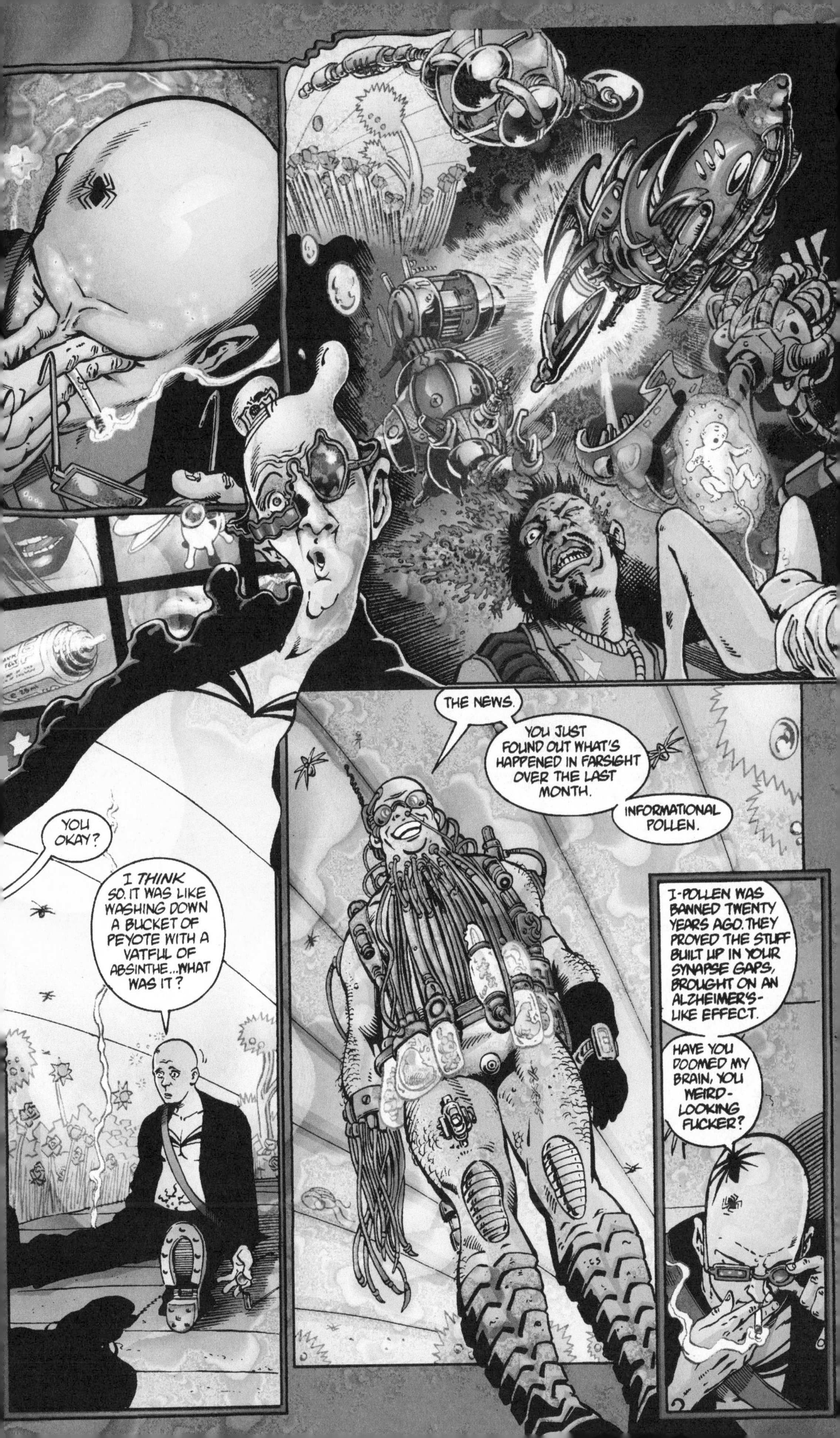
YOU OKAY?
I THINK SO. IT WAS LIKE WASHING DOWN A BUCKET OF PEYOTE WITH A VATFUL OF ABSINTHE...WHAT WAS IT?
THE NEWS.
YOU JUST FOUND OUT WHAT'S HAPPENED IN FARSIGHT OVER THE LAST MONTH.
INFORMATIONAL POLLEN.
I-POLLEN WAS BANNED TWENTY YEARS AGO. THEY PROVED THE STUFF BUILT UP IN YOUR SYNAPSE GAPS, BROUGHT ON AN ALZHEIMER'S-LIKE EFFECT.
HAVE YOU DOOMED MY BRAIN, YOU WEIRD-LOOKING FUCKER?

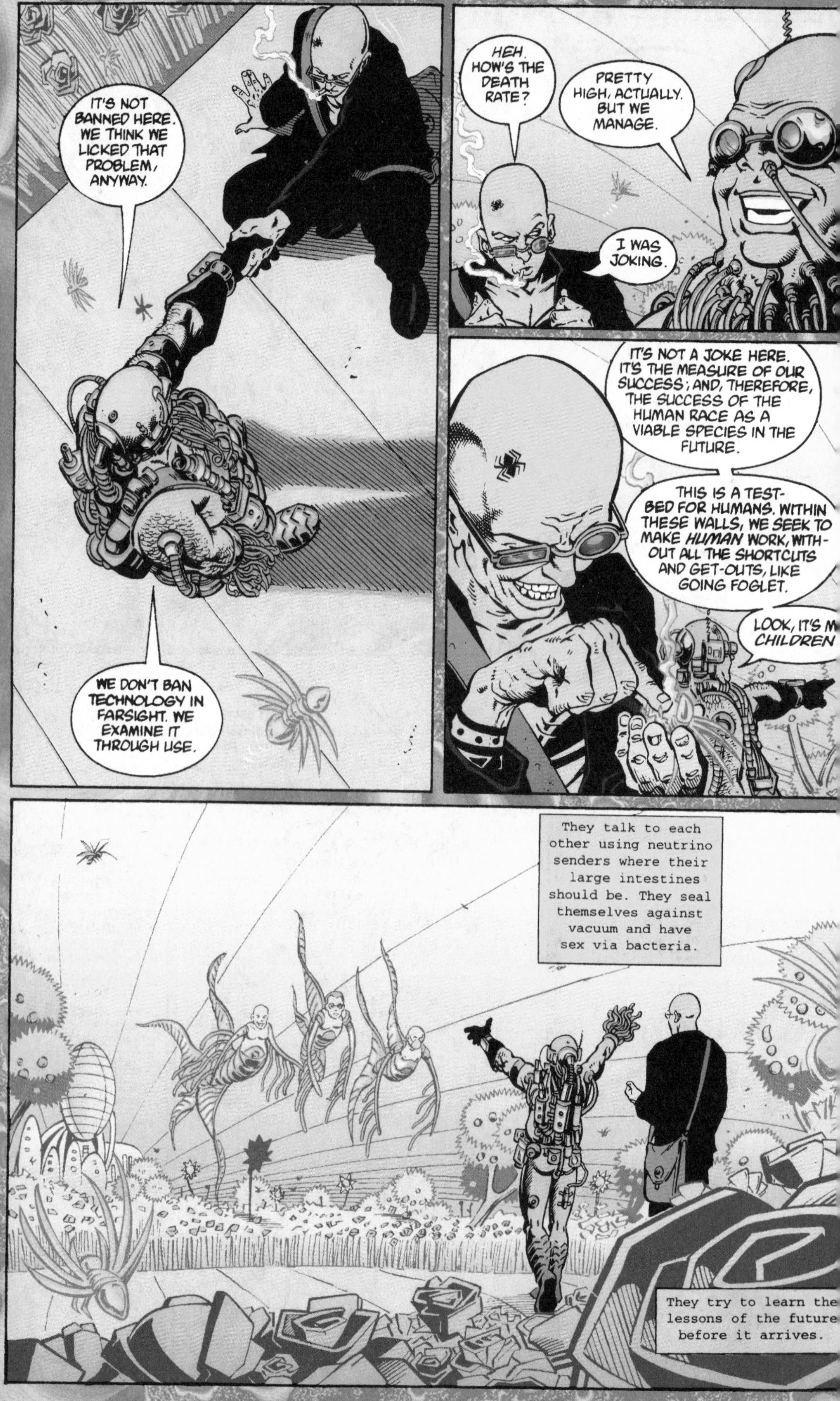
IT'S NOT BANNED HERE. WE THINK WE LICKED THAT PROBLEM, ANYWAY.
WE DON'T BAN TECHNOLOGY IN FARSIGHT. WE EXAMINE IT THROUGH USE.
HEH. HOW'S THE DEATH RATE?
PRETTY HIGH, ACTUALLY. BUT WE MANAGE.
I WAS JOKING.
IT'S NOT A JOKE HERE. IT'S THE MEASURE OF OUR SUCCESS; AND, THEREFORE, THE SUCCESS OF THE HUMAN RACE AS A VIABLE SPECIES IN THE FUTURE.
THIS IS A TEST-BED FOR HUMANS. WITHIN THESE WALLS, WE SEEK TO MAKE HUMAN WORK, WITH-OUT ALL THE SHORTCUTS AND GET-OUTS, LIKE GOING FOGLET.
They talk to each other using neutrino senders where their large intestines should be. They seal themselves against vacuum and have sex via bacteria.
They try to learn the lessons of the future before it arrives.

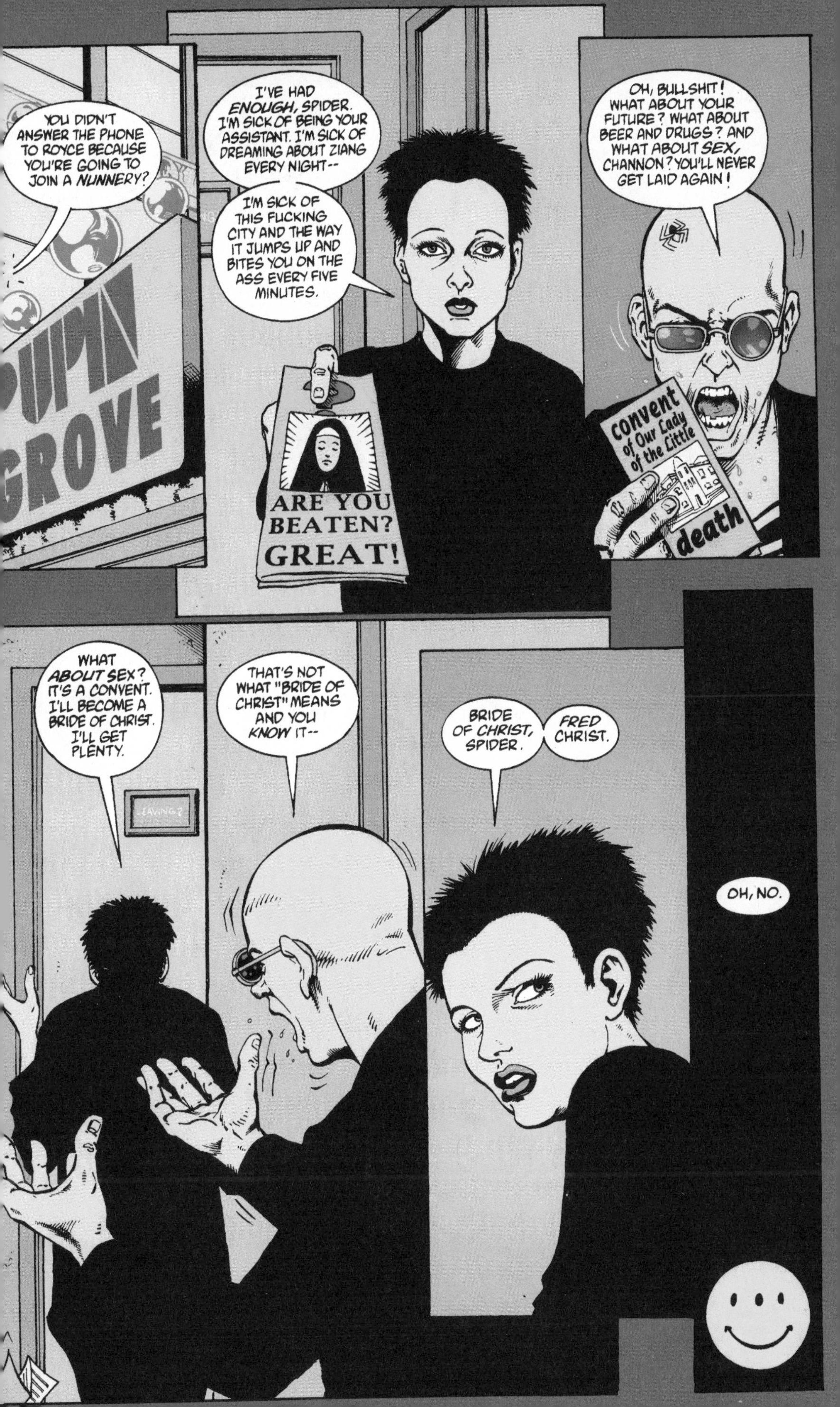
YOU DIDN'T ANSWER THE PHONE TO ROYCE BECAUSE YOU'RE GOING TO JOIN A NUNNERY?
I'VE HAD ENOUGH, SPIDER. I'M SICK OF BEING YOUR ASSISTANT. I'M SICK OF DREAMING ABOUT ZIANG EVERY NIGHT--
I'M SICK OF THIS FUCKING CITY AND THE WAY IT JUMPS UP AND BITES YOU ON THE ASS EVERY FIVE MINUTES.
GROVE
ARE YOU BEATEN? GREAT!
OH, BULLSHIT! WHAT ABOUT YOUR FUTURE? WHAT ABOUT BEER AND DRUGS? AND WHAT ABOUT SEX, CHANNON? YOU'LL NEVER GET LAID AGAIN!
convent of Our Lady of the Little death
WHAT ABOUT SEX? IT'S A CONVENT. I'LL BECOME A BRIDE OF CHRIST. I'LL GET PLENTY.
LEAVING?
THAT'S NOT WHAT "BRIDE OF CHRIST" MEANS AND YOU KNOW IT--
BRIDE OF CHRIST, SPIDER.
FRED CHRIST.
OH, NO.

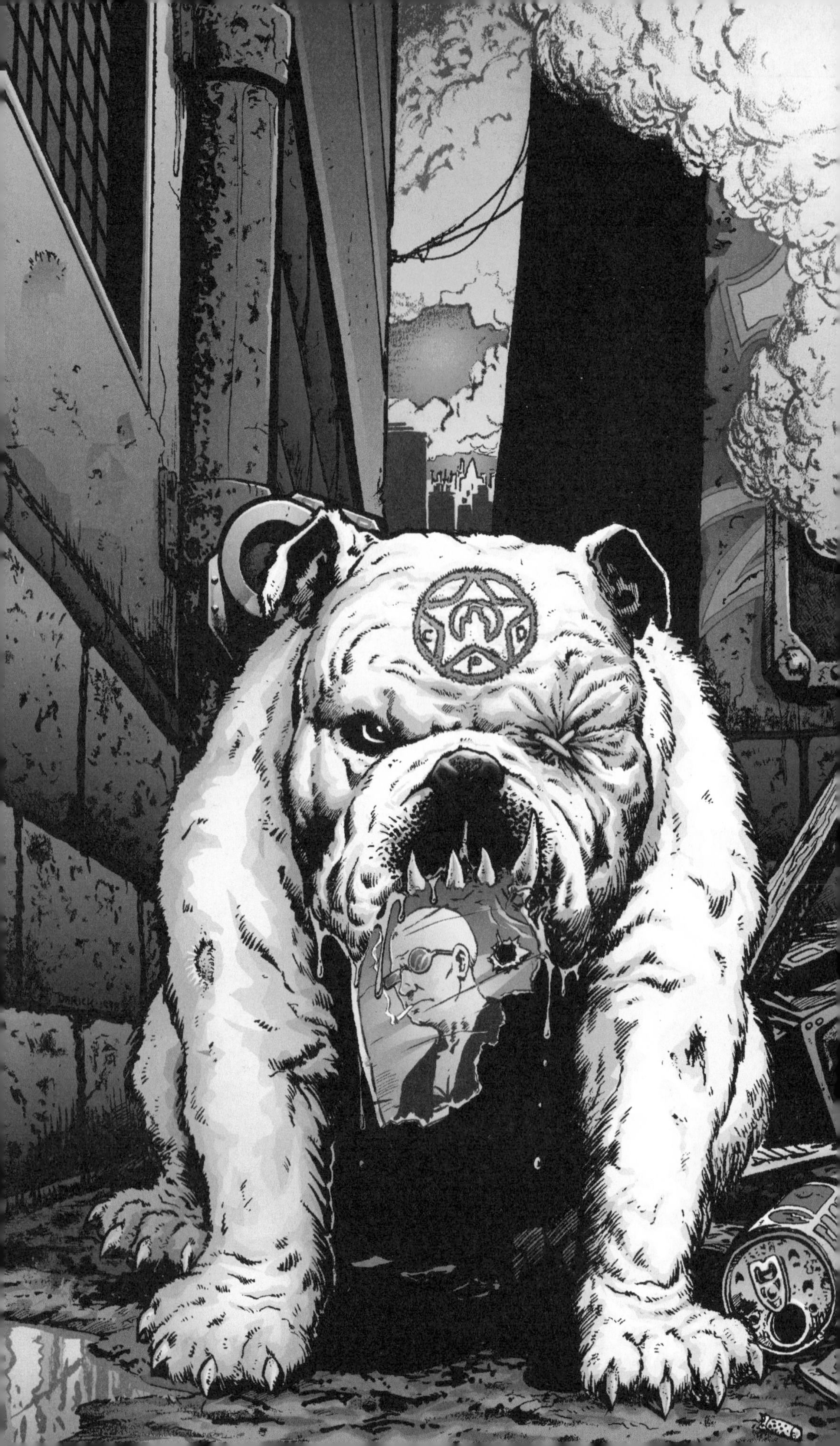

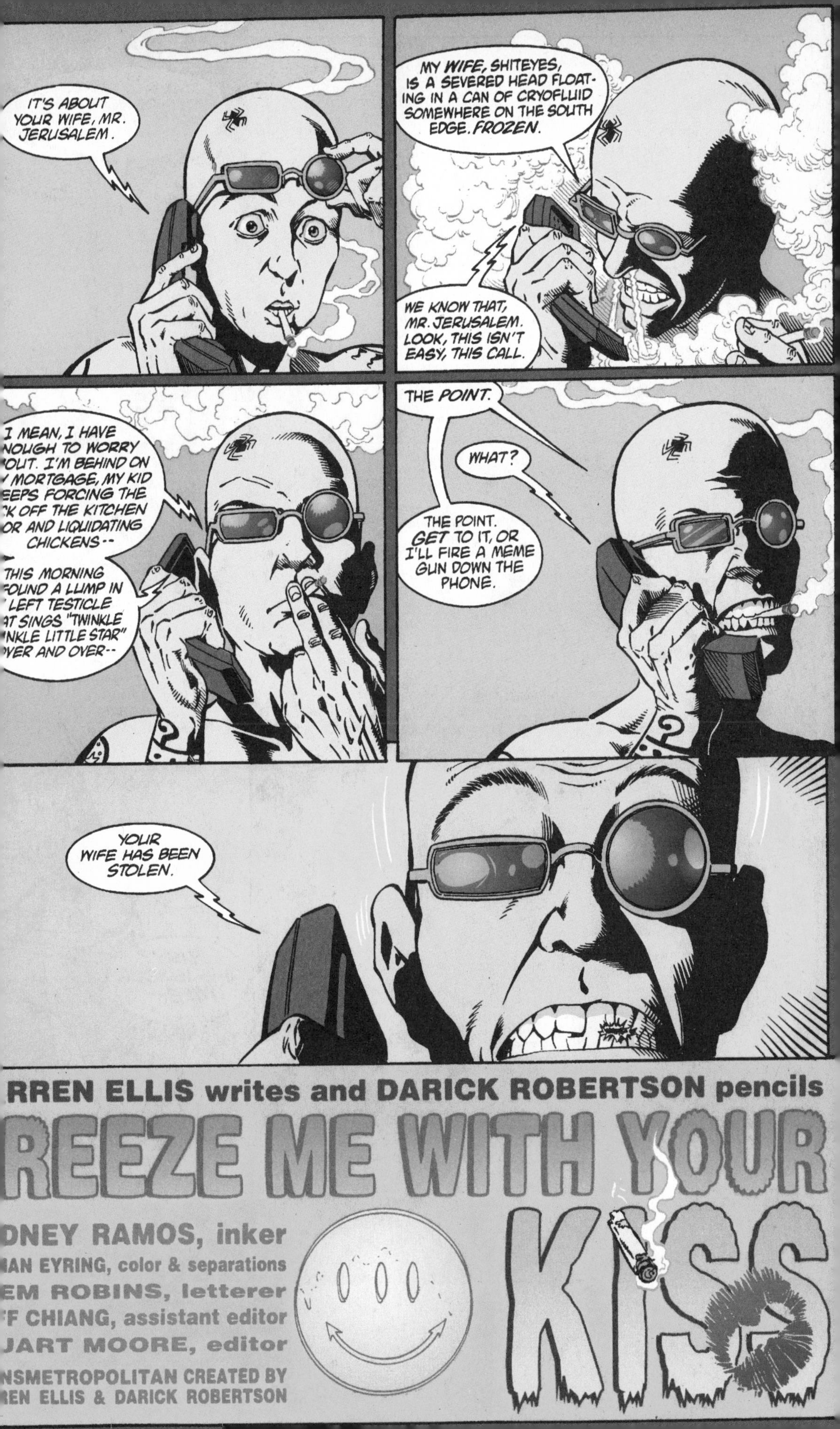
IT'S ABOUT YOUR WIFE, MR. JERUSALEM.
MY WIFE, SHITEYES, IS A SEVERED HEAD FLOATING IN A CAN OF CRYOFLUID SOMEWHERE ON THE SOUTH EDGE. FROZEN.
WE KNOW THAT, MR. JERUSALEM. LOOK, THIS ISN'T EASY, THIS CALL.
I MEAN, I HAVE NOUGH TO WORRY OUT. I'M BEHIND ON MORTGAGE, MY KID EEPS FORCING THE CK OFF THE KITCHEN OR AND LIQUIDATING CHICKENS--
THIS MORNING FOUND A LUMP IN LEFT TESTICLE AT SINGS "TWINKLE NKLE LITTLE STAR" VER AND OVER--
THE POINT.
WHAT?
THE POINT. GET TO IT, OR I'LL FIRE A MEME GUN DOWN THE PHONE.
YOUR WIFE HAS BEEN STOLEN.
RREN ELLIS writes and DARICK ROBERTSON pencils
REEZE ME WITH YOUR KISS
ONEY RAMOS, inker
AN EYRING, color & separations
EM ROBINS, letterer
F CHIANG, assistant editor
JART MOORE, editor
NSMETROPOLITAN CREATED BY
REN ELLIS & DARICK ROBERTSON

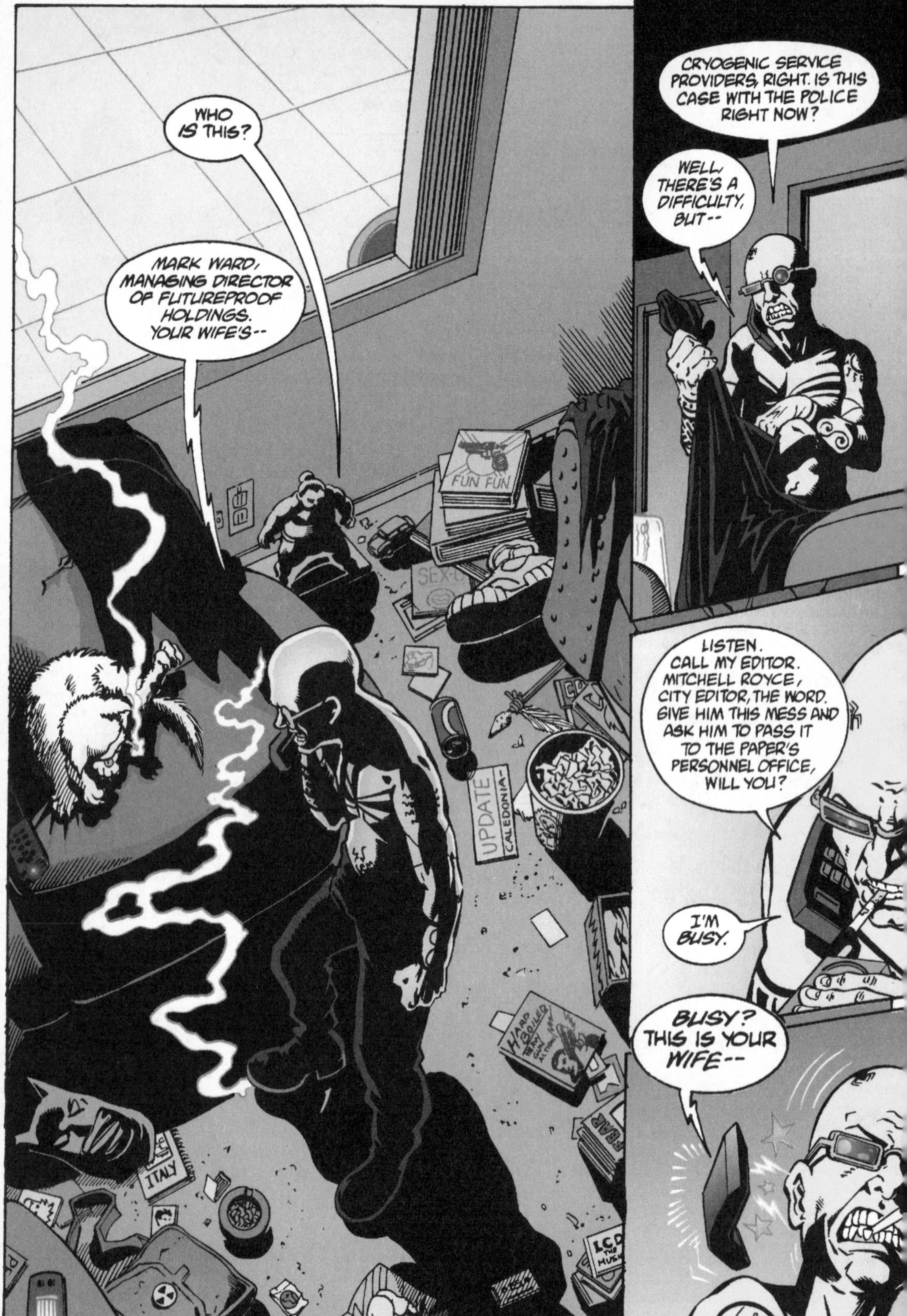

WHO IS THIS?
MARK WARD, MANAGING DIRECTOR OF FUTUREPROOF HOLDINGS. YOUR WIFE'S--
CRYOGENIC SERVICE PROVIDERS, RIGHT. IS THIS CASE WITH THE POLICE RIGHT NOW?
WELL, THERE'S A DIFFICULTY, BUT--
LISTEN. CALL MY EDITOR. MITCHELL ROYCE, CITY EDITOR, THE WORD. GIVE HIM THIS MESS AND ASK HIM TO PASS IT TO THE PAPER'S PERSONNEL OFFICE, WILL YOU?
I'M BUSY.
BUSY? THIS IS YOUR WIFE--
FUN FUN
UPDATE
CALEDONIA
ITALY
SWING

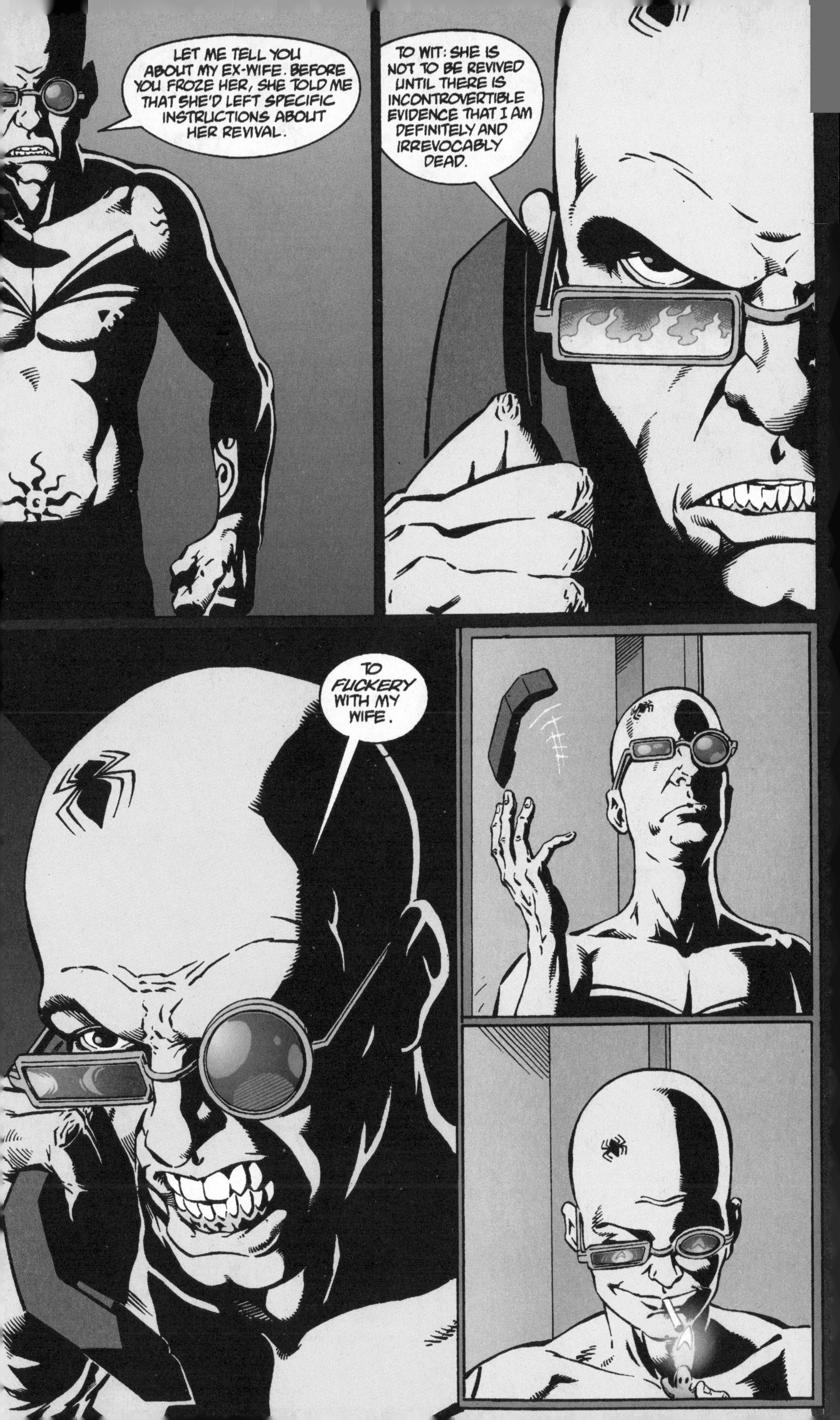
LET ME TELL YOU ABOUT MY EX-WIFE. BEFORE YOU FROZE HER, SHE TOLD ME THAT SHE'D LEFT SPECIFIC INSTRUCTIONS ABOUT HER REVIVAL.
TO WIT: SHE IS NOT TO BE REVIVED UNTIL THERE IS INCONTROVERTIBLE EVIDENCE THAT I AM DEFINITELY AND IRREVOCABLY DEAD.
TO FUCKERY WITH MY WIFE.

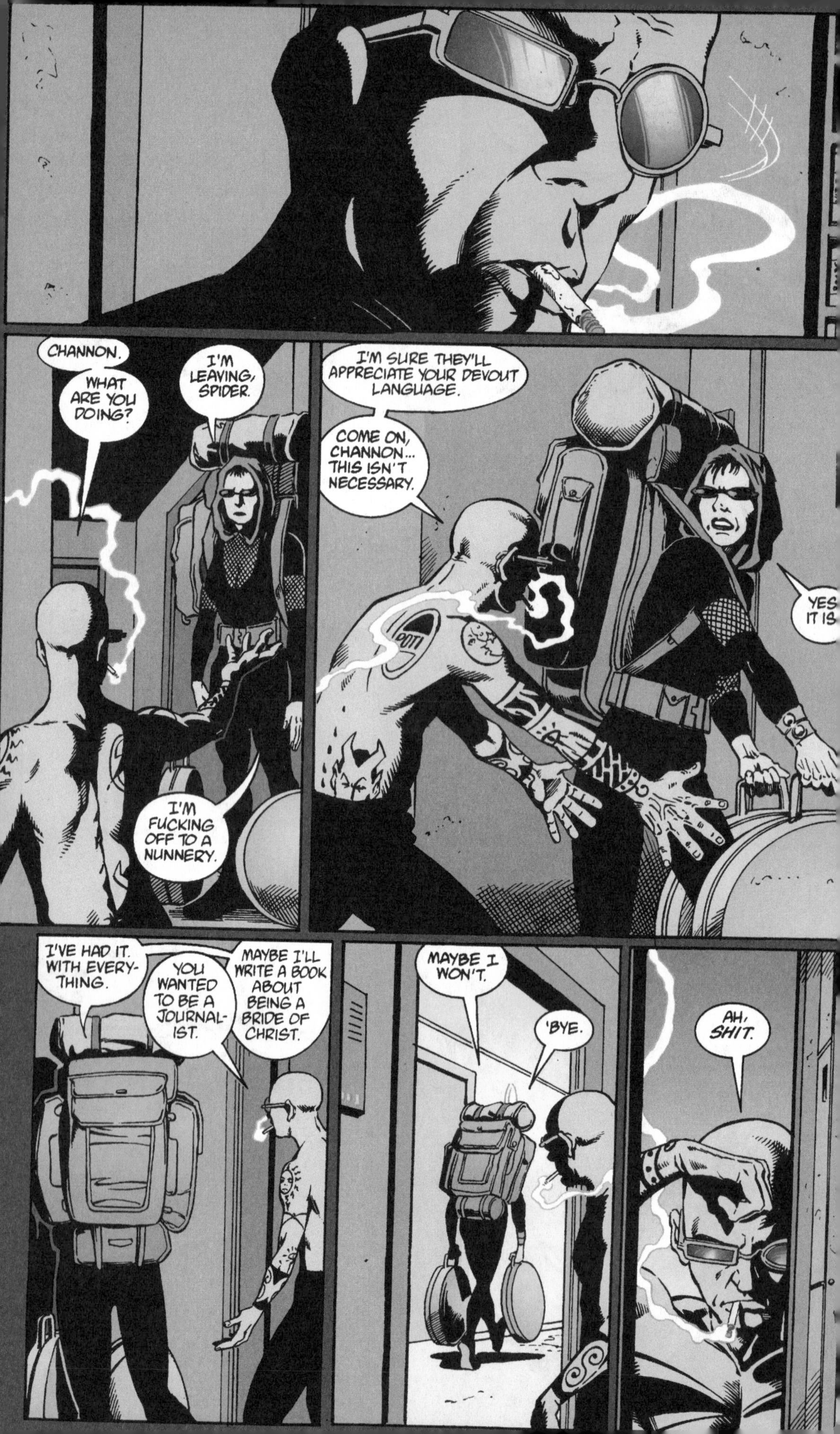
CHANNON.
WHAT ARE YOU DOING?
I'M LEAVING, SPIDER.
I'M FUCKING OFF TO A NUNNERY.
I'M SURE THEY'LL APPRECIATE YOUR DEVOUT LANGUAGE.
COME ON, CHANNON... THIS ISN'T NECESSARY.
YES IT IS
I'VE HAD IT. WITH EVERY-THING.
YOU WANTED TO BE A JOURNAL-IST.
MAYBE I'LL WRITE A BOOK ABOUT BEING A BRIDE OF CHRIST.
MAYBE I WON'T.
'BYE.
AH, SHIT.

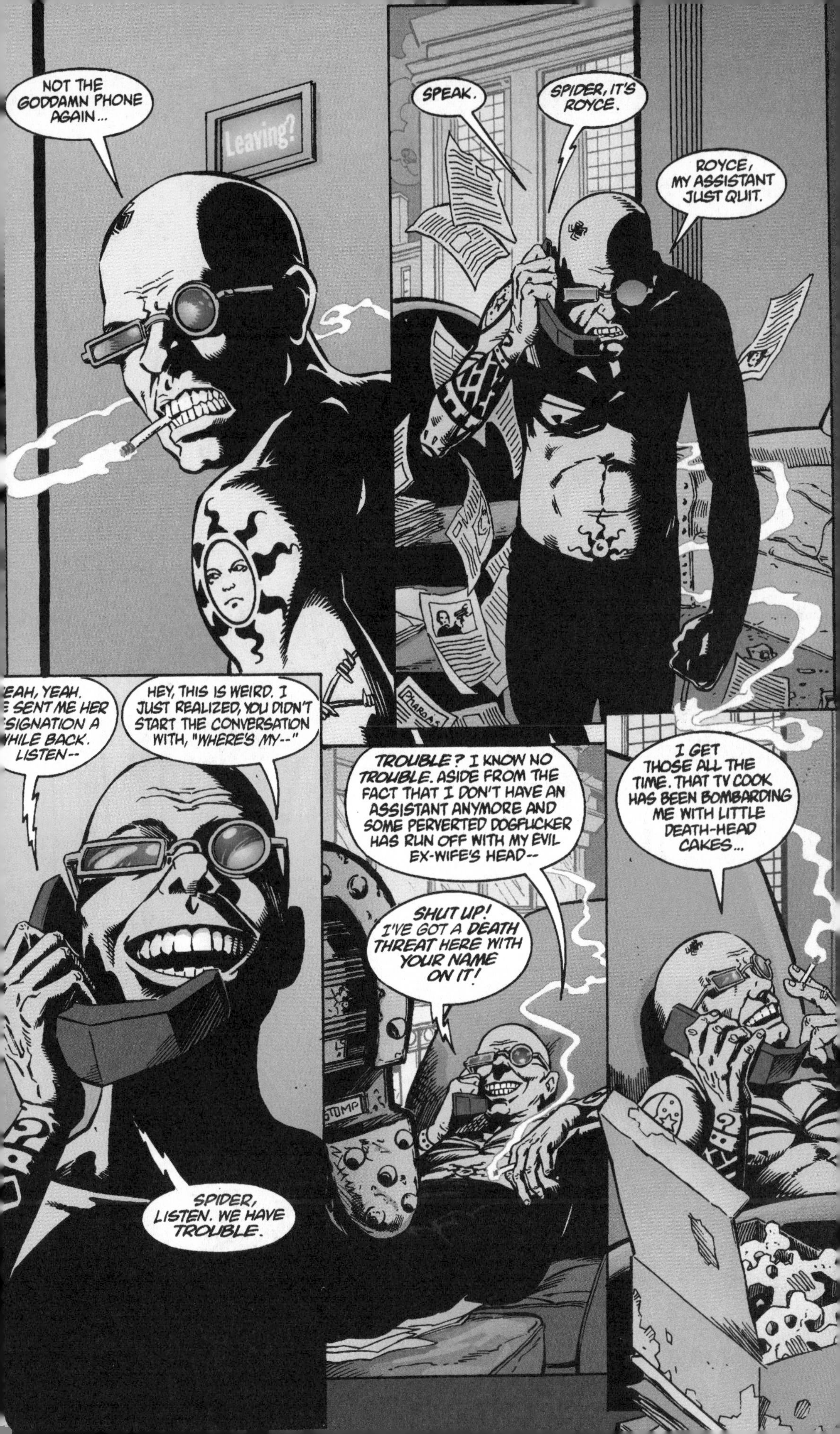

NOT THE GODDAMN PHONE AGAIN...
Leaving?
SPEAK.
SPIDER, IT'S ROYCE.
ROYCE, MY ASSISTANT JUST QUIT.
EAH, YEAH. E SENT ME HER SIGNATION A WHILE BACK. LISTEN--
HEY, THIS IS WEIRD. I JUST REALIZED, YOU DIDN'T START THE CONVERSATION WITH, "WHERE'S MY--"
SPIDER, LISTEN. WE HAVE TROUBLE.
TROUBLE? I KNOW NO TROUBLE. ASIDE FROM THE FACT THAT I DON'T HAVE AN ASSISTANT ANYMORE AND SOME PERVERTED DOGFUCKER HAS RUN OFF WITH MY EVIL EX-WIFE'S HEAD--
SHUT UP! I'VE GOT A DEATH THREAT HERE WITH YOUR NAME ON IT!
I GET THOSE ALL THE TIME. THAT TV COOK HAS BEEN BOMBARDING ME WITH LITTLE DEATH-HEAD CAKES...

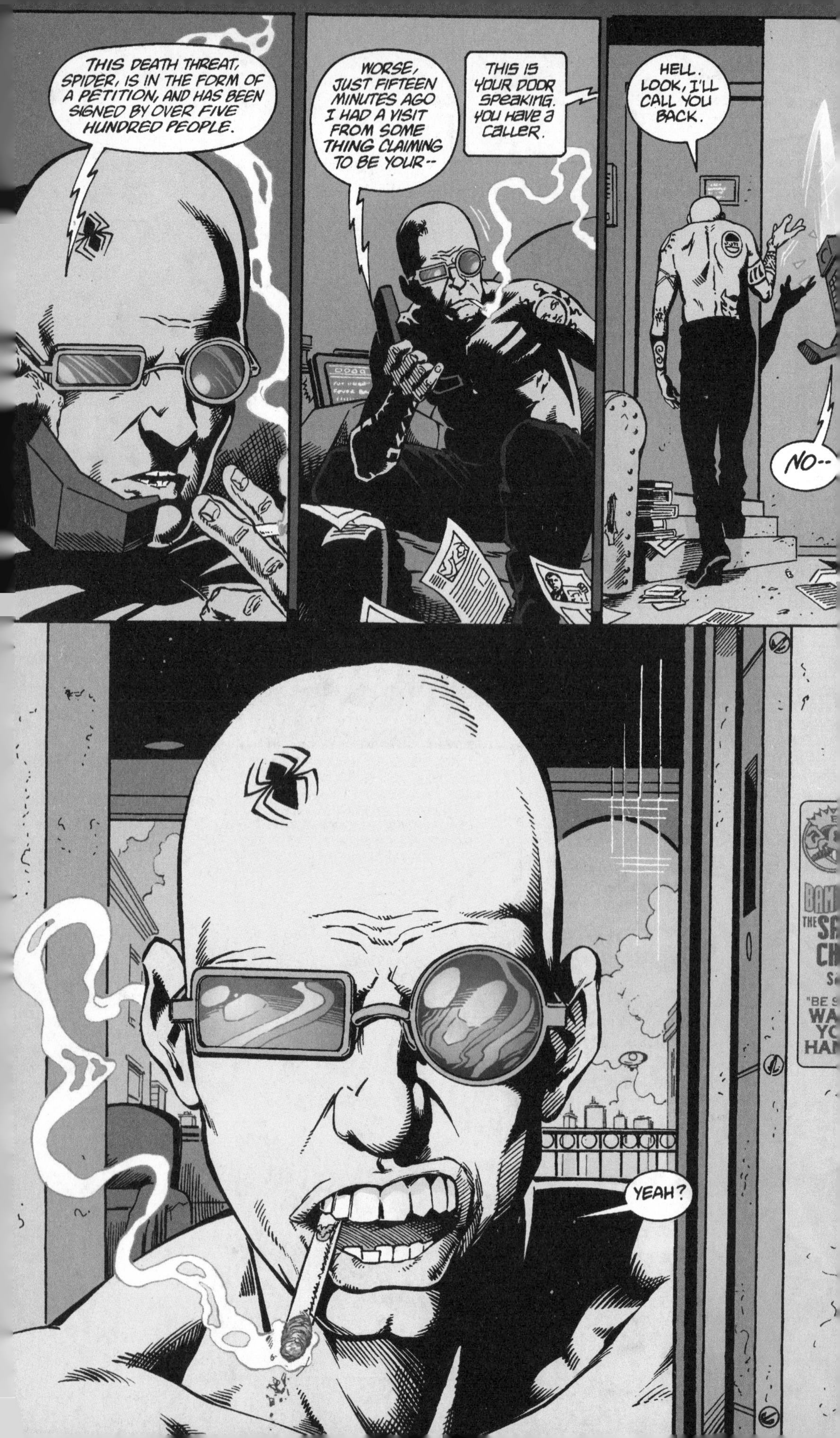
THIS DEATH THREAT, SPIDER, IS IN THE FORM OF A PETITION, AND HAS BEEN SIGNED BY OVER FIVE HUNDRED PEOPLE.
WORSE, JUST FIFTEEN MINUTES AGO I HAD A VISIT FROM SOME THING CLAIMING TO BE YOUR--
THIS IS YOUR DOOR SPEAKING. YOU HAVE A CALLER.
HELL. LOOK, I'LL CALL YOU BACK.
NO--
YEAH?

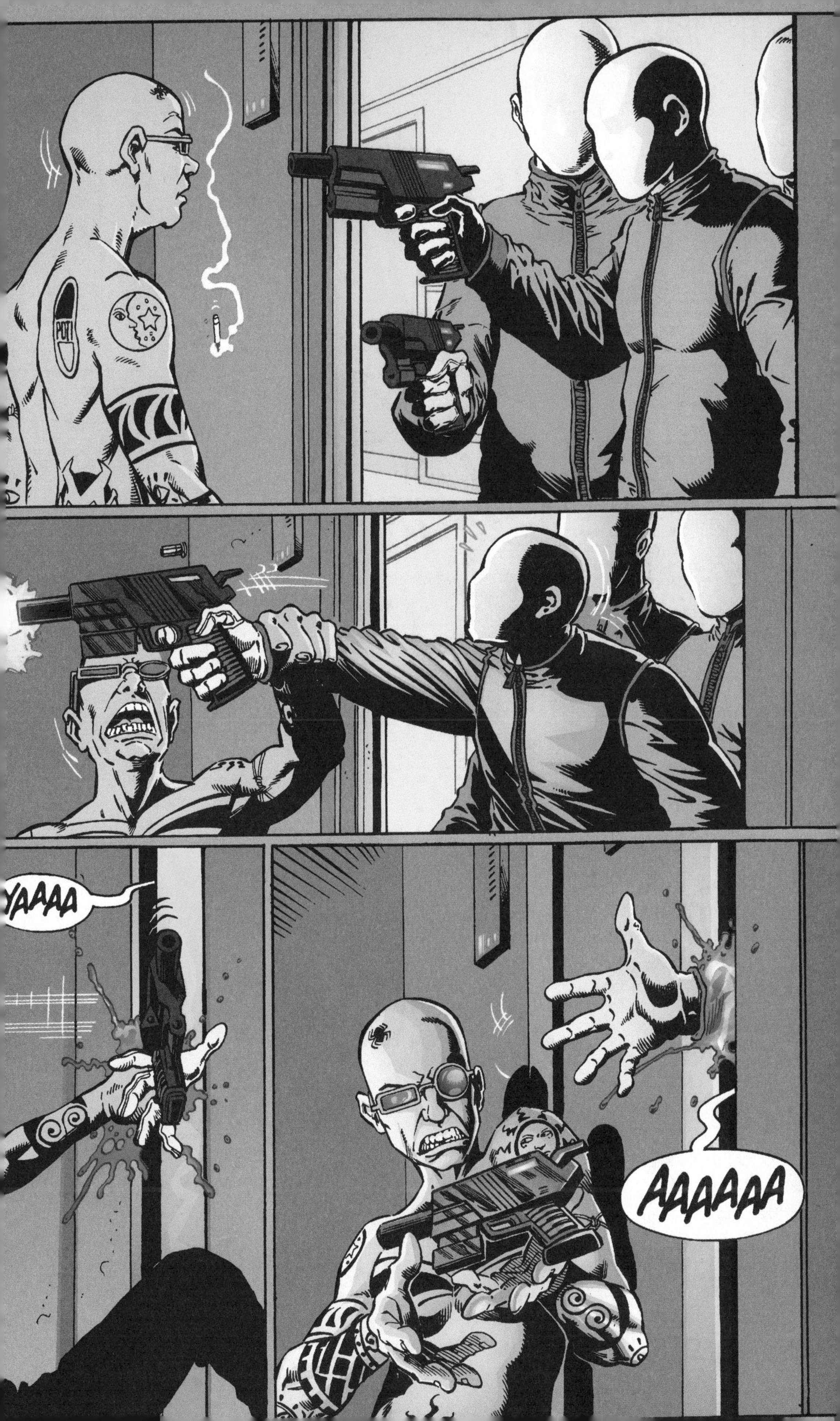
POTI
YAAAA
AAAAAA

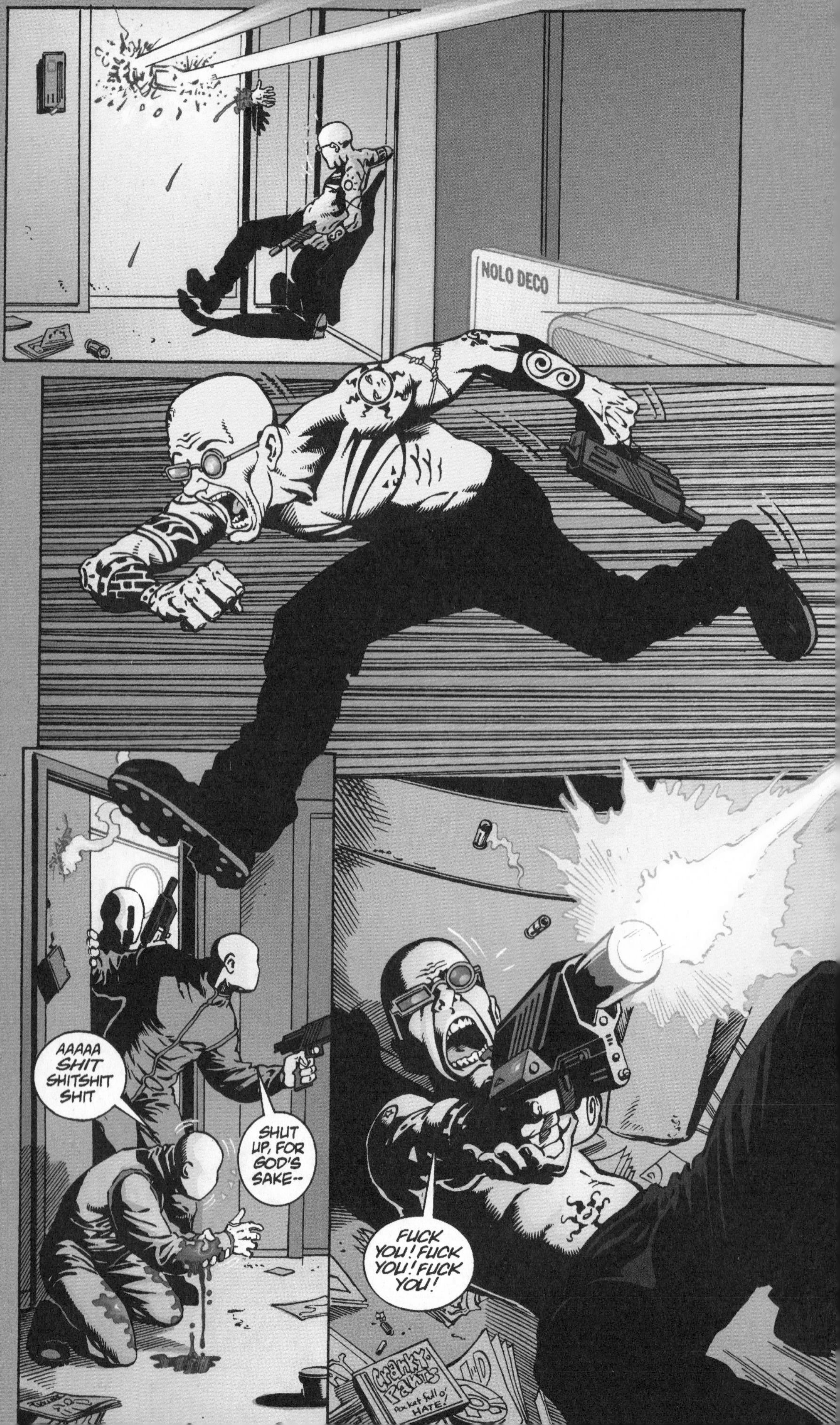
NOLO DECO
AAAAA SHIT SHITSHIT SHIT
SHUT UP, FOR GOD'S SAKE--
FUCK YOU! FUCK YOU! FUCK YOU!
Cranky Pants
Pocket full o' HATE!

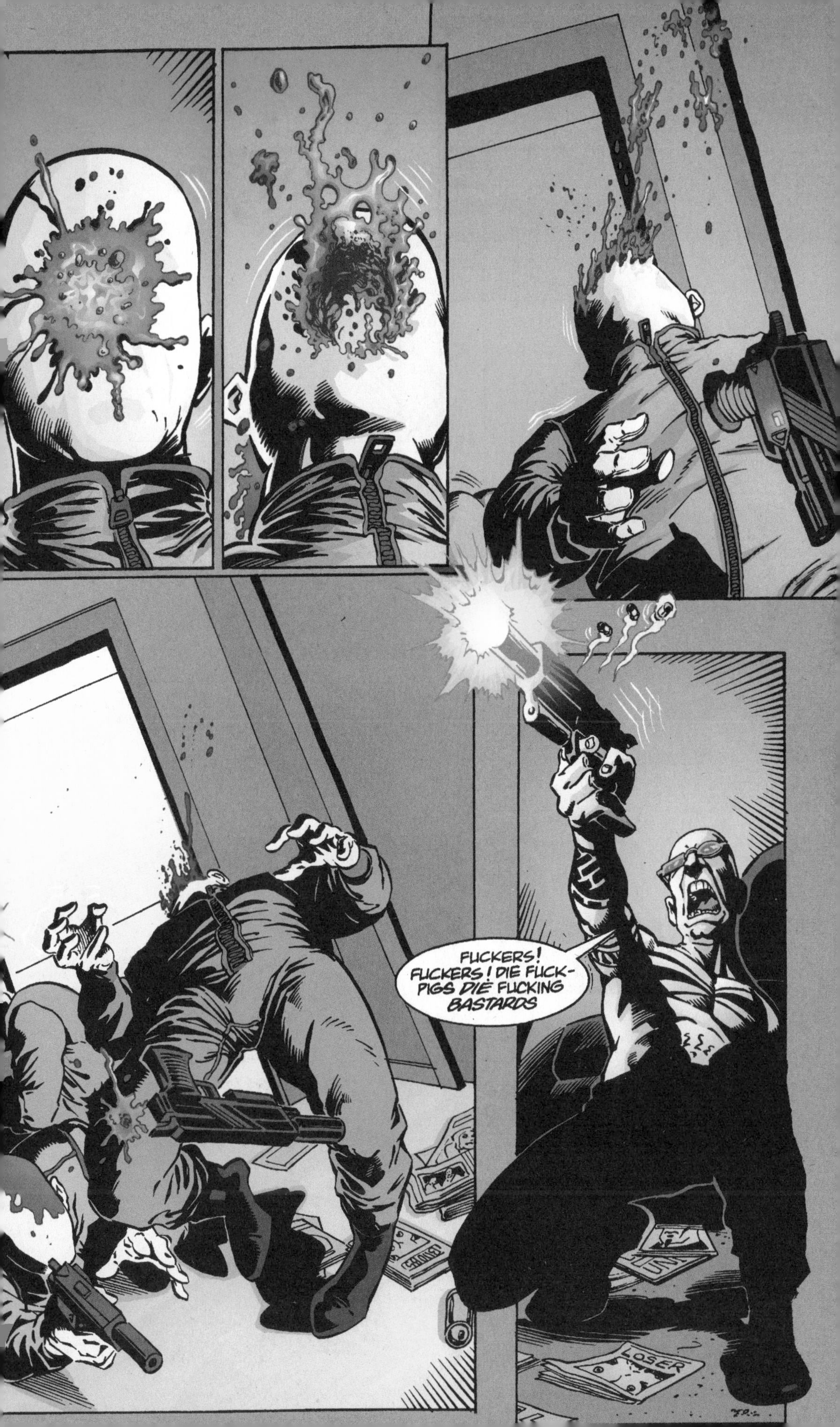
FUCKERS! FUCKERS! DIE FUCK-PIGS *DIE* FUCKING *BASTARDS*
LOSER

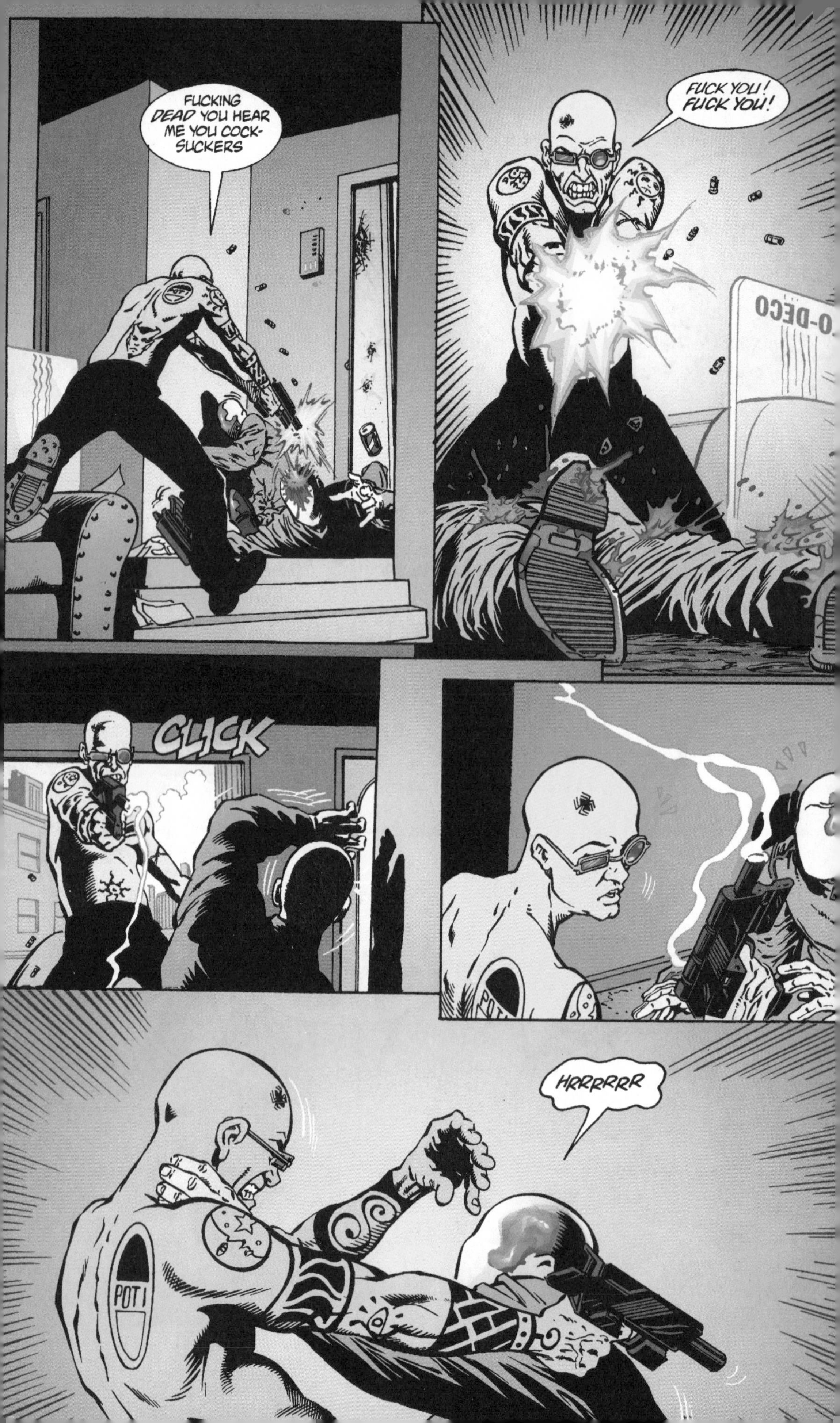
FUCKING
DEAD YOU HEAR
ME YOU COCK-
SUCKERS
FUCK YOU!
FUCK YOU!
CLICK
HRRRRRR

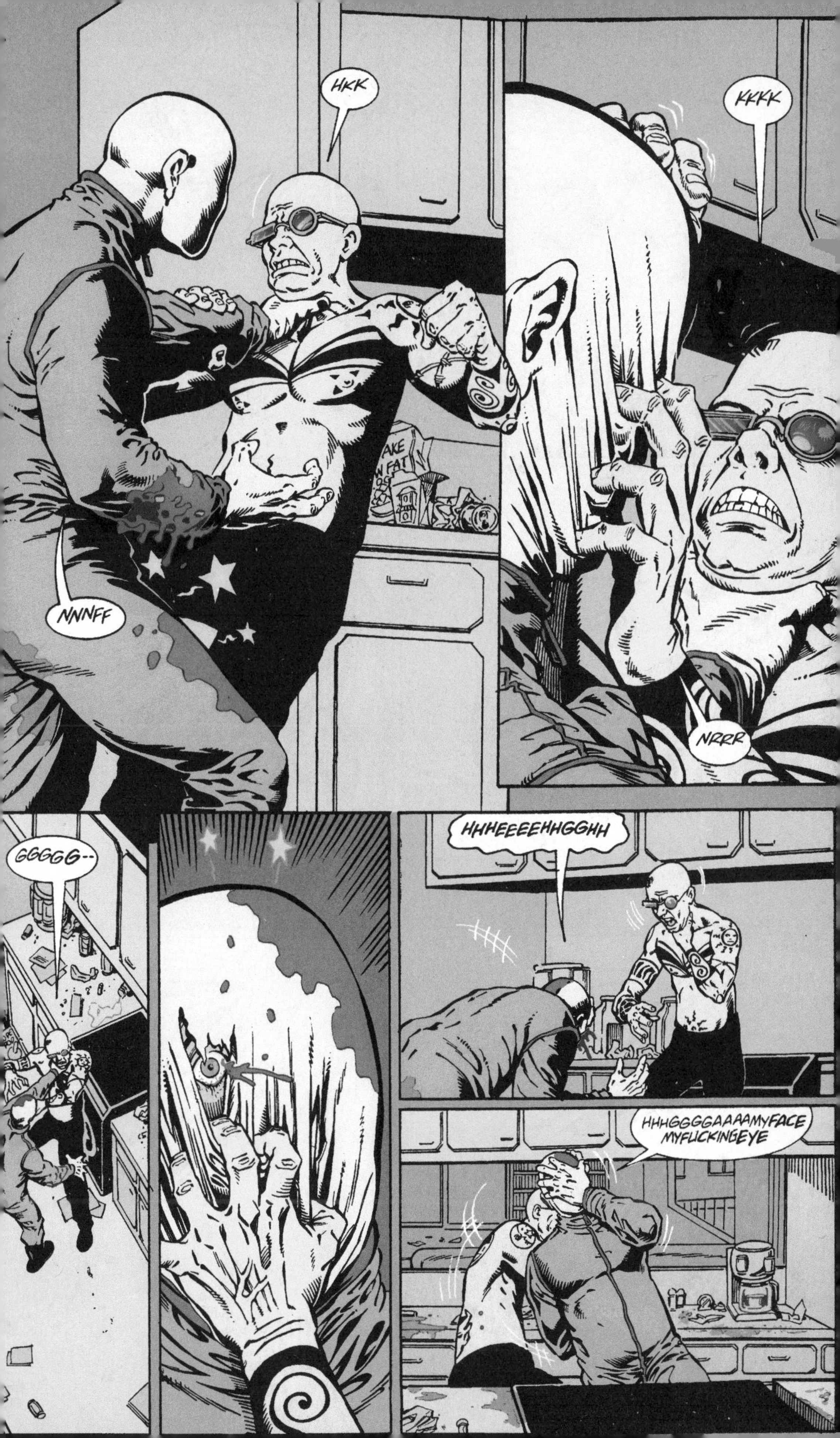
HKK
NNNFF
KKKK
NRRR
GGGGG--
HHHEEEEHHGGHH
HHHGGGAAAAMYFACE MYFUCKINGEYE

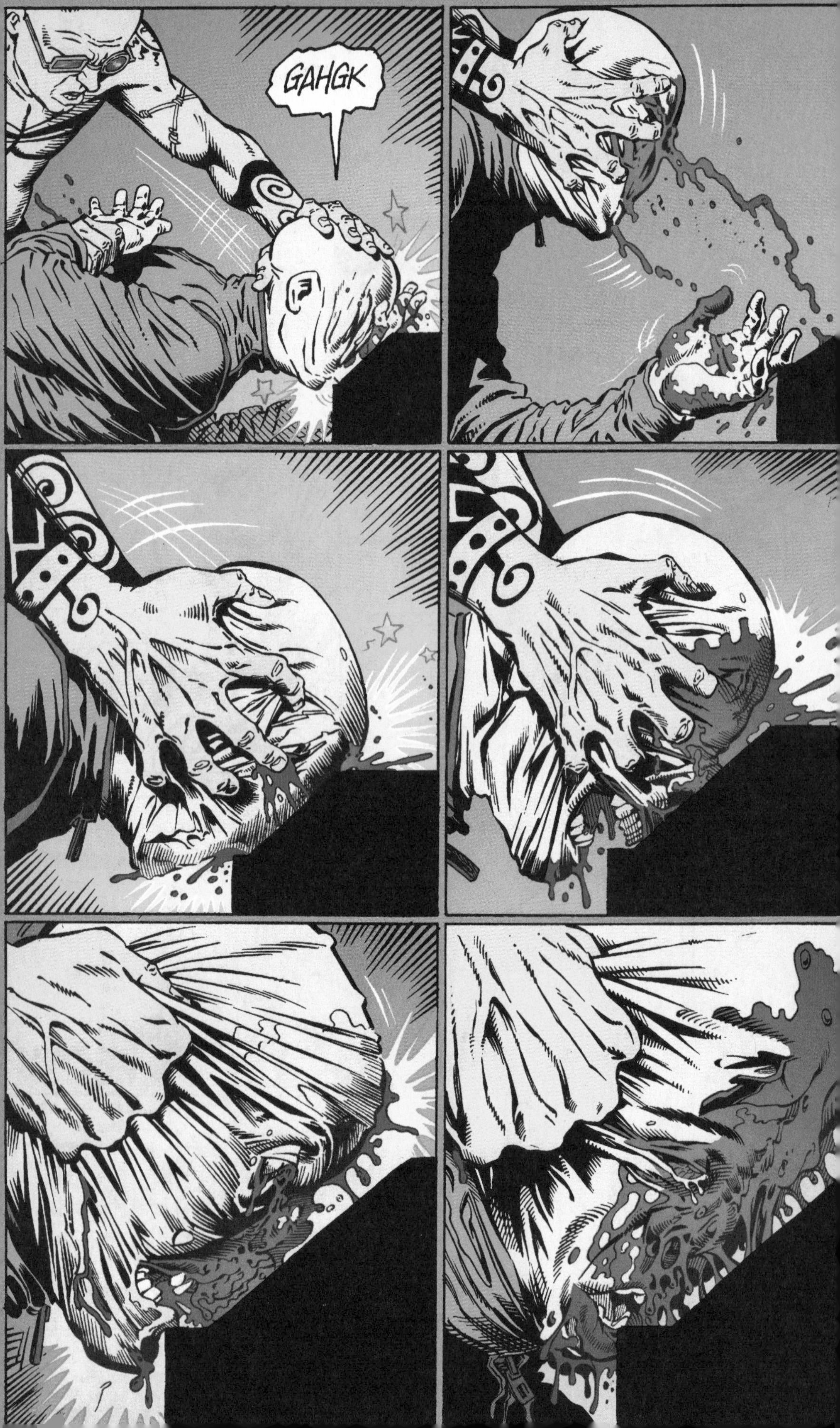
GAHGK

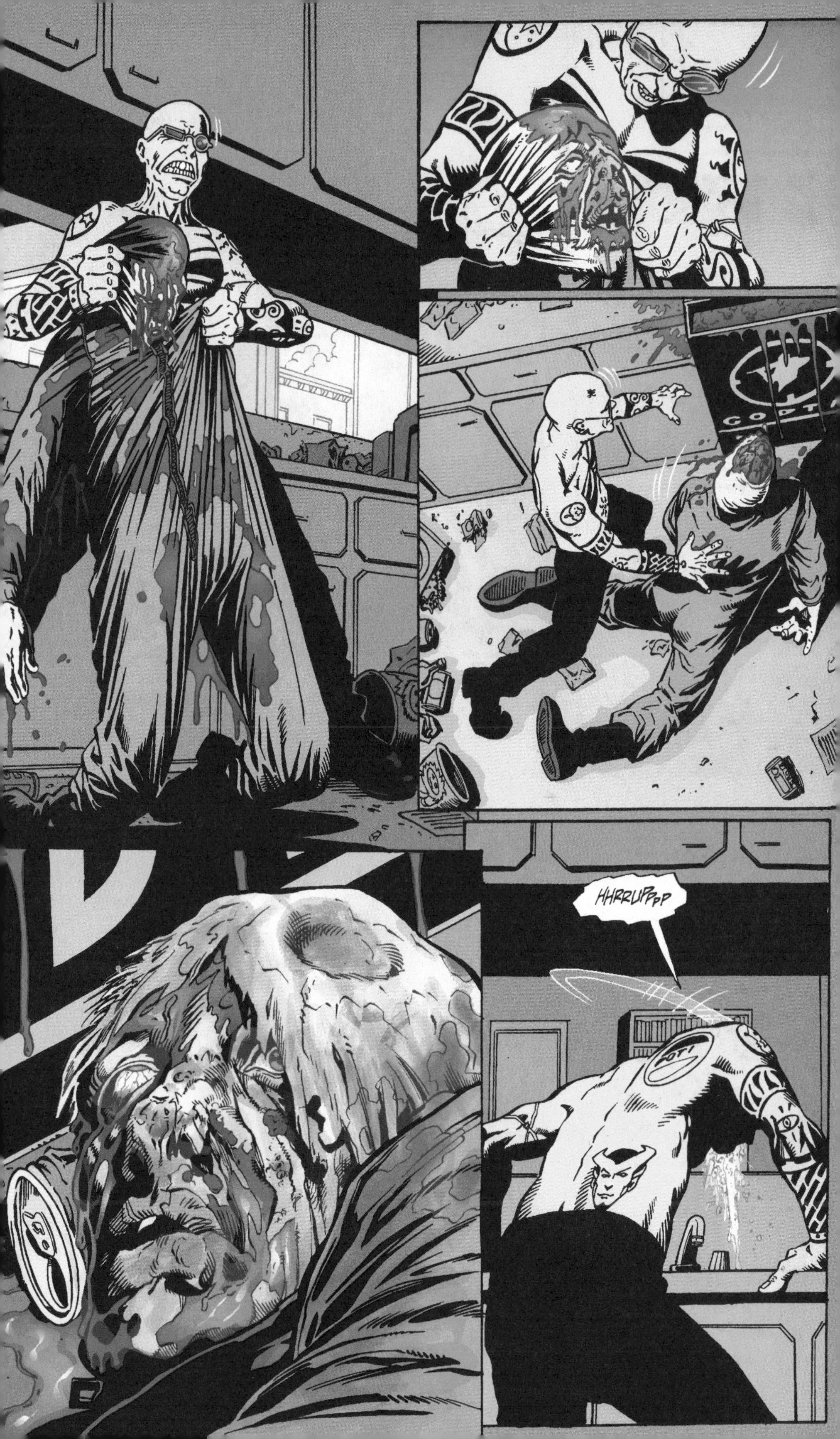
HHRRUPPPP

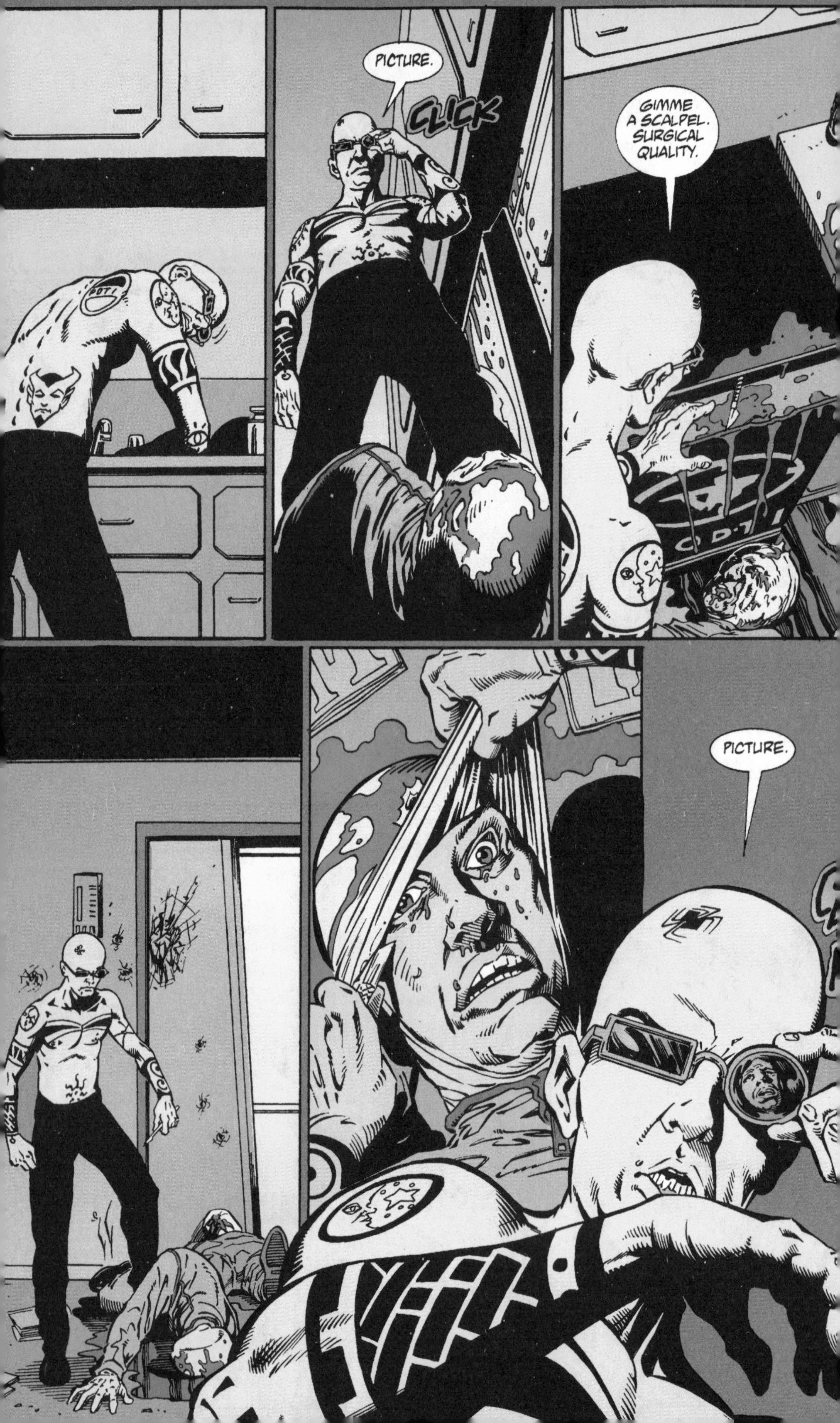
PICTURE.
CLICK
GIMME A SCALPEL. SURGICAL QUALITY.
PICTURE.

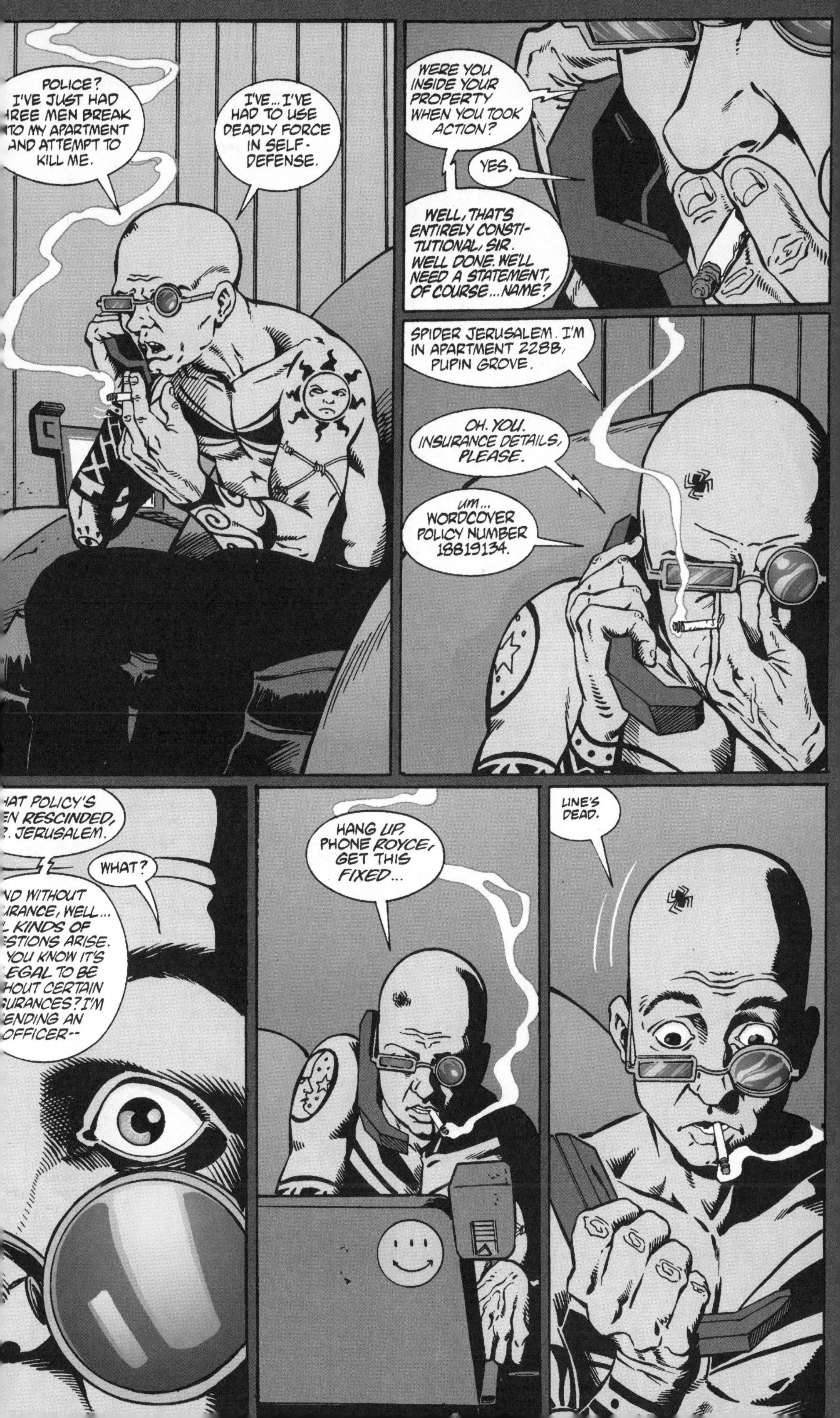
POLICE? I'VE JUST HAD HREE MEN BREAK TO MY APARTMENT AND ATTEMPT TO KILL ME.
I'VE... I'VE HAD TO USE DEADLY FORCE IN SELF-DEFENSE.
WERE YOU INSIDE YOUR PROPERTY WHEN YOU TOOK ACTION?
YES.
WELL, THAT'S ENTIRELY CONSTI-TUTIONAL, SIR. WELL DONE. WE'LL NEED A STATEMENT, OF COURSE... NAME?
SPIDER JERUSALEM. I'M IN APARTMENT 228B, PUPIN GROVE.
OH. YOU. INSURANCE DETAILS, PLEASE.
UM... WORDCOVER POLICY NUMBER 18819134.
HAT POLICY'S EN RESCINDED, R. JERUSALEM.
WHAT?
ND WITHOUT URANCE, WELL... L KINDS OF ESTIONS ARISE. YOU KNOW IT'S EGAL TO BE HOUT CERTAIN URANCES? I'M ENDING AN OFFICER--
HANG UP, PHONE ROYCE, GET THIS FIXED...
LINE'S DEAD.

"THE POLICE DOG"

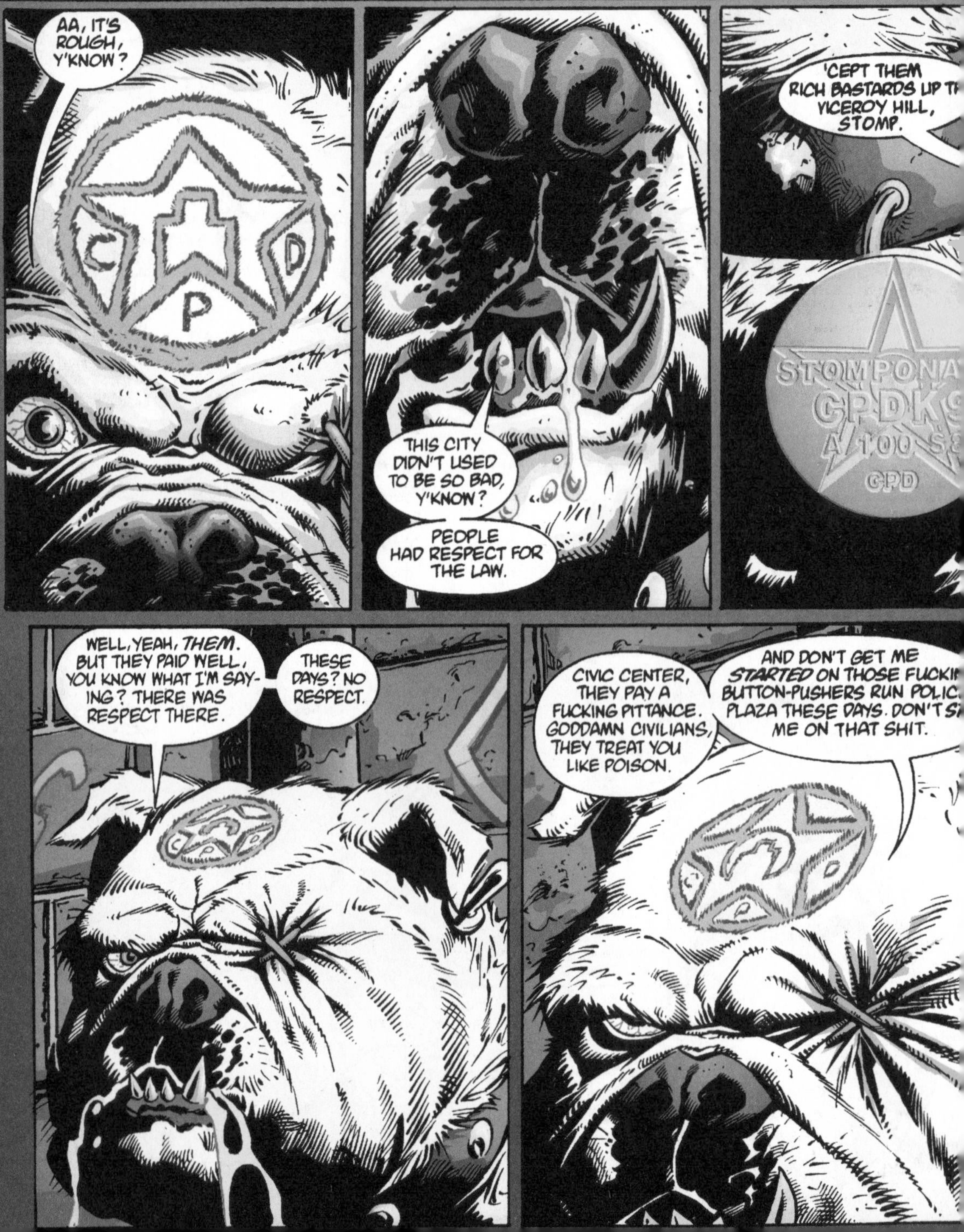

AA, IT'S ROUGH, Y'KNOW?
C P D
THIS CITY DIDN'T USED TO BE SO BAD, Y'KNOW?
PEOPLE HAD RESPECT FOR THE LAW.
'CEPT THEM RICH BASTARDS UP TH VICEROY HILL, STOMP.
STOMPONA CPDK9 A 100 S3 CPD
WELL, YEAH, THEM. BUT THEY PAID WELL, YOU KNOW WHAT I'M SAYING? THERE WAS RESPECT THERE.
THESE DAYS? NO RESPECT.
CIVIC CENTER, THEY PAY A FUCKING PITTANCE. GODDAMN CIVILIANS, THEY TREAT YOU LIKE POISON.
AND DON'T GET ME STARTED ON THOSE FUCKIN BUTTON-PUSHERS RUN POLIC PLAZA THESE DAYS. DON'T S ME ON THAT SHIT.

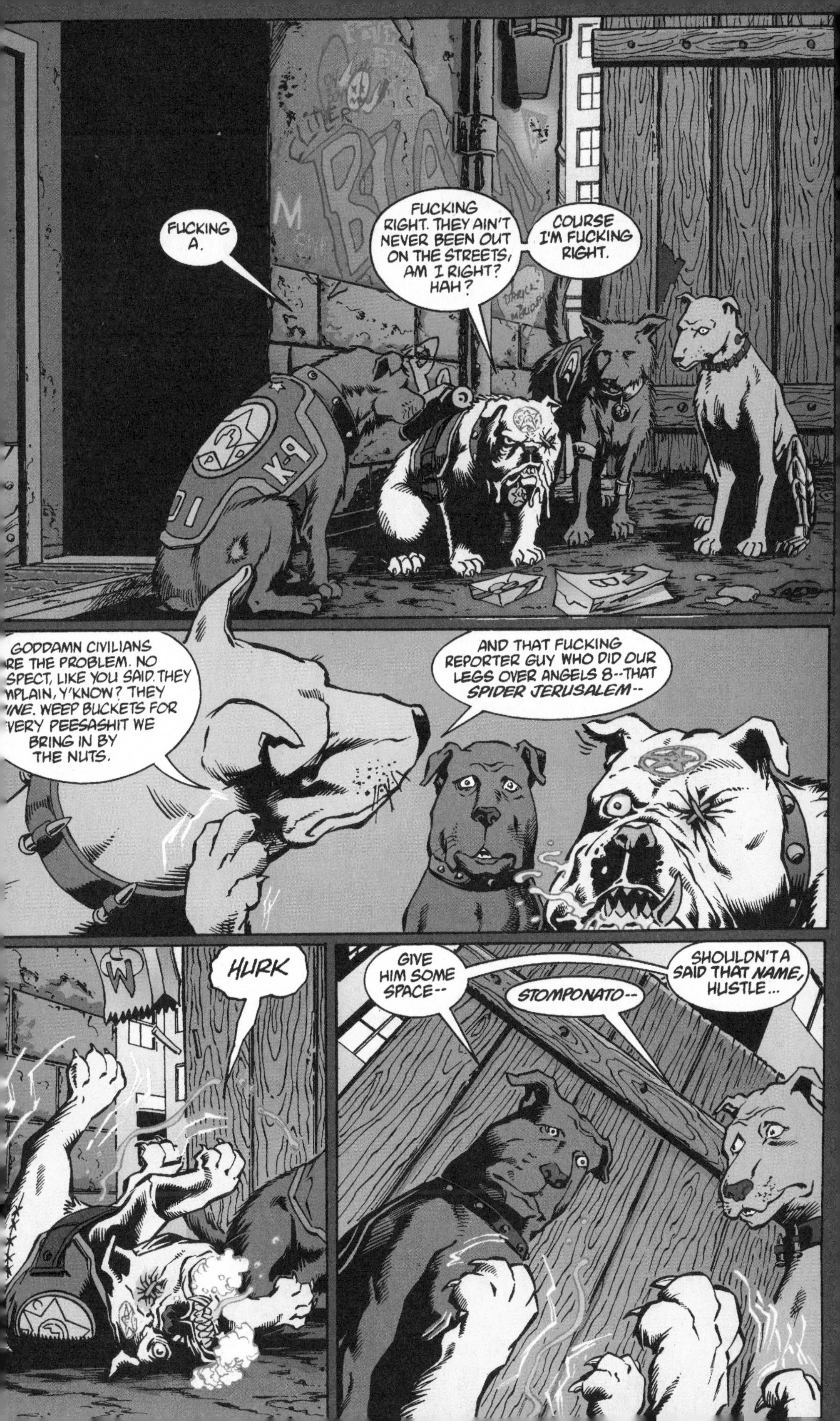
FUCKING A.
FUCKING RIGHT. THEY AIN'T NEVER BEEN OUT ON THE STREETS, AM I RIGHT? HAH?
COURSE I'M FUCKING RIGHT.
GODDAMN CIVILIANS ARE THE PROBLEM. NO SPECT, LIKE YOU SAID. THEY MPLAIN, Y'KNOW? THEY INE. WEEP BUCKETS FOR VERY PEESASHIT WE BRING IN BY THE NUTS.
AND THAT FUCKING REPORTER GUY WHO DID OUR LEGS OVER ANGELS 8--THAT SPIDER JERUSALEM--
HURK
GIVE HIM SOME SPACE--
STOMPONATO--
SHOULDN'TA SAID THAT NAME, HUSTLE...

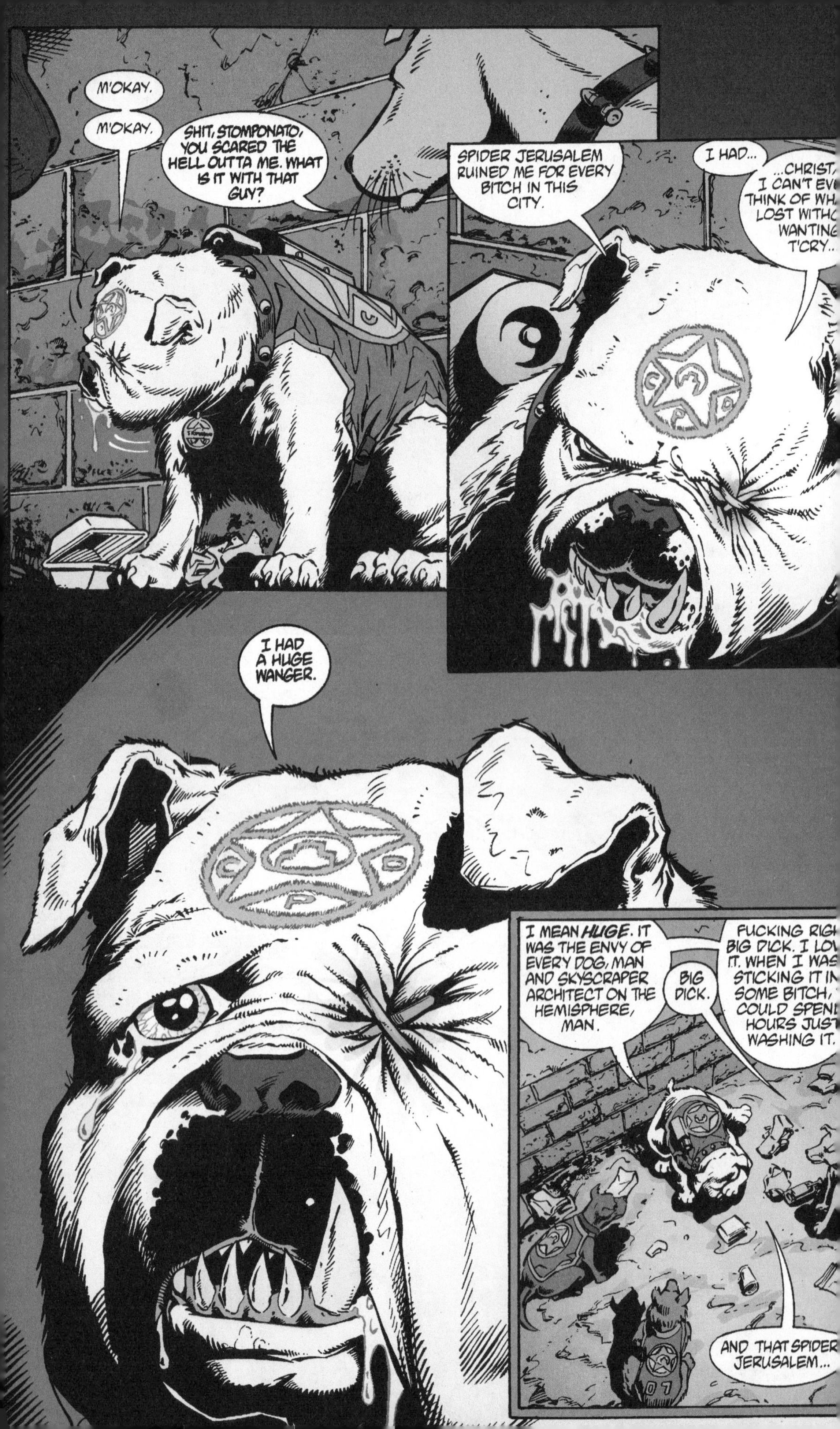

M'OKAY.
M'OKAY.
SHIT, STOMPONATO, YOU SCARED THE HELL OUTTA ME. WHAT IS IT WITH THAT GUY?
SPIDER JERUSALEM RUINED ME FOR EVERY BITCH IN THIS CITY.
I HAD...
...CHRIST, I CAN'T EV THINK OF WHA LOST WITHO WANTING T'CRY...
I HAD A HUGE WANGER.
I MEAN *HUGE*. IT WAS THE ENVY OF EVERY DOG, MAN AND SKYSCRAPER ARCHITECT ON THE HEMISPHERE, MAN.
BIG DICK.
FUCKING RIG BIG DICK. I LOV IT. WHEN I WAS STICKING IT IN SOME BITCH, COULD SPEN HOURS JUST WASHING IT.
AND THAT SPIDER JERUSALEM...

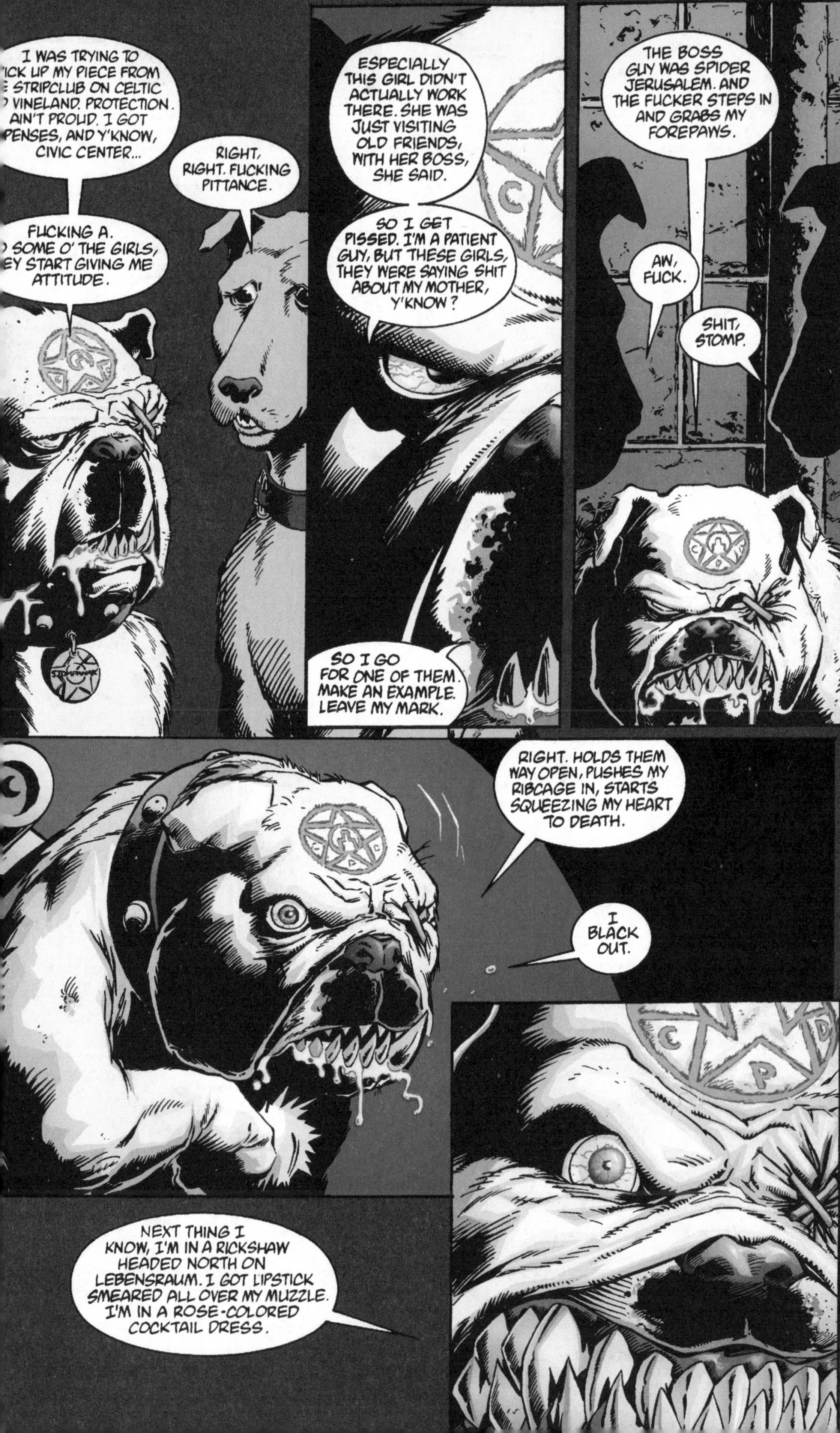
I WAS TRYING TO 'ICK UP MY PIECE FROM E STRIPCLUB ON CELTIC D VINELAND. PROTECTION AIN'T PROUD. I GOT PENSES, AND Y'KNOW, CIVIC CENTER...
RIGHT, RIGHT. FUCKING PITTANCE.
FUCKING A. D SOME O' THE GIRLS, EY START GIVING ME ATTITUDE.
ESPECIALLY THIS GIRL DIDN'T ACTUALLY WORK THERE. SHE WAS JUST VISITING OLD FRIENDS, WITH HER BOSS, SHE SAID.
SO I GET PISSED. I'M A PATIENT GUY, BUT THESE GIRLS, THEY WERE SAYING SHIT ABOUT MY MOTHER, Y'KNOW?
SO I GO FOR ONE OF THEM. MAKE AN EXAMPLE. LEAVE MY MARK.
THE BOSS GUY WAS SPIDER JERUSALEM. AND THE FUCKER STEPS IN AND GRABS MY FOREPAWS.
AW, FUCK.
SHIT, STOMP.
RIGHT. HOLDS THEM WAY OPEN, PUSHES MY RIBCAGE IN, STARTS SQUEEZING MY HEART TO DEATH.
I BLACK OUT.
NEXT THING I KNOW, I'M IN A RICKSHAW HEADED NORTH ON LEBENSRAUM. I GOT LIPSTICK SMEARED ALL OVER MY MUZZLE. I'M IN A ROSE-COLORED COCKTAIL DRESS.

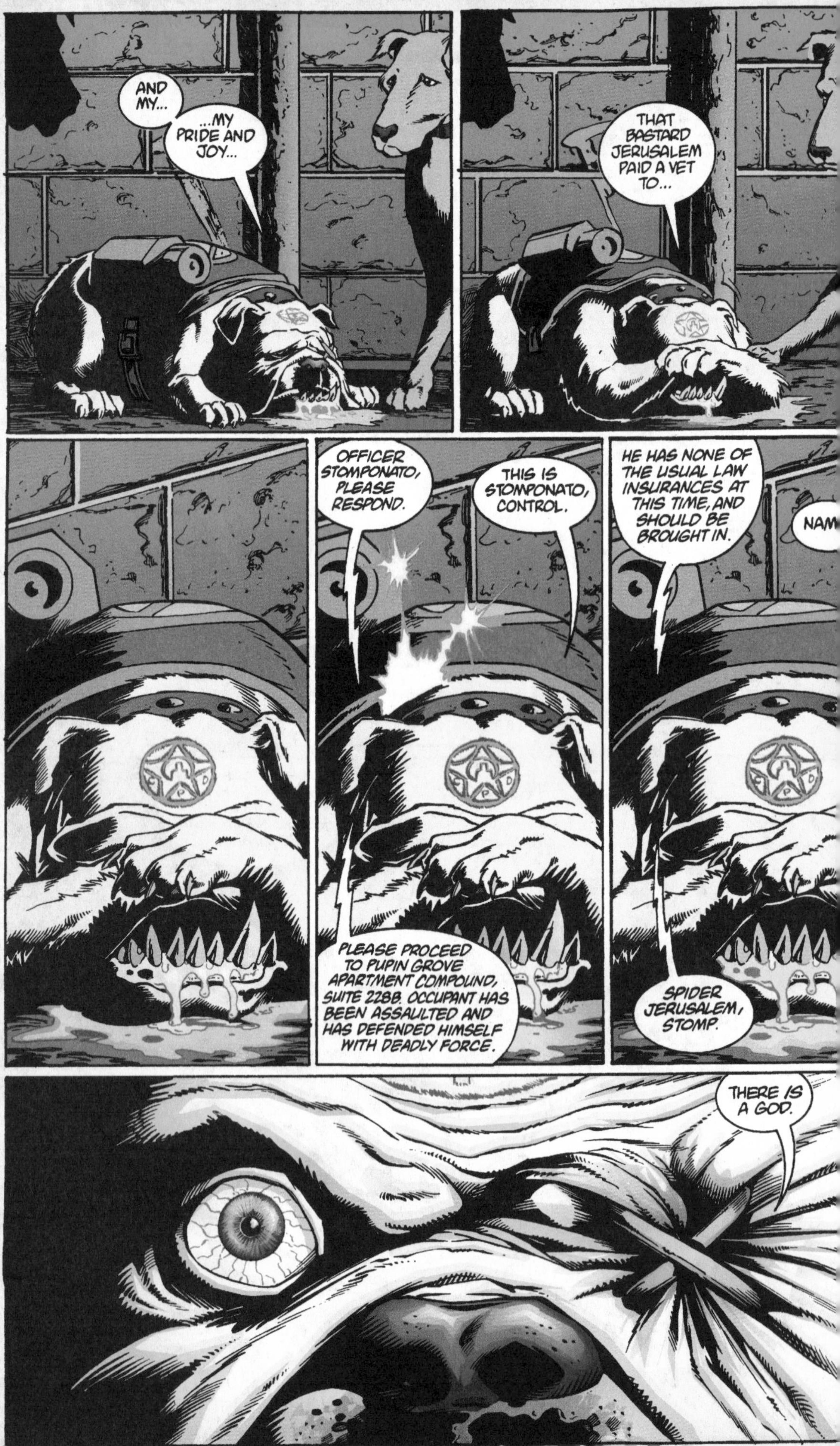
AND MY...
...MY PRIDE AND JOY...
THAT BASTARD JERUSALEM PAID A VET TO...
OFFICER STOMPONATO, PLEASE RESPOND.
THIS IS STOMPONATO, CONTROL.
PLEASE PROCEED TO PUPIN GROVE APARTMENT COMPOUND, SUITE 228B. OCCUPANT HAS BEEN ASSAULTED AND HAS DEFENDED HIMSELF WITH DEADLY FORCE.
HE HAS NONE OF THE USUAL LAW INSURANCES AT THIS TIME, AND SHOULD BE BROUGHT IN.
NAM
SPIDER JERUSALEM, STOMP.
THERE IS A GOD.

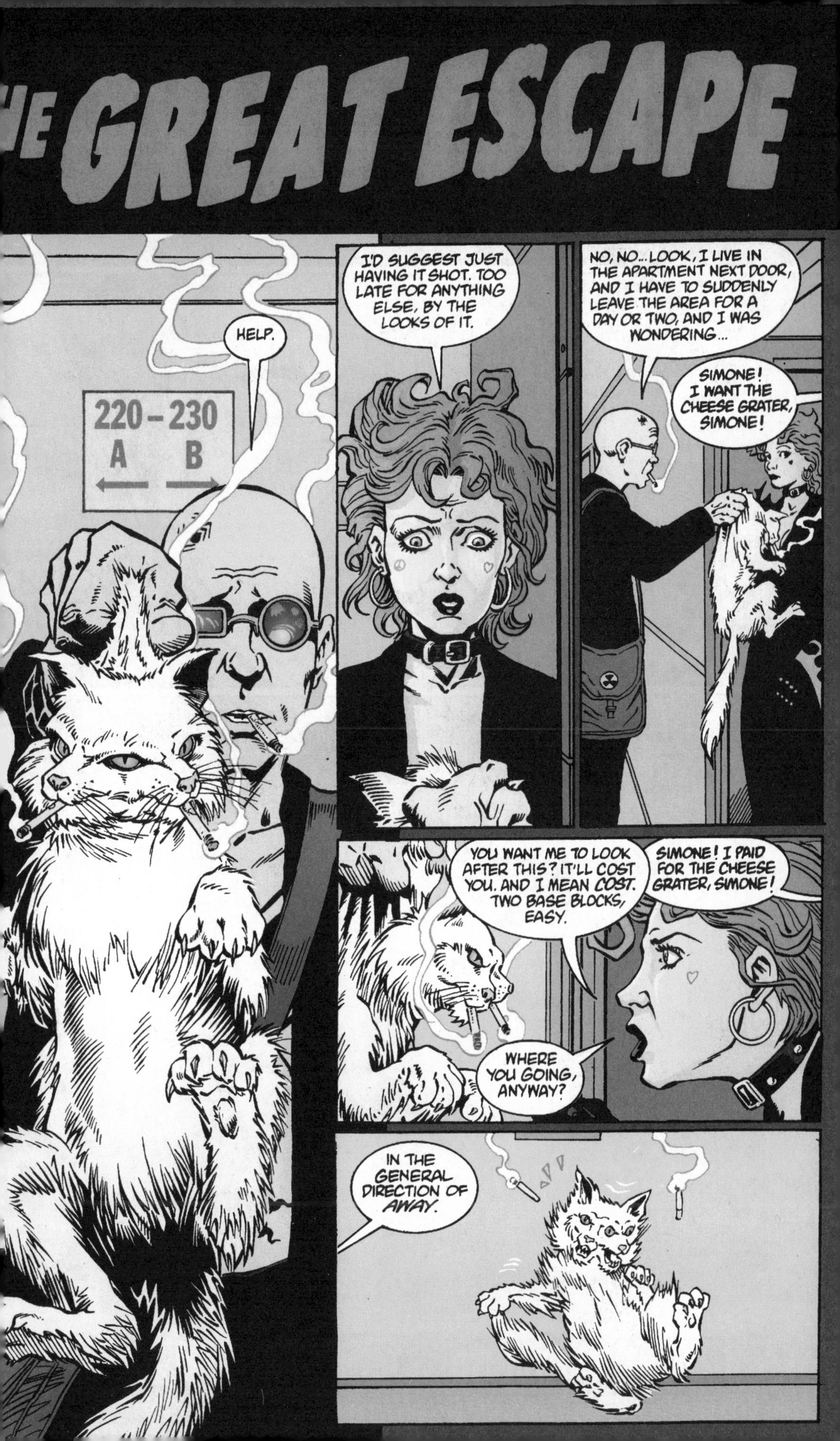
GREAT ESCAPE
HELP.
220 – 230
A B
I'D SUGGEST JUST HAVING IT SHOT. TOO LATE FOR ANYTHING ELSE, BY THE LOOKS OF IT.
NO, NO... LOOK, I LIVE IN THE APARTMENT NEXT DOOR, AND I HAVE TO SUDDENLY LEAVE THE AREA FOR A DAY OR TWO, AND I WAS WONDERING...
SIMONE! I WANT THE CHEESE GRATER, SIMONE!
YOU WANT ME TO LOOK AFTER THIS? IT'LL COST YOU. AND I MEAN *COST*. TWO BASE BLOCKS, EASY.
SIMONE! I PAID FOR THE CHEESE GRATER, SIMONE!
WHERE YOU GOING, ANYWAY?
IN THE GENERAL DIRECTION OF *AWAY*.

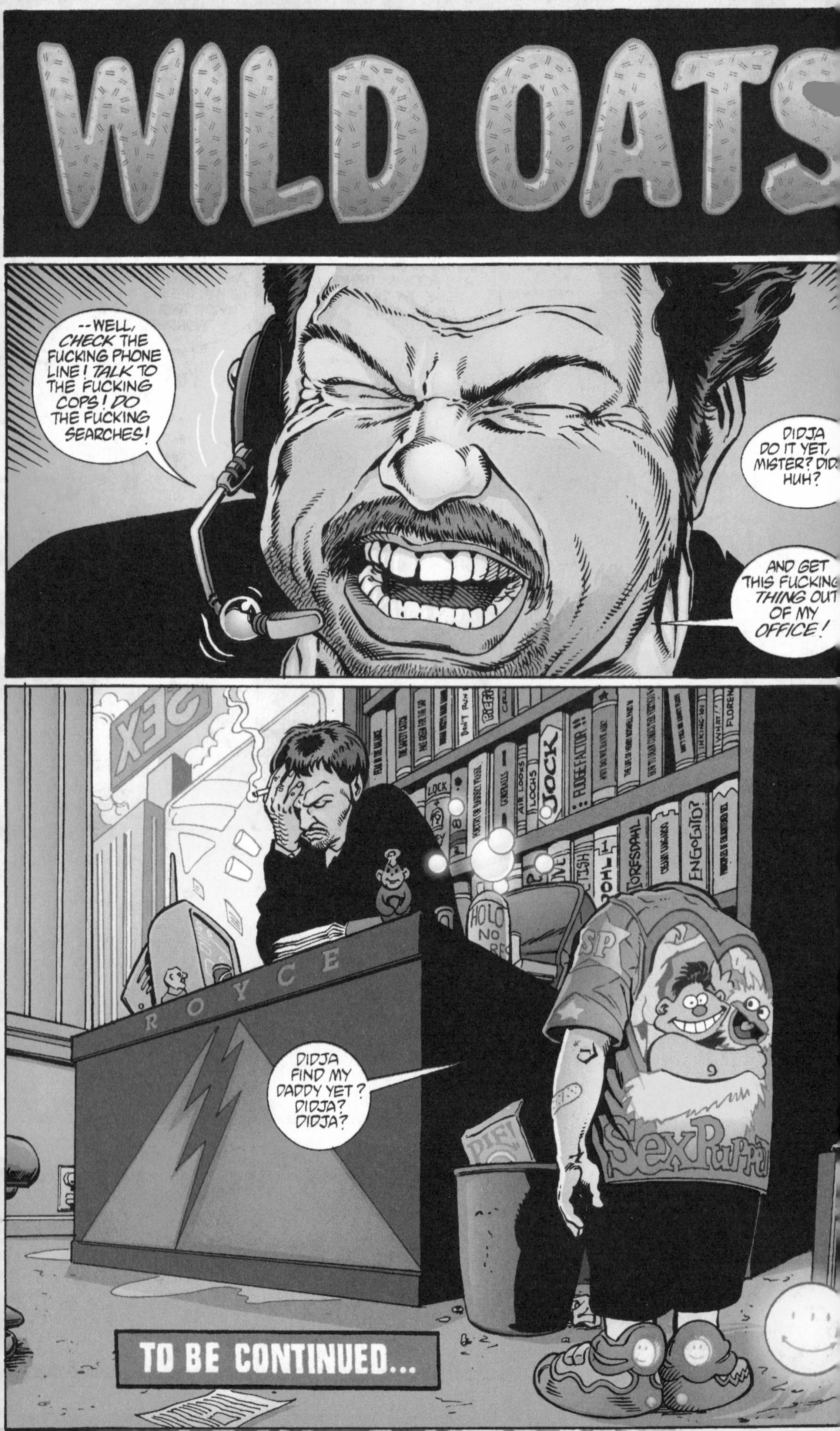
WILD OATS
--WELL, CHECK THE FUCKING PHONE LINE! TALK TO THE FUCKING COPS! DO THE FUCKING SEARCHES!
DIDJA DO IT YET, MISTER? DID. HUH?
AND GET THIS FUCKING THING OUT OF MY OFFICE!
ROYCE
DIDJA FIND MY DADDY YET? DIDJA? DIDJA?
TO BE CONTINUED...

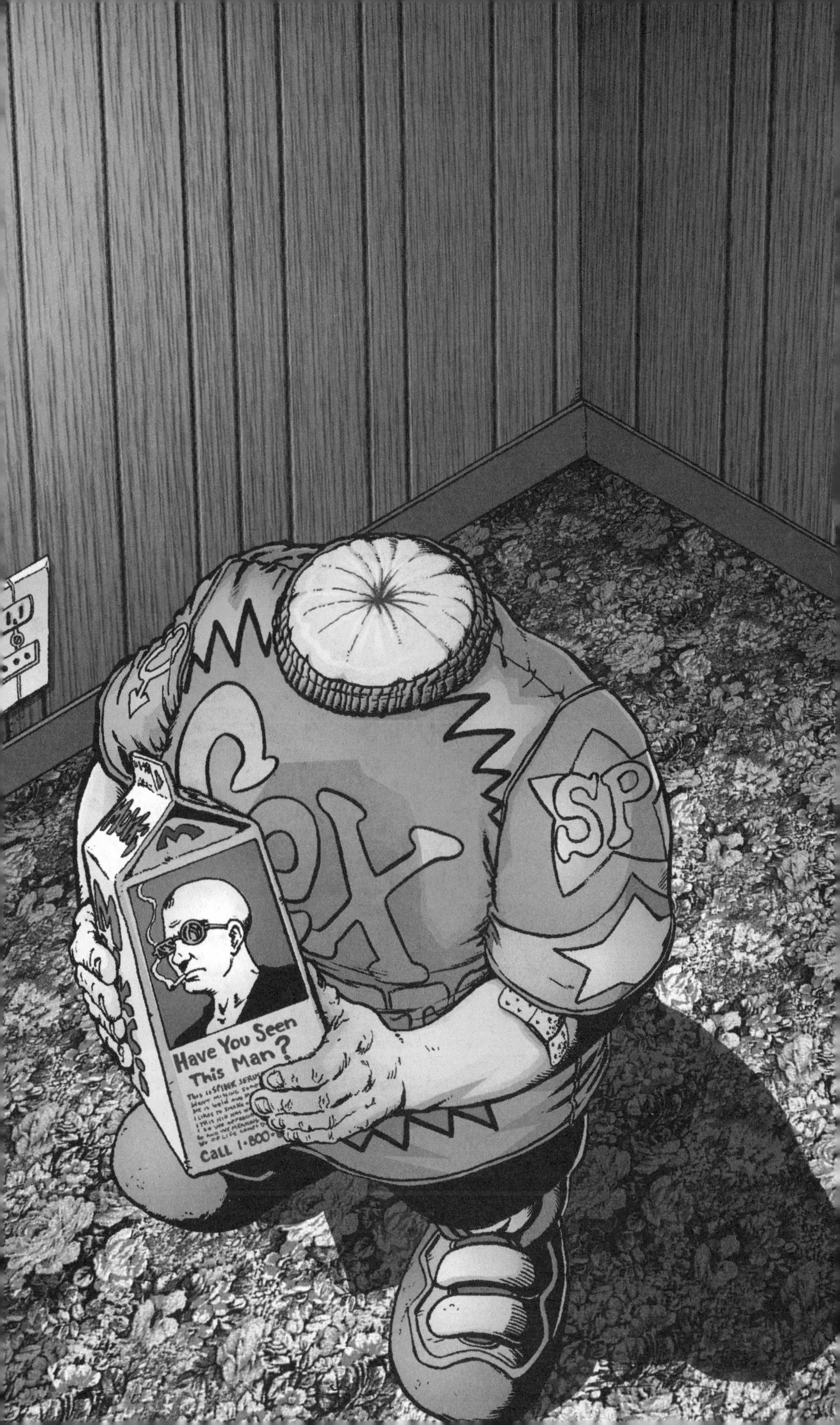
Have You Seen This Man?
CALL 1-800-

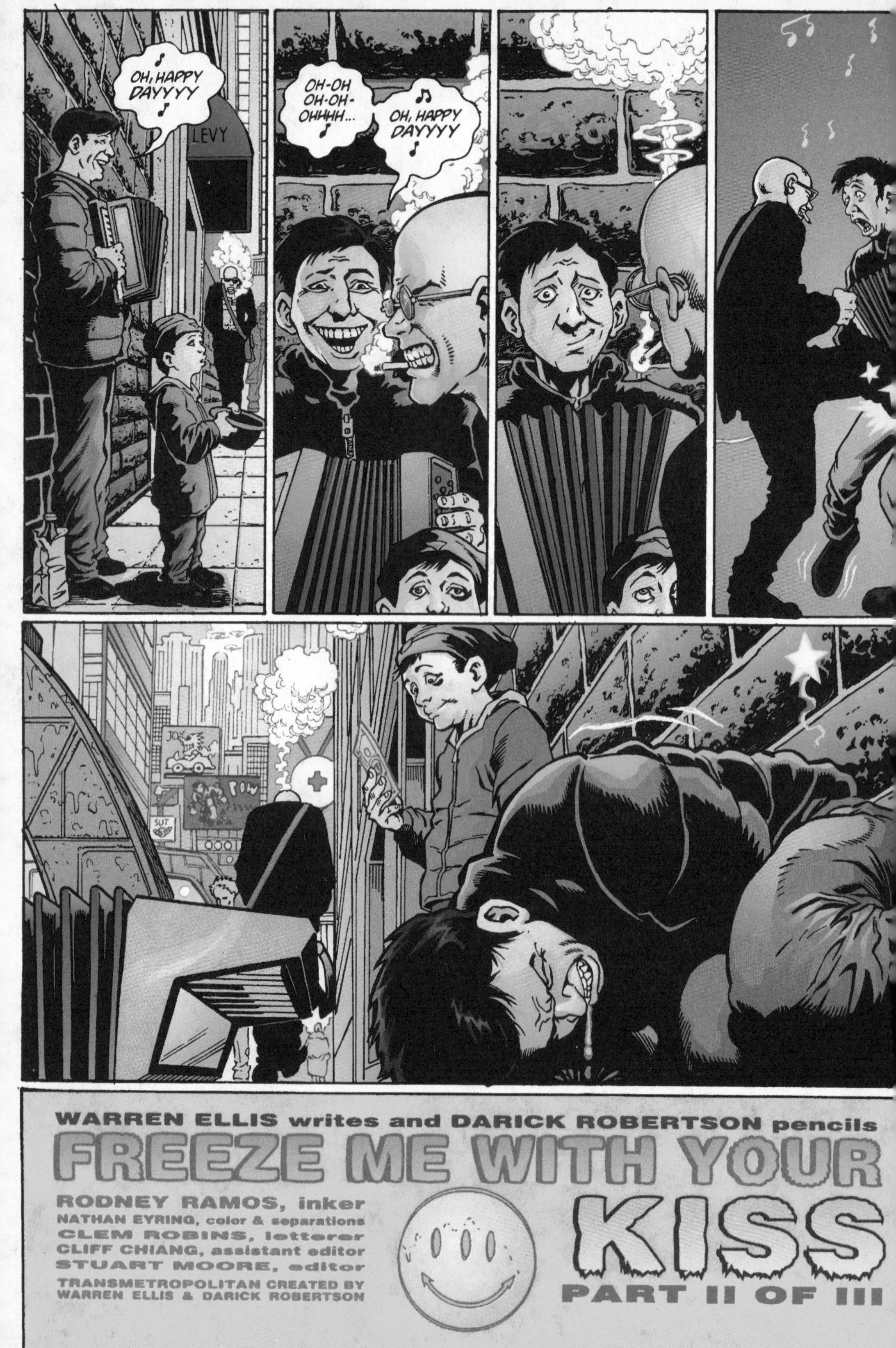

OH, HAPPY DAYYYY
LEVY
OH-OH OH-OH-OHHHH...
OH, HAPPY DAYYYY

WARREN ELLIS writes and **DARICK ROBERTSON** pencils

FREEZE ME WITH YOUR KISS

PART II OF III

RODNEY RAMOS, inker
NATHAN EYRING, color & separations
CLEM ROBINS, letterer
CLIFF CHIANG, assistant editor
STUART MOORE, editor
TRANSMETROPOLITAN CREATED BY WARREN ELLIS & DARICK ROBERTSON

the last time this happened...

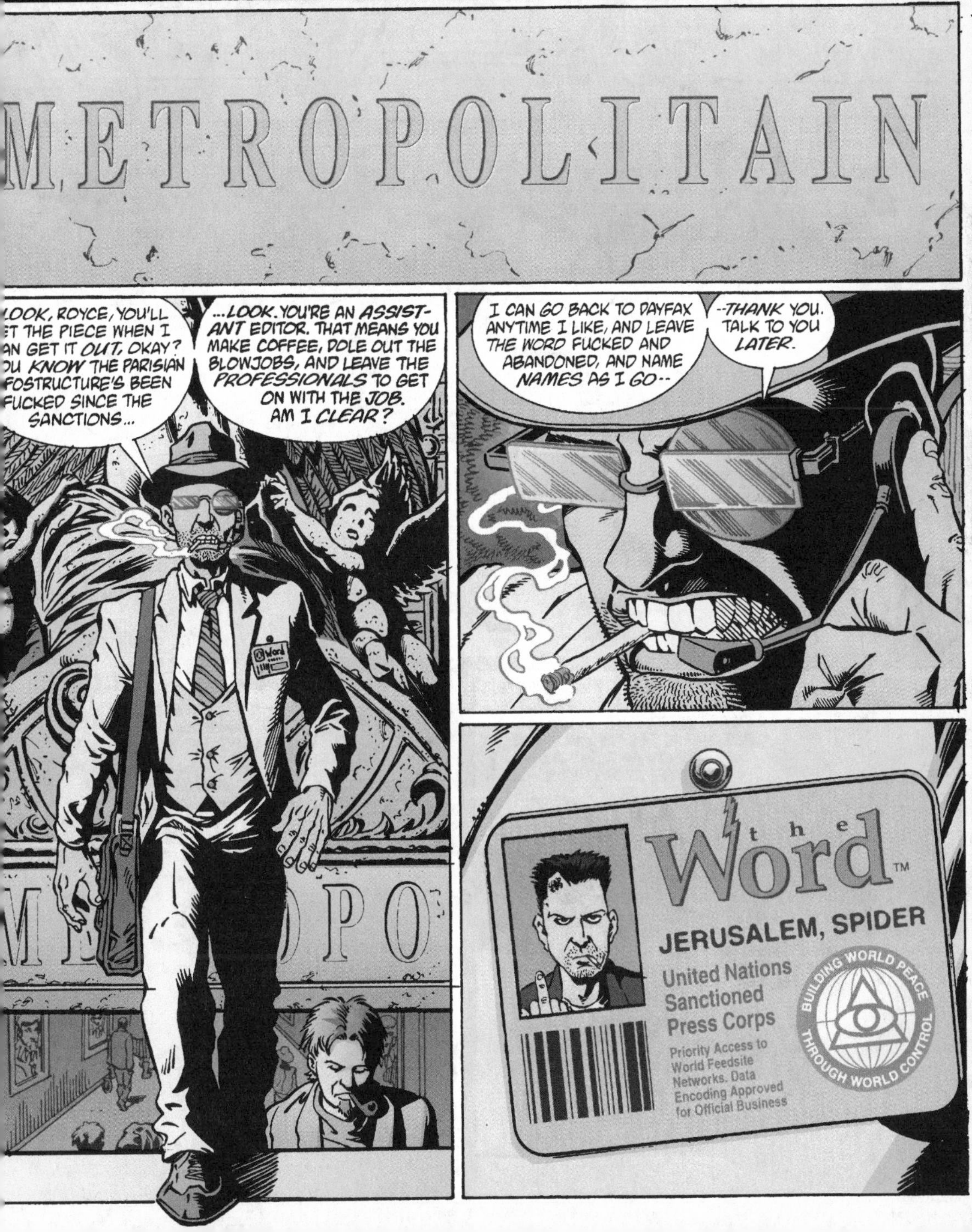
METROPOLITAIN
OOK, ROYCE, YOU'LL ET THE PIECE WHEN I AN GET IT OUT, OKAY? OU KNOW THE PARISIAN FOSTRUCTURE'S BEEN FUCKED SINCE THE SANCTIONS...
...LOOK. YOU'RE AN ASSIST-ANT EDITOR. THAT MEANS YOU MAKE COFFEE, DOLE OUT THE BLOWJOBS, AND LEAVE THE PROFESSIONALS TO GET ON WITH THE JOB. AM I CLEAR?
I CAN GO BACK TO DAYFAX ANYTIME I LIKE, AND LEAVE THE WORD FUCKED AND ABANDONED, AND NAME NAMES AS I GO--
--THANK YOU. TALK TO YOU LATER.
the Word™
JERUSALEM, SPIDER
United Nations Sanctioned Press Corps
Priority Access to World Feedsite Networks. Data Encoding Approved for Official Business
BUILDING WORLD PEACE THROUGH WORLD CONTROL

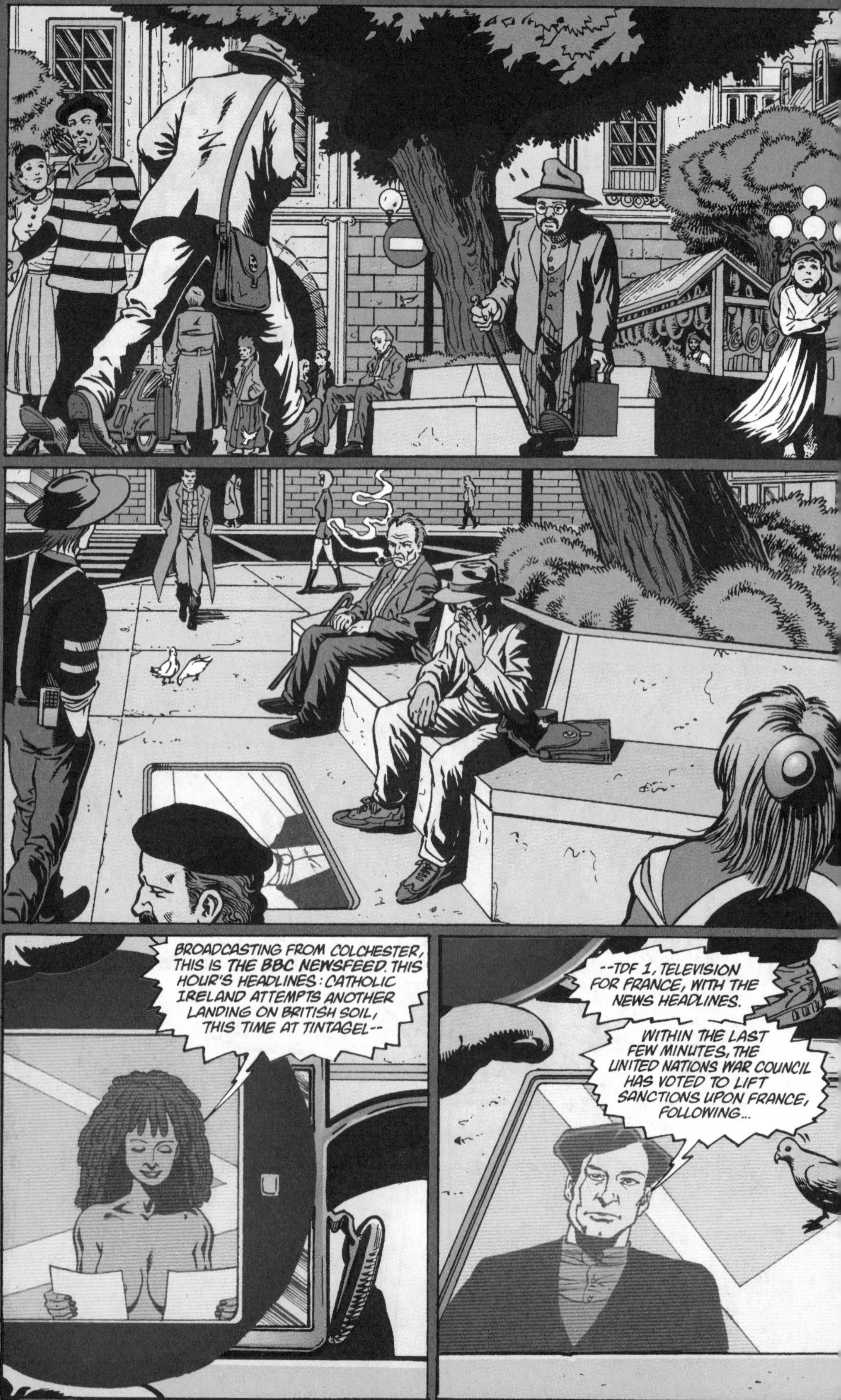
BROADCASTING FROM COLCHESTER, THIS IS THE BBC NEWSFEED. THIS HOUR'S HEADLINES: CATHOLIC IRELAND ATTEMPTS ANOTHER LANDING ON BRITISH SOIL, THIS TIME AT TINTAGEL--
--TDF 1, TELEVISION FOR FRANCE, WITH THE NEWS HEADLINES.
WITHIN THE LAST FEW MINUTES, THE UNITED NATIONS WAR COUNCIL HAS VOTED TO LIFT SANCTIONS UPON FRANCE, FOLLOWING...

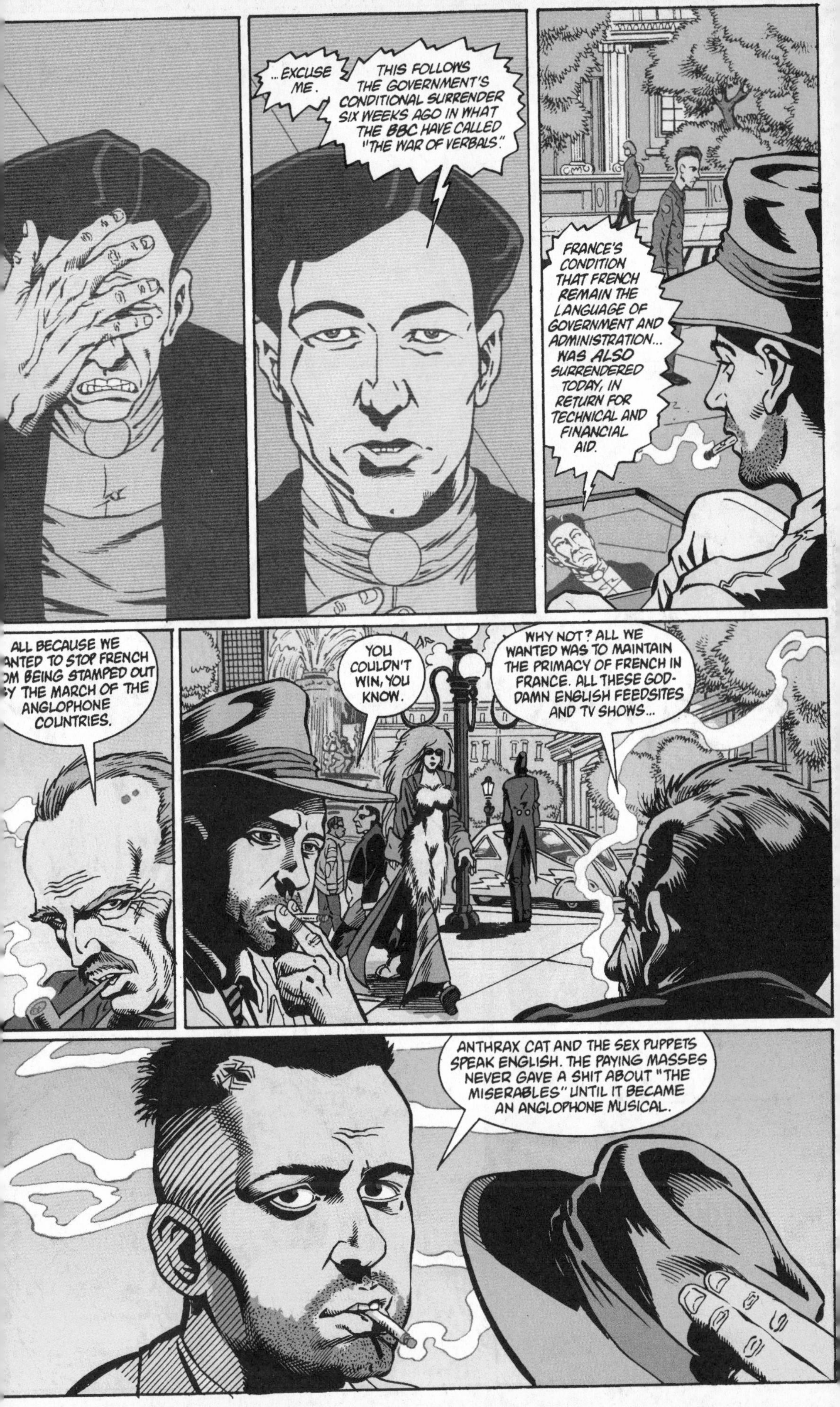
...EXCUSE ME.
THIS FOLLOWS THE GOVERNMENT'S CONDITIONAL SURRENDER SIX WEEKS AGO IN WHAT THE BBC HAVE CALLED "THE WAR OF VERBALS".
FRANCE'S CONDITION THAT FRENCH REMAIN THE LANGUAGE OF GOVERNMENT AND ADMINISTRATION... WAS ALSO SURRENDERED TODAY, IN RETURN FOR TECHNICAL AND FINANCIAL AID.
ALL BECAUSE WE ANTED TO STOP FRENCH OM BEING STAMPED OUT Y THE MARCH OF THE ANGLOPHONE COUNTRIES.
YOU COULDN'T WIN, YOU KNOW.
WHY NOT? ALL WE WANTED WAS TO MAINTAIN THE PRIMACY OF FRENCH IN FRANCE. ALL THESE GOD-DAMN ENGLISH FEEDSITES AND TV SHOWS...
ANTHRAX CAT AND THE SEX PUPPETS SPEAK ENGLISH. THE PAYING MASSES NEVER GAVE A SHIT ABOUT "THE MISERABLES" UNTIL IT BECAME AN ANGLOPHONE MUSICAL.

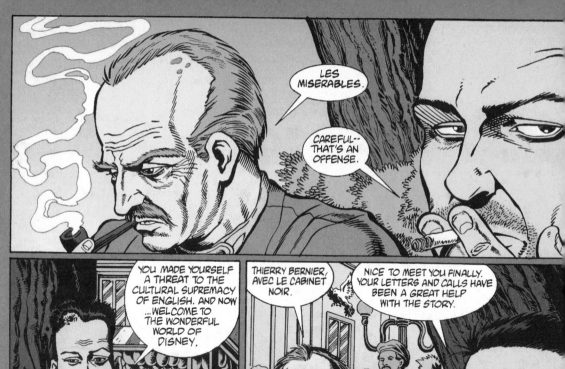

LES MISERABLES.

CAREFUL-- THAT'S AN OFFENSE.

YOU MADE YOURSELF A THREAT TO THE CULTURAL SUPREMACY OF ENGLISH. AND NOW ...WELCOME TO THE WONDERFUL WORLD OF DISNEY.

THIERRY BERNIER, AVEC LE CABINET NOIR.

NICE TO MEET YOU FINALLY. YOUR LETTERS AND CALLS HAVE BEEN A GREAT HELP WITH THE STORY.

YOU'VE MADE YOURSELF ENEMIES IN PARIS WITH YOUR REPORTAGE, MR. JERUSALEM.

YOU NEVER CITED ME IN YOUR REPORTS, AND COVERED ME IN SECURITY WELL. I OWE YOU, SO I'M HERE TO WARN YOU.

MY COLLEAGUES IN THE SECRET SERVICE ARE...WELL, SOME OF THEM ARE REACTIONARY AND TOO LOYAL TO BE DESCRIBED AS SANE.

YOU DESCRIBED OUR PREMIER AS A POLITICAL TAPEWORM AND LYING PERVERT MADDENED BY CRACK VISIONS OF HIS NAME IN HISTORY BOOKS, AN OBSESSIVE FETISH FOR MEDIA TIME, AND A SICK ADDICTION TO KISSING BABIES USING HIS TONGUE.

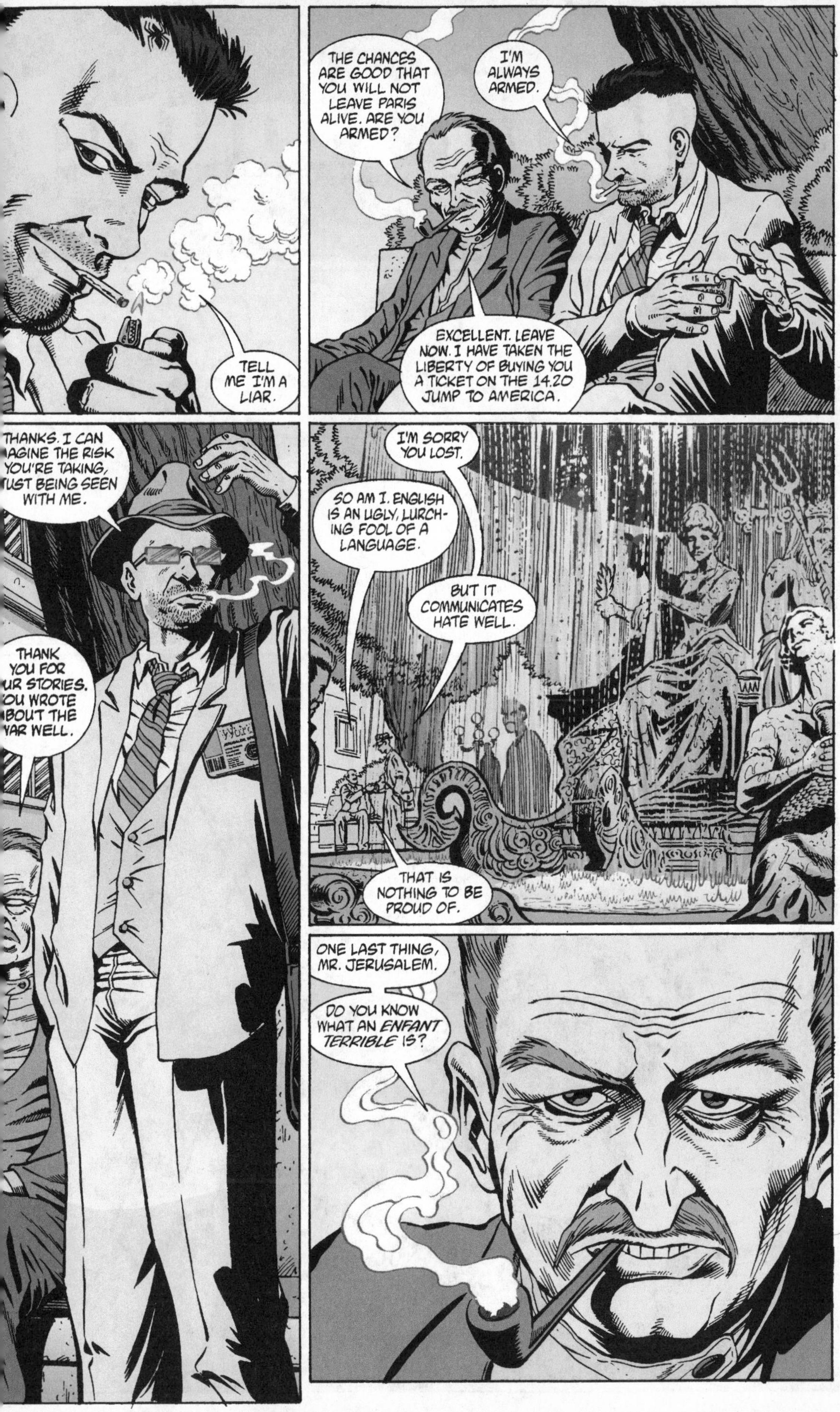
TELL ME I'M A LIAR.
THE CHANCES ARE GOOD THAT YOU WILL NOT LEAVE PARIS ALIVE. ARE YOU ARMED?
I'M ALWAYS ARMED.
EXCELLENT. LEAVE NOW. I HAVE TAKEN THE LIBERTY OF BUYING YOU A TICKET ON THE 14.20 JUMP TO AMERICA.
THANKS. I CAN AGINE THE RISK YOU'RE TAKING, UST BEING SEEN WITH ME.
THANK YOU FOR UR STORIES. OU WROTE BOUT THE VAR WELL.
I'M SORRY YOU LOST.
SO AM I. ENGLISH IS AN UGLY, LURCHING FOOL OF A LANGUAGE.
BUT IT COMMUNICATES HATE WELL.
THAT IS NOTHING TO BE PROUD OF.
ONE LAST THING, MR. JERUSALEM.
DO YOU KNOW WHAT AN *ENFANT TERRIBLE* IS?

Blood Hound

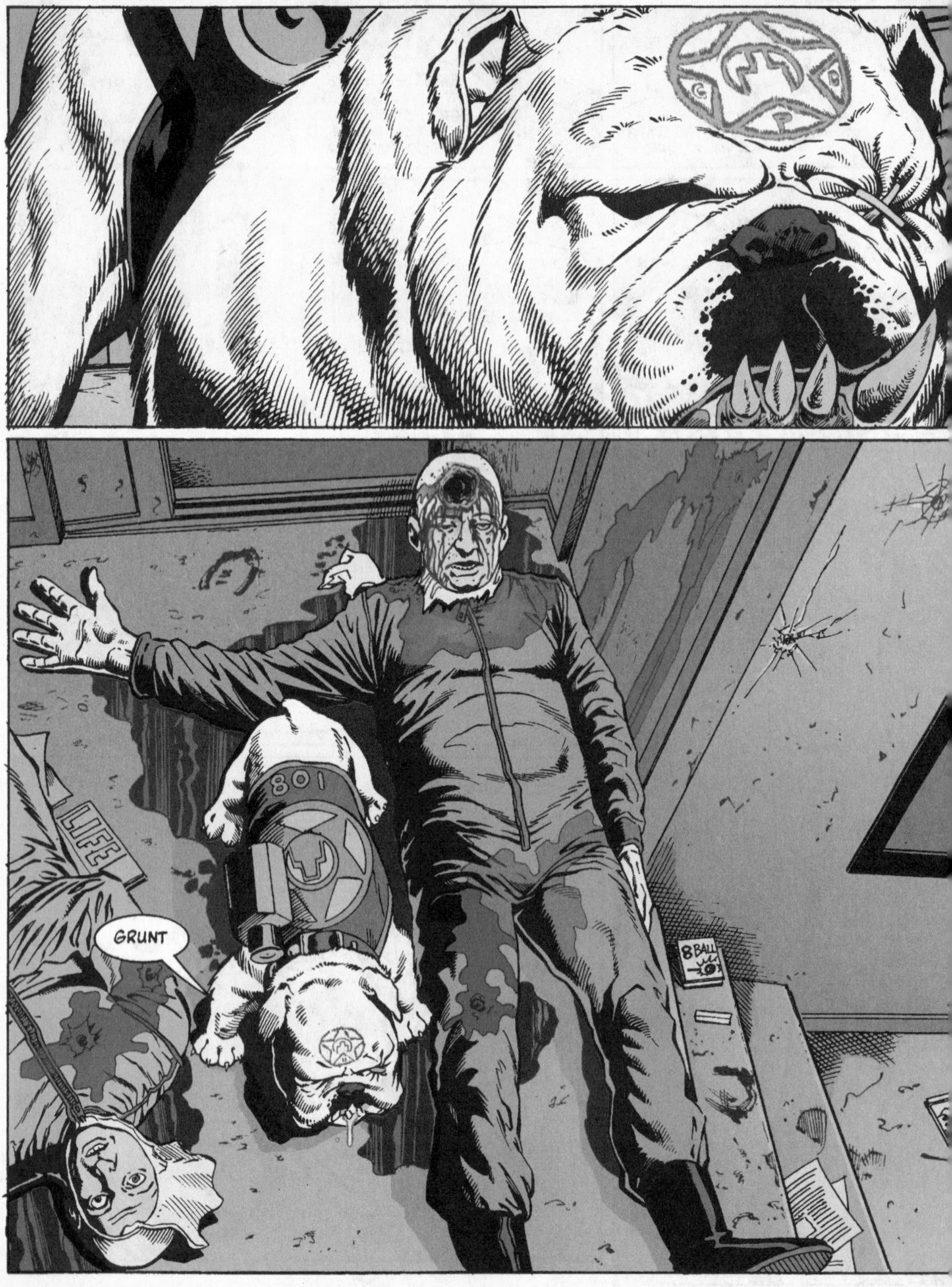
801
LIFE
GRUNT
8 BALL

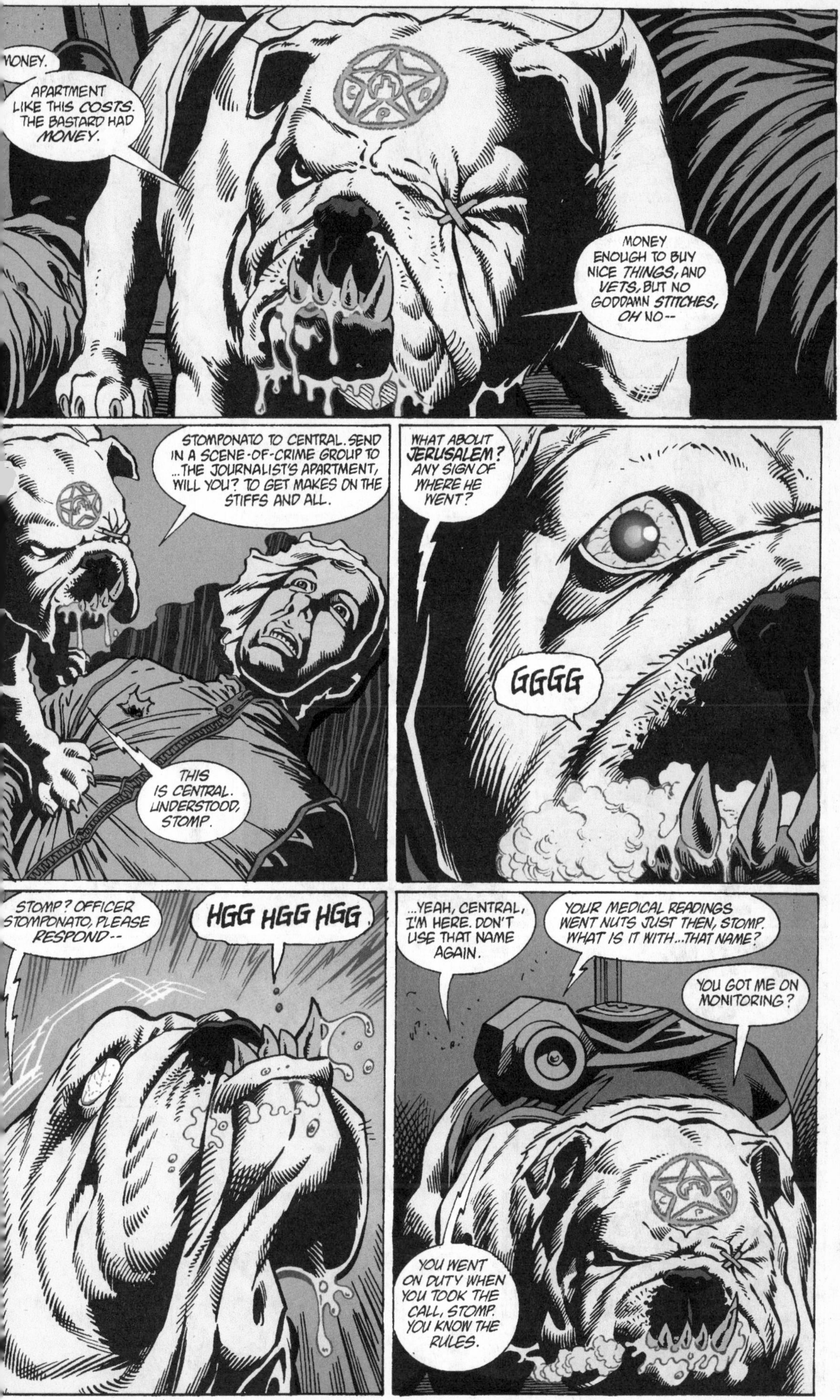
MONEY.
APARTMENT LIKE THIS COSTS. THE BASTARD HAD MONEY.
MONEY ENOUGH TO BUY NICE THINGS, AND VETS, BUT NO GODDAMN STITCHES, OH NO--
STOMPONATO TO CENTRAL. SEND IN A SCENE-OF-CRIME GROUP TO ...THE JOURNALIST'S APARTMENT, WILL YOU? TO GET MAKES ON THE STIFFS AND ALL.
THIS IS CENTRAL. UNDERSTOOD, STOMP.
WHAT ABOUT JERUSALEM? ANY SIGN OF WHERE HE WENT?
GGGG
STOMP? OFFICER STOMPONATO, PLEASE RESPOND--
HGG HGG HGG
...YEAH, CENTRAL, I'M HERE. DON'T USE THAT NAME AGAIN.
YOUR MEDICAL READINGS WENT NUTS JUST THEN, STOMP. WHAT IS IT WITH...THAT NAME?
YOU GOT ME ON MONITORING?
YOU WENT ON DUTY WHEN YOU TOOK THE CALL, STOMP. YOU KNOW THE RULES.

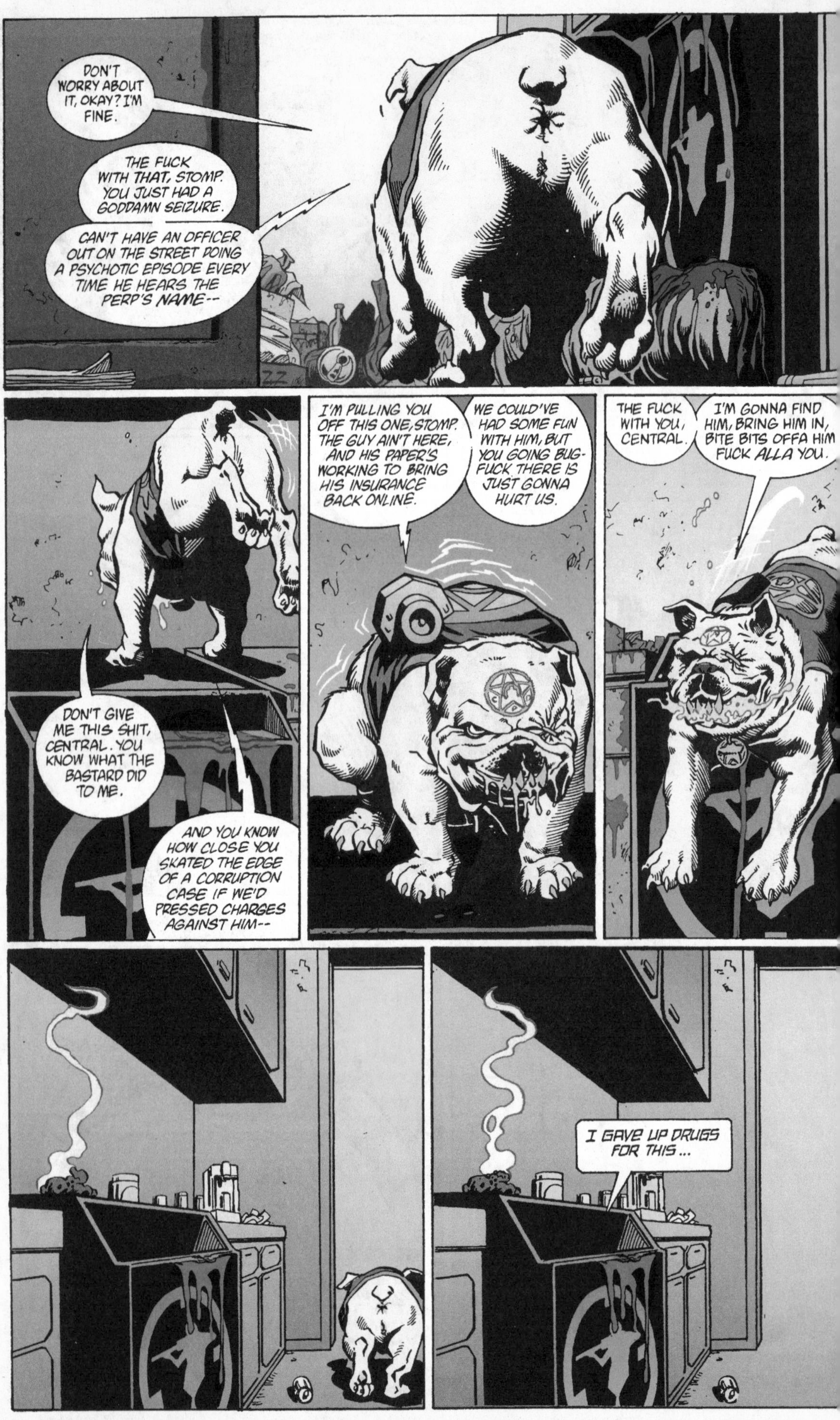
DON'T WORRY ABOUT IT, OKAY? I'M FINE.
THE FUCK WITH THAT, STOMP. YOU JUST HAD A GODDAMN SEIZURE.
CAN'T HAVE AN OFFICER OUT ON THE STREET DOING A PSYCHOTIC EPISODE EVERY TIME HE HEARS THE PERP'S NAME--
DON'T GIVE ME THIS SHIT, CENTRAL. YOU KNOW WHAT THE BASTARD DID TO ME.
AND YOU KNOW HOW CLOSE YOU SKATED THE EDGE OF A CORRUPTION CASE IF WE'D PRESSED CHARGES AGAINST HIM--
I'M PULLING YOU OFF THIS ONE, STOMP. THE GUY AIN'T HERE, AND HIS PAPER'S WORKING TO BRING HIS INSURANCE BACK ONLINE.
WE COULD'VE HAD SOME FUN WITH HIM, BUT YOU GOING BUG-FUCK THERE IS JUST GONNA HURT US.
THE FUCK WITH YOU, CENTRAL.
I'M GONNA FIND HIM, BRING HIM IN, BITE BITS OFFA HIM FUCK ALLA YOU.
I GAVE UP DRUGS FOR THIS ...

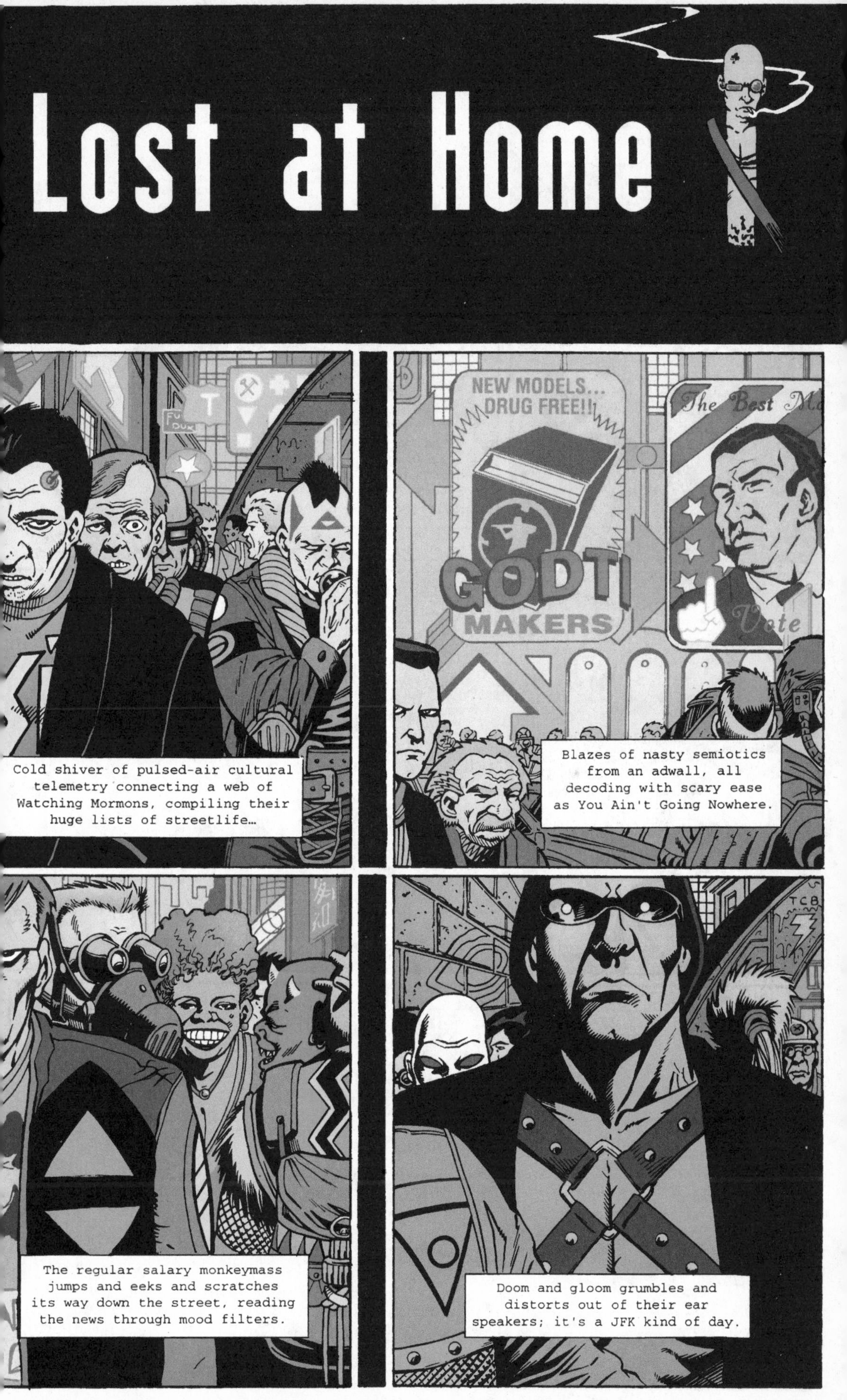
Lost at Home
NEW MODELS...
DRUG FREE!!
GODTI
MAKERS
The Best M
Vote
Cold shiver of pulsed-air cultural telemetry connecting a web of Watching Mormons, compiling their huge lists of streetlife…
Blazes of nasty semiotics from an adwall, all decoding with scary ease as You Ain't Going Nowhere.
The regular salary monkeymass jumps and eeks and scratches its way down the street, reading the news through mood filters.
TCB
Doom and gloom grumbles and distorts out of their ear speakers; it's a JFK kind of day.

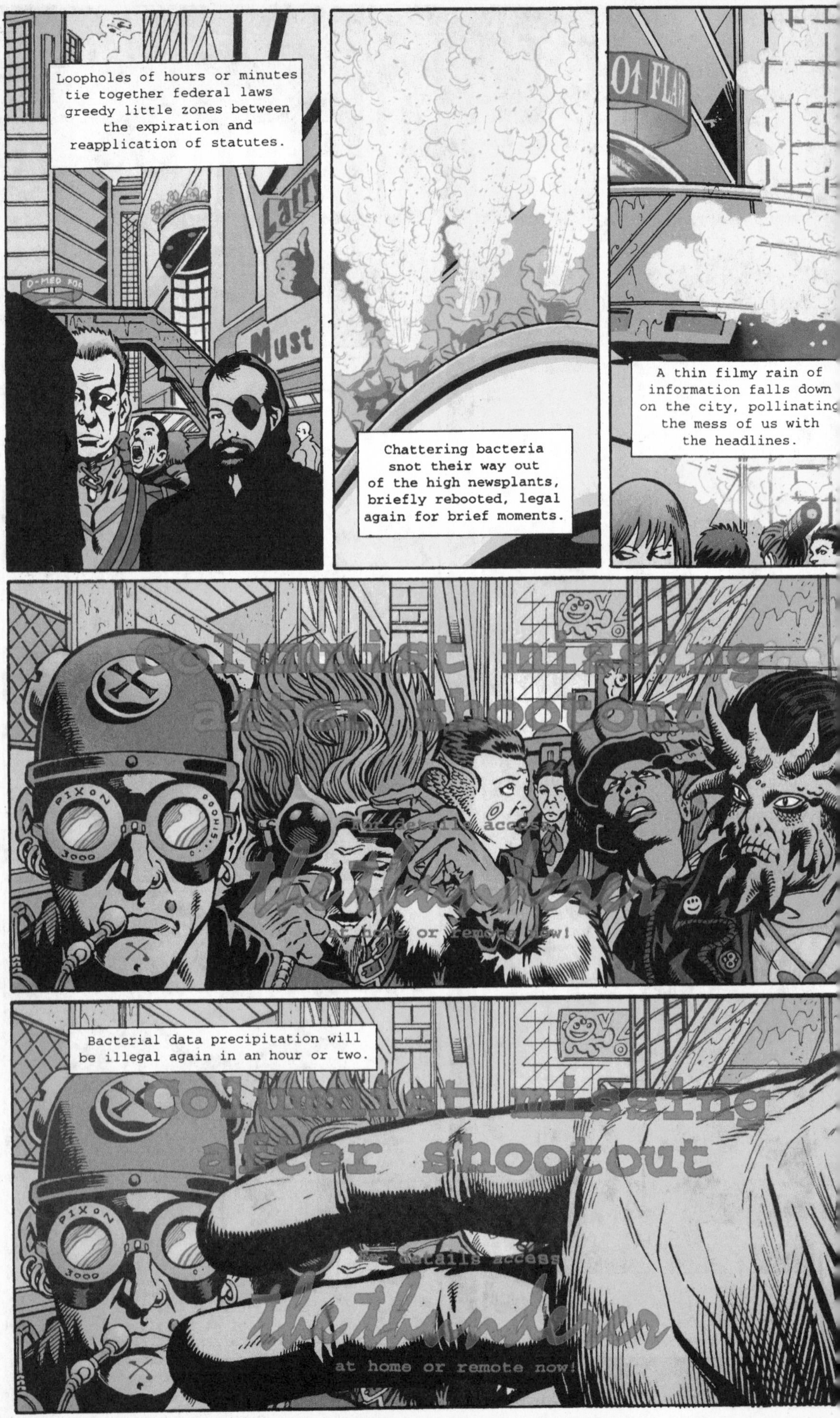
Loopholes of hours or minutes tie together federal laws greedy little zones between the expiration and reapplication of statutes.
Larry
Must
Chattering bacteria snot their way out of the high newsplants, briefly rebooted, legal again for brief moments.
A thin filmy rain of information falls down on the city, pollinating the mess of us with the headlines.
PIXON
3000
Bacterial data precipitation will be illegal again in an hour or two.
Columnist missing after shootout
details access
thethunderer
at home or remote now!

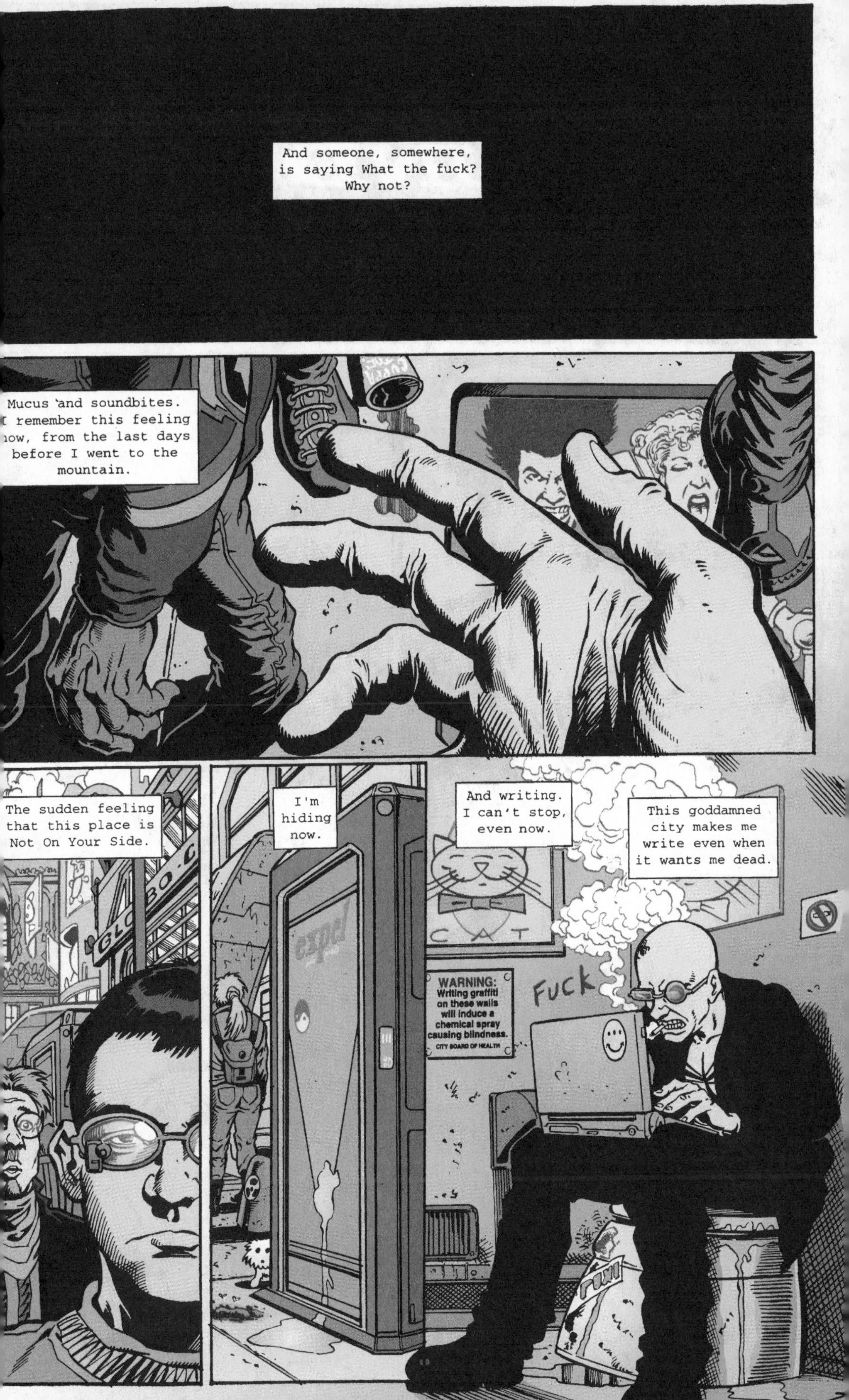
And someone, somewhere, is saying What the fuck? Why not?
Mucus 'and soundbites. I remember this feeling now, from the last days before I went to the mountain.
The sudden feeling that this place is Not On Your Side.
I'm hiding now.
And writing. I can't stop, even now.
This goddamned city makes me write even when it wants me dead.
CAT
WARNING: Writing graffiti on these walls will induce a chemical spray causing blindness.
CITY BOARD OF HEALTH
FUCK
expel

A VOYAGE ROUND MY FATHER

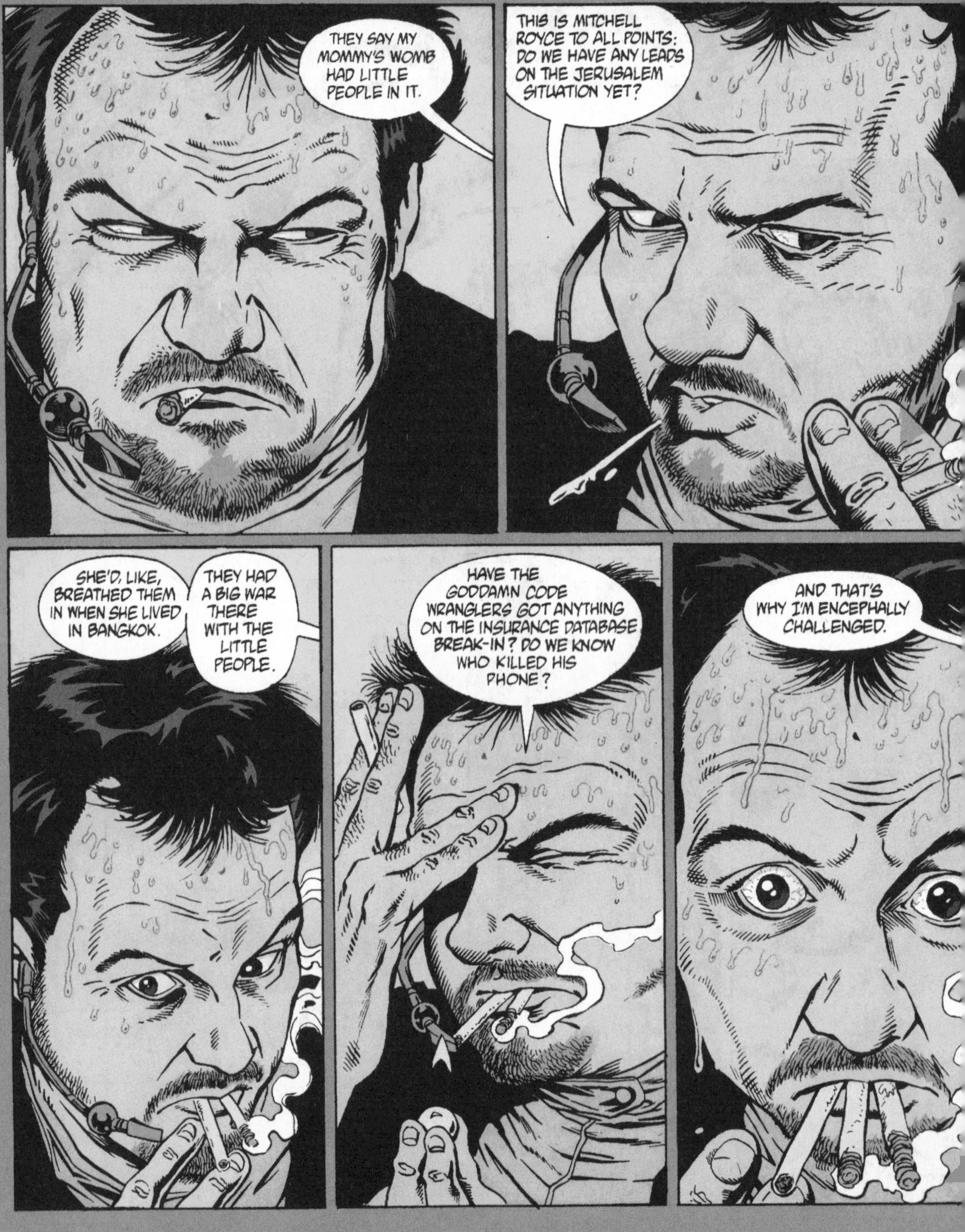
THEY SAY MY MOMMY'S WOMB HAD LITTLE PEOPLE IN IT.
THIS IS MITCHELL ROYCE TO ALL POINTS: DO WE HAVE ANY LEADS ON THE JERUSALEM SITUATION YET?
SHE'D, LIKE, BREATHED THEM IN WHEN SHE LIVED IN BANGKOK.
THEY HAD A BIG WAR THERE WITH THE LITTLE PEOPLE.
HAVE THE GODDAMN CODE WRANGLERS GOT ANYTHING ON THE INSURANCE DATABASE BREAK-IN? DO WE KNOW WHO KILLED HIS PHONE?
AND THAT'S WHY I'M ENCEPHALLY CHALLENGED.

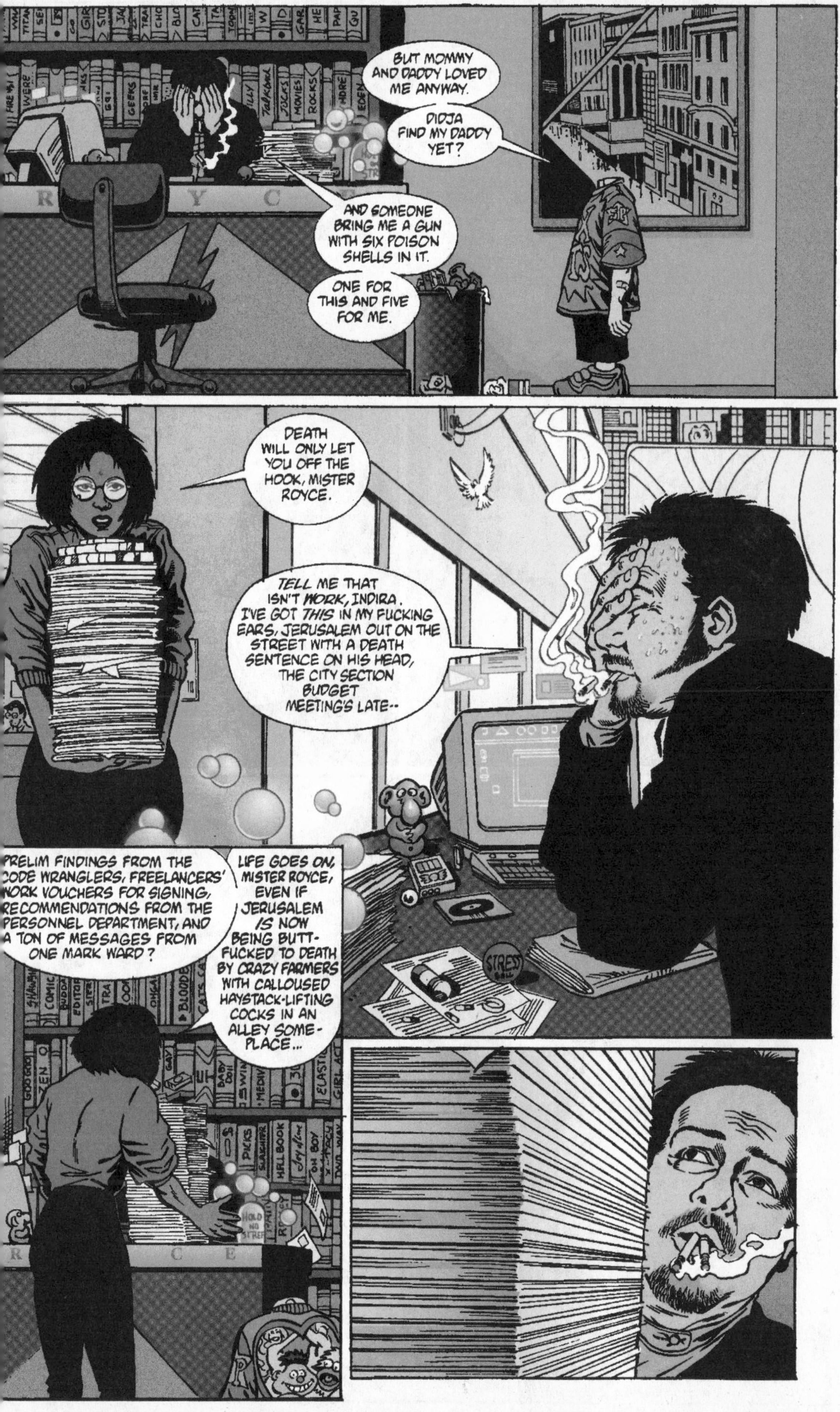
BUT MOMMY AND DADDY LOVED ME ANYWAY.
DIDJA FIND MY DADDY YET?
AND SOMEONE BRING ME A GUN WITH SIX POISON SHELLS IN IT.
ONE FOR THIS AND FIVE FOR ME.
DEATH WILL ONLY LET YOU OFF THE HOOK, MISTER ROYCE.
TELL ME THAT ISN'T WORK, INDIRA. I'VE GOT THIS IN MY FUCKING EARS, JERUSALEM OUT ON THE STREET WITH A DEATH SENTENCE ON HIS HEAD, THE CITY SECTION BUDGET MEETING'S LATE--
PRELIM FINDINGS FROM THE CODE WRANGLERS, FREELANCERS' WORK VOUCHERS FOR SIGNING, RECOMMENDATIONS FROM THE PERSONNEL DEPARTMENT, AND A TON OF MESSAGES FROM ONE MARK WARD?
LIFE GOES ON, MISTER ROYCE, EVEN IF JERUSALEM IS NOW BEING BUTT-FUCKED TO DEATH BY CRAZY FARMERS WITH CALLOUSED HAYSTACK-LIFTING COCKS IN AN ALLEY SOME-PLACE...

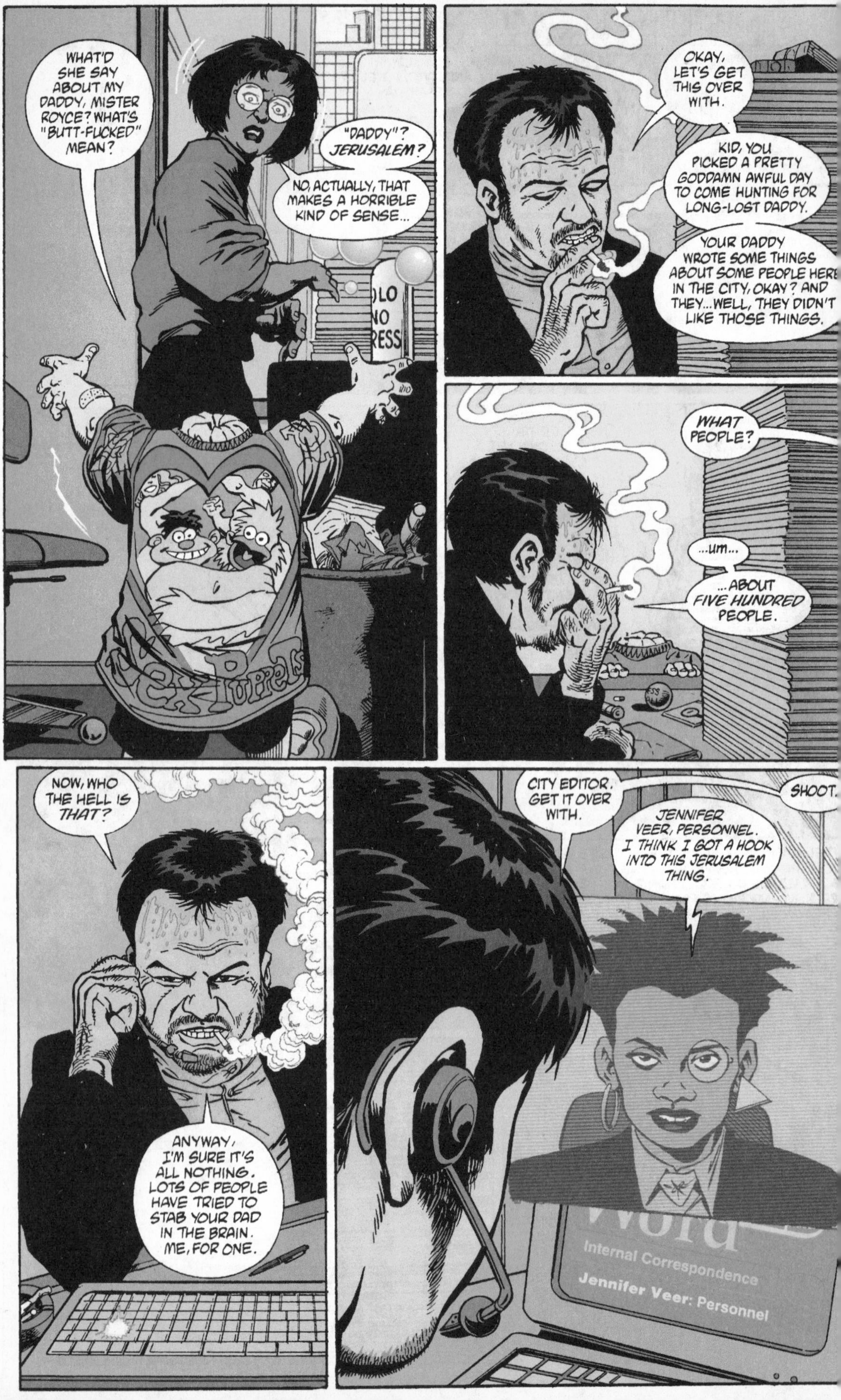
WHAT'D SHE SAY ABOUT MY DADDY, MISTER ROYCE? WHAT'S "BUTT-FUCKED" MEAN?
"DADDY"? JERUSALEM?
NO, ACTUALLY, THAT MAKES A HORRIBLE KIND OF SENSE...
OLO
NO
RESS
OKAY, LET'S GET THIS OVER WITH.
KID, YOU PICKED A PRETTY GODDAMN AWFUL DAY TO COME HUNTING FOR LONG-LOST DADDY.
YOUR DADDY WROTE SOME THINGS ABOUT SOME PEOPLE HERE IN THE CITY, OKAY? AND THEY...WELL, THEY DIDN'T LIKE THOSE THINGS.
WHAT PEOPLE?
...um...
...ABOUT FIVE HUNDRED PEOPLE.
NOW, WHO THE HELL IS THAT?
ANYWAY, I'M SURE IT'S ALL NOTHING. LOTS OF PEOPLE HAVE TRIED TO STAB YOUR DAD IN THE BRAIN. ME, FOR ONE.
CITY EDITOR. GET IT OVER WITH.
SHOOT.
JENNIFER VEER, PERSONNEL. I THINK I GOT A HOOK INTO THIS JERUSALEM THING.
Internal Correspondence
Jennifer Veer: Personnel

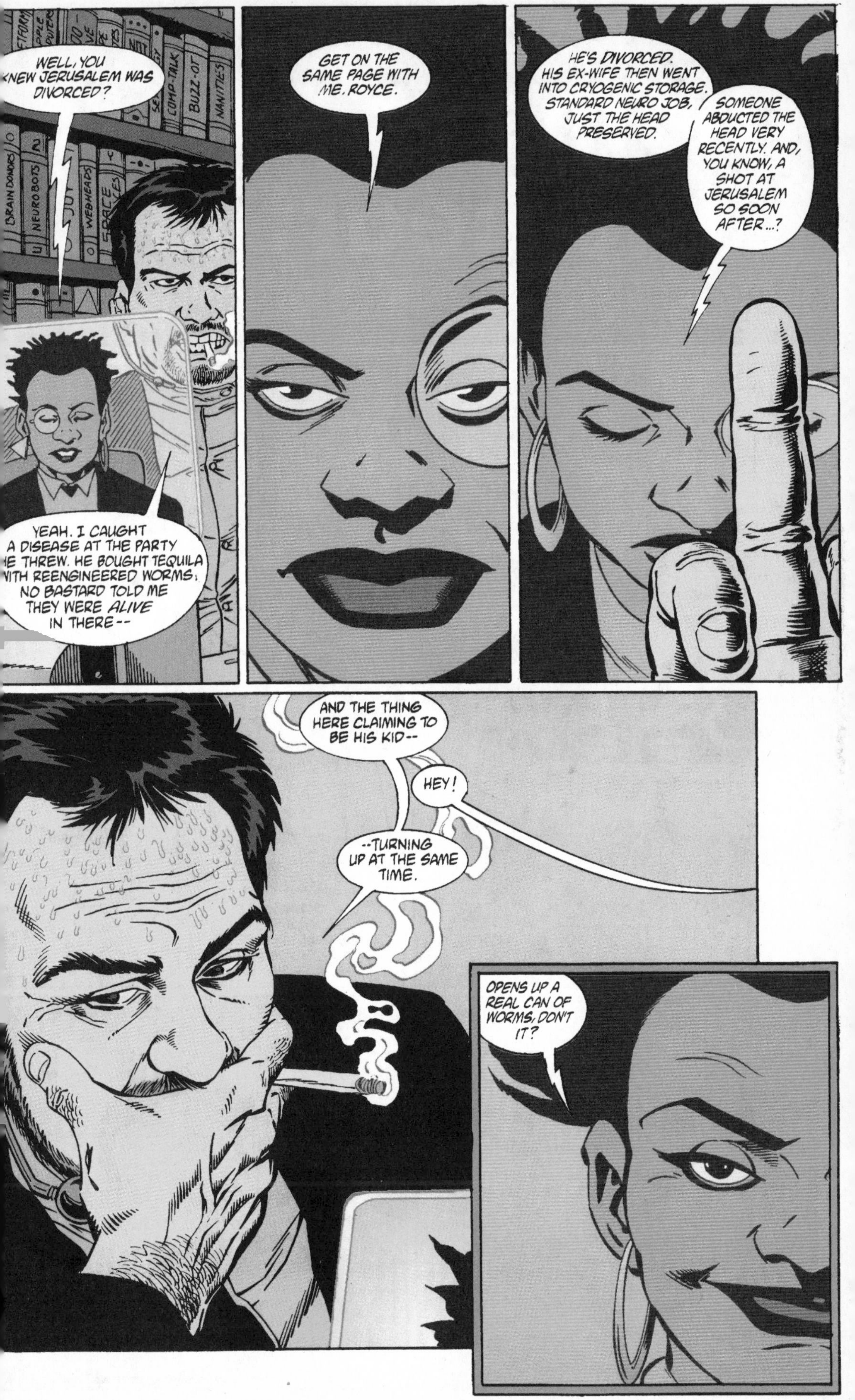
WELL, YOU KNEW JERUSALEM WAS DIVORCED?
YEAH. I CAUGHT A DISEASE AT THE PARTY HE THREW. HE BOUGHT TEQUILA WITH REENGINEERED WORMS; NO BASTARD TOLD ME THEY WERE ALIVE IN THERE--
GET ON THE SAME PAGE WITH ME, ROYCE.
HE'S DIVORCED. HIS EX-WIFE THEN WENT INTO CRYOGENIC STORAGE. STANDARD NEURO JOB, JUST THE HEAD PRESERVED.
SOMEONE ABDUCTED THE HEAD VERY RECENTLY. AND, YOU KNOW, A SHOT AT JERUSALEM SO SOON AFTER...?
AND THE THING HERE CLAIMING TO BE HIS KID--
HEY!
--TURNING UP AT THE SAME TIME.
OPENS UP A REAL CAN OF WORMS, DON'T IT?

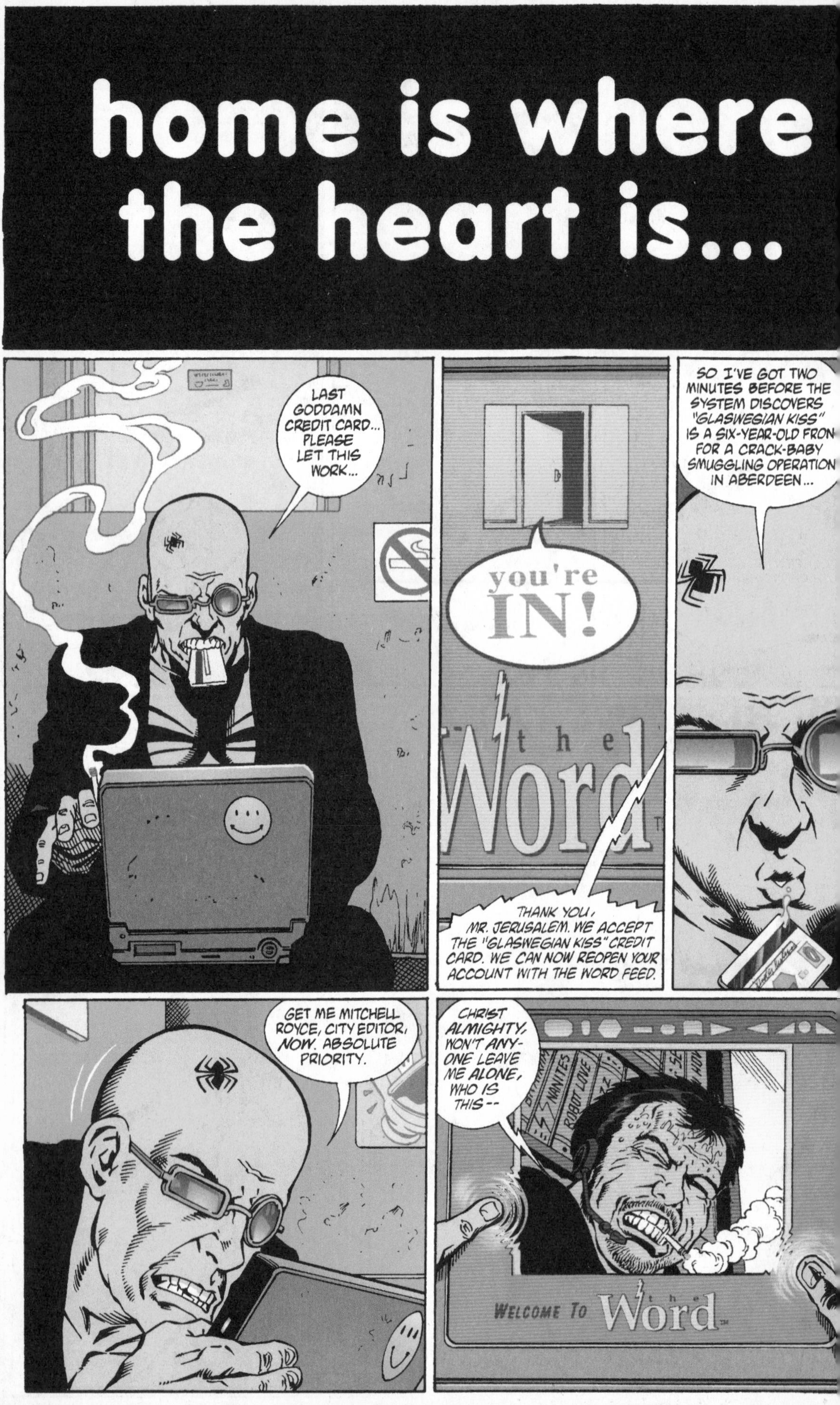
home is where the heart is...
LAST GODDAMN CREDIT CARD... PLEASE LET THIS WORK...
you're IN!
the Word
THANK YOU, MR. JERUSALEM. WE ACCEPT THE "GLASWEGIAN KISS" CREDIT CARD. WE CAN NOW REOPEN YOUR ACCOUNT WITH THE WORD FEED.
SO I'VE GOT TWO MINUTES BEFORE THE SYSTEM DISCOVERS "GLASWEGIAN KISS" IS A SIX-YEAR-OLD FRON FOR A CRACK-BABY SMUGGLING OPERATION IN ABERDEEN...
GET ME MITCHELL ROYCE, CITY EDITOR, NOW. ABSOLUTE PRIORITY.
CHRIST ALMIGHTY, WON'T ANYONE LEAVE ME ALONE, WHO IS THIS --
NANITES
ROBOT LOVE
WELCOME TO the Word

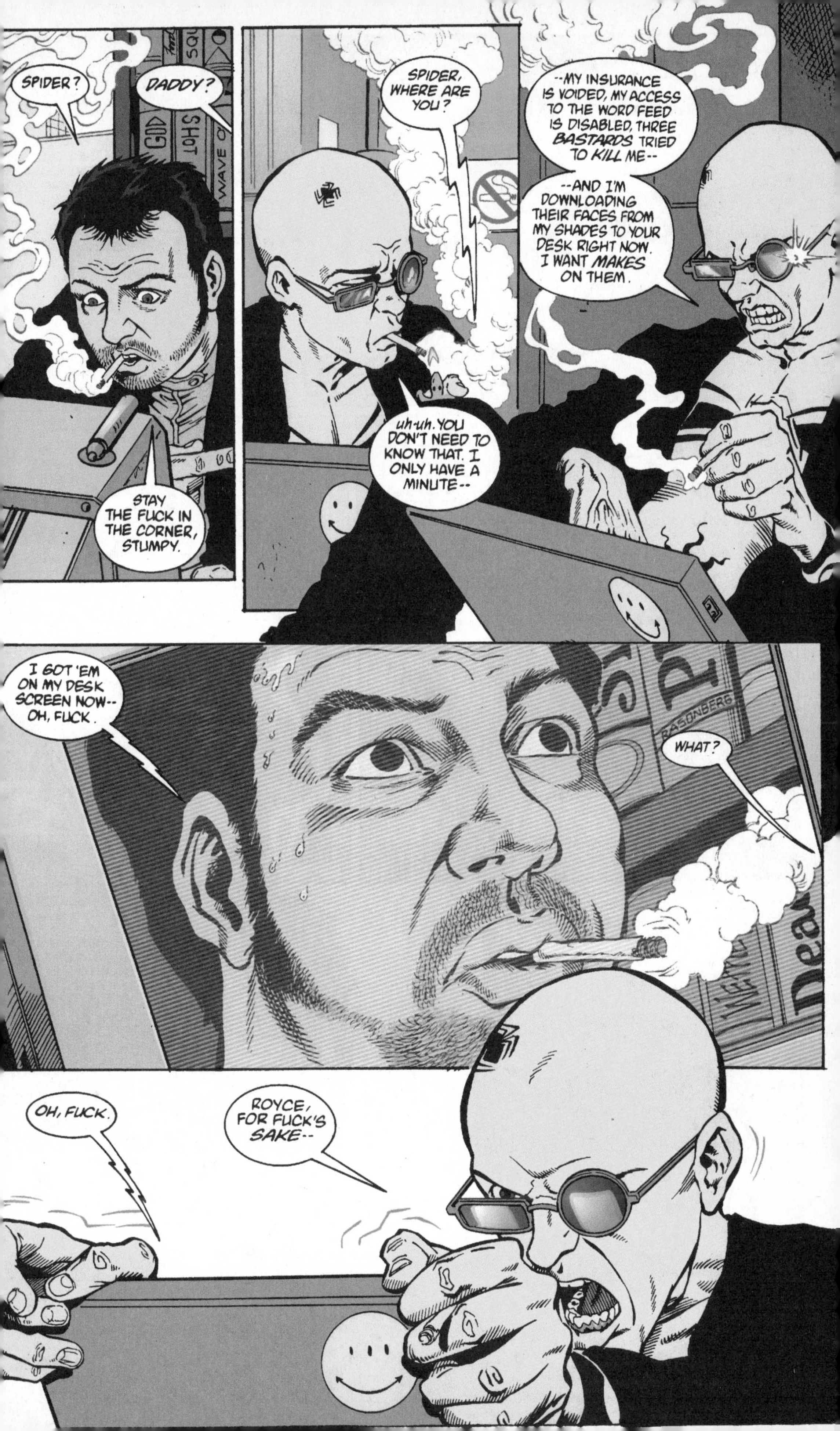
SPIDER?
DADDY?
STAY THE FUCK IN THE CORNER, STUMPY.
SPIDER, WHERE ARE YOU?
uh-uh. YOU DON'T NEED TO KNOW THAT. I ONLY HAVE A MINUTE--
--MY INSURANCE IS VOIDED, MY ACCESS TO THE WORD FEED IS DISABLED, THREE BASTARDS TRIED TO KILL ME--
--AND I'M DOWNLOADING THEIR FACES FROM MY SHADES TO YOUR DESK RIGHT NOW. I WANT MAKES ON THEM.
I GOT 'EM ON MY DESK SCREEN NOW-- OH, FUCK.
WHAT?
OH, FUCK.
ROYCE, FOR FUCK'S SAKE--

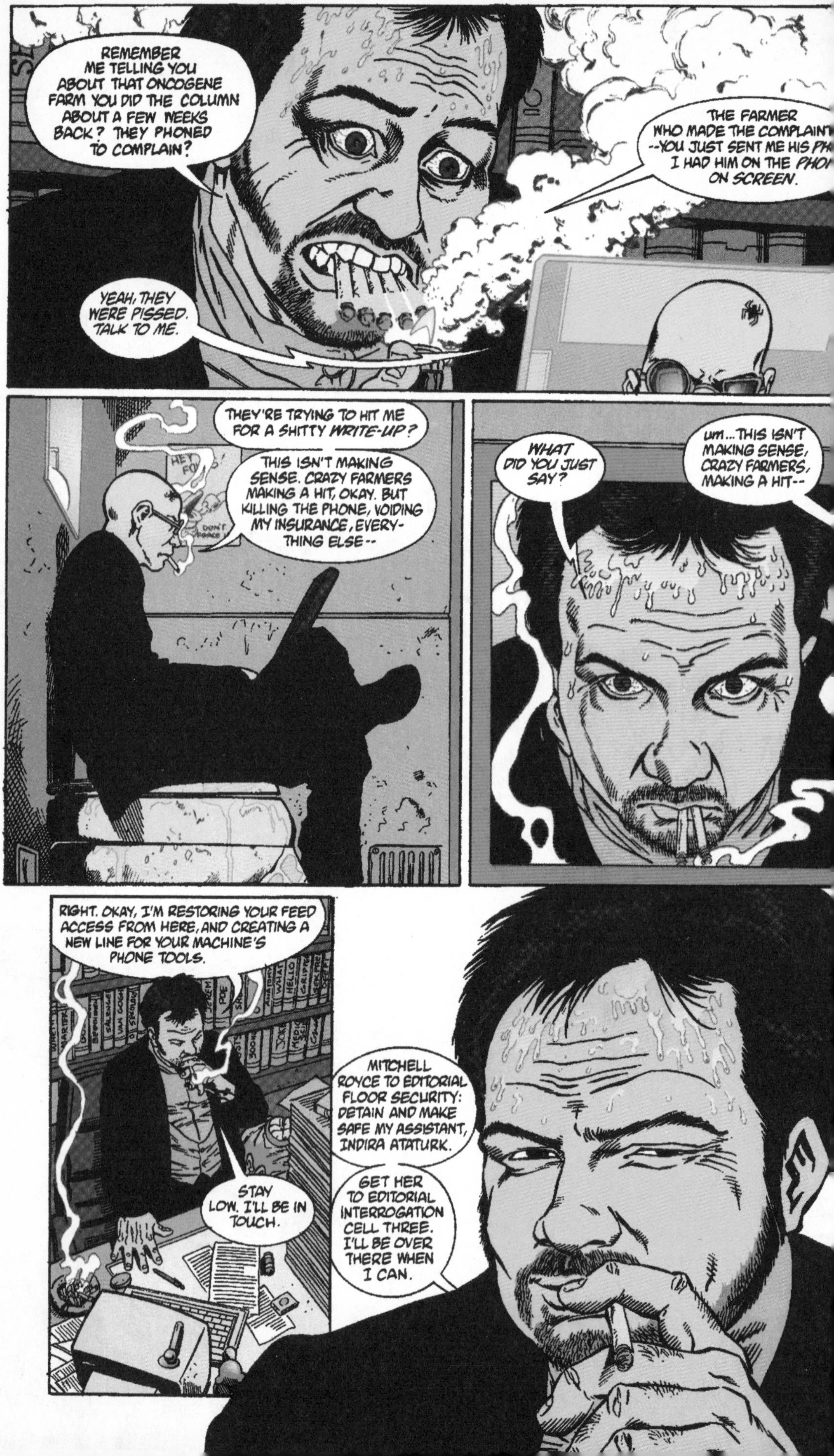
REMEMBER ME TELLING YOU ABOUT THAT ONCOGENE FARM YOU DID THE COLUMN ABOUT A FEW WEEKS BACK? THEY PHONED TO COMPLAIN?
YEAH, THEY WERE PISSED. TALK TO ME.
THE FARMER WHO MADE THE COMPLAINT --YOU JUST SENT ME HIS PH I HAD HIM ON THE PHO ON SCREEN.
THEY'RE TRYING TO HIT ME FOR A SHITTY WRITE-UP?
THIS ISN'T MAKING SENSE. CRAZY FARMERS MAKING A HIT, OKAY. BUT KILLING THE PHONE, VOIDING MY INSURANCE, EVERYTHING ELSE--
WHAT DID YOU JUST SAY?
um...THIS ISN'T MAKING SENSE, CRAZY FARMERS, MAKING A HIT--
RIGHT. OKAY, I'M RESTORING YOUR FEED ACCESS FROM HERE, AND CREATING A NEW LINE FOR YOUR MACHINE'S PHONE TOOLS.
STAY LOW. I'LL BE IN TOUCH.
MITCHELL ROYCE TO EDITORIAL FLOOR SECURITY: DETAIN AND MAKE SAFE MY ASSISTANT, INDIRA ATATURK.
GET HER TO EDITORIAL INTERROGATION CELL THREE. I'LL BE OVER THERE WHEN I CAN.

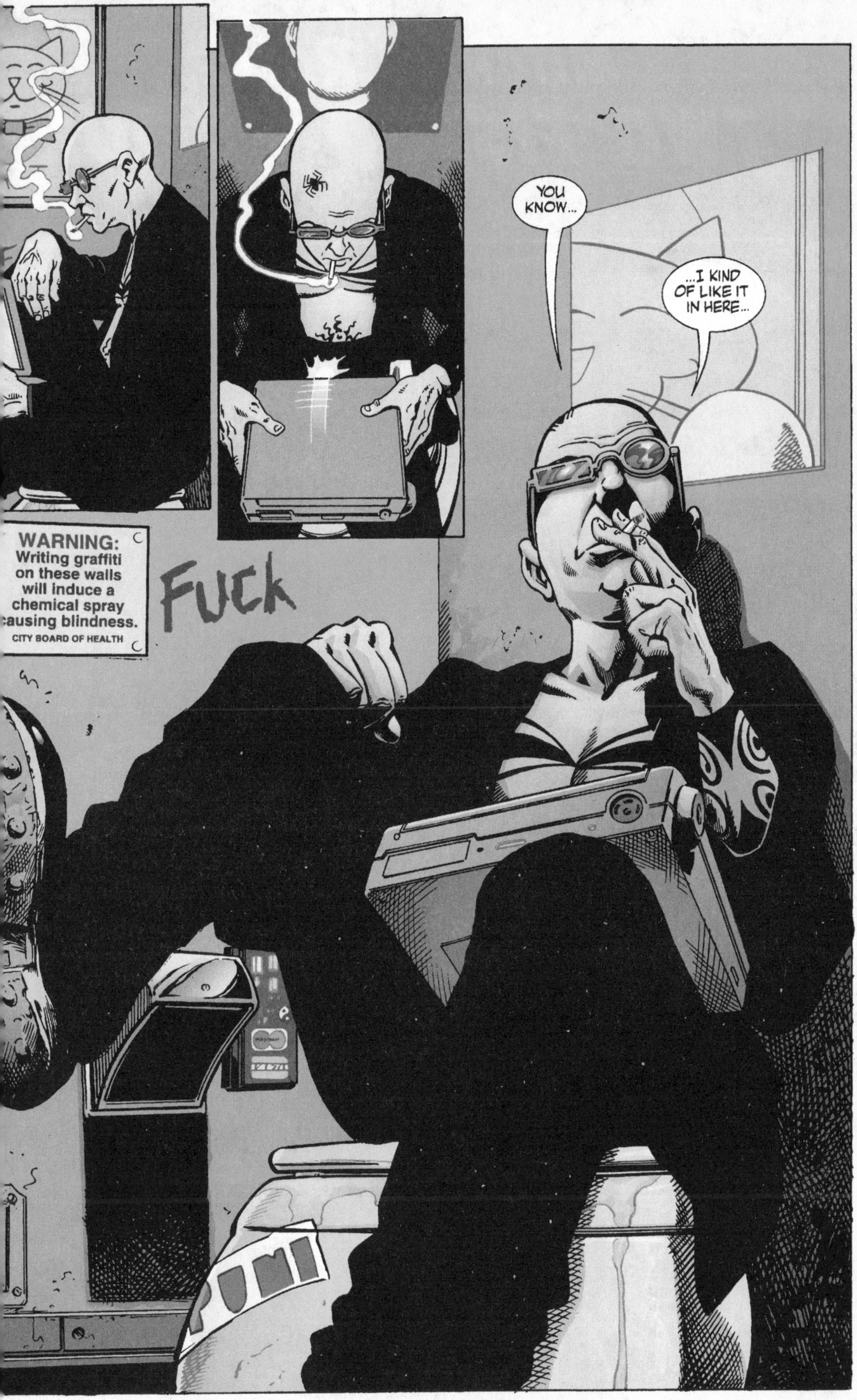
WARNING:
Writing graffiti on these walls will induce a chemical spray causing blindness.
CITY BOARD OF HEALTH
FUCK
YOU KNOW...
...I KIND OF LIKE IT IN HERE...

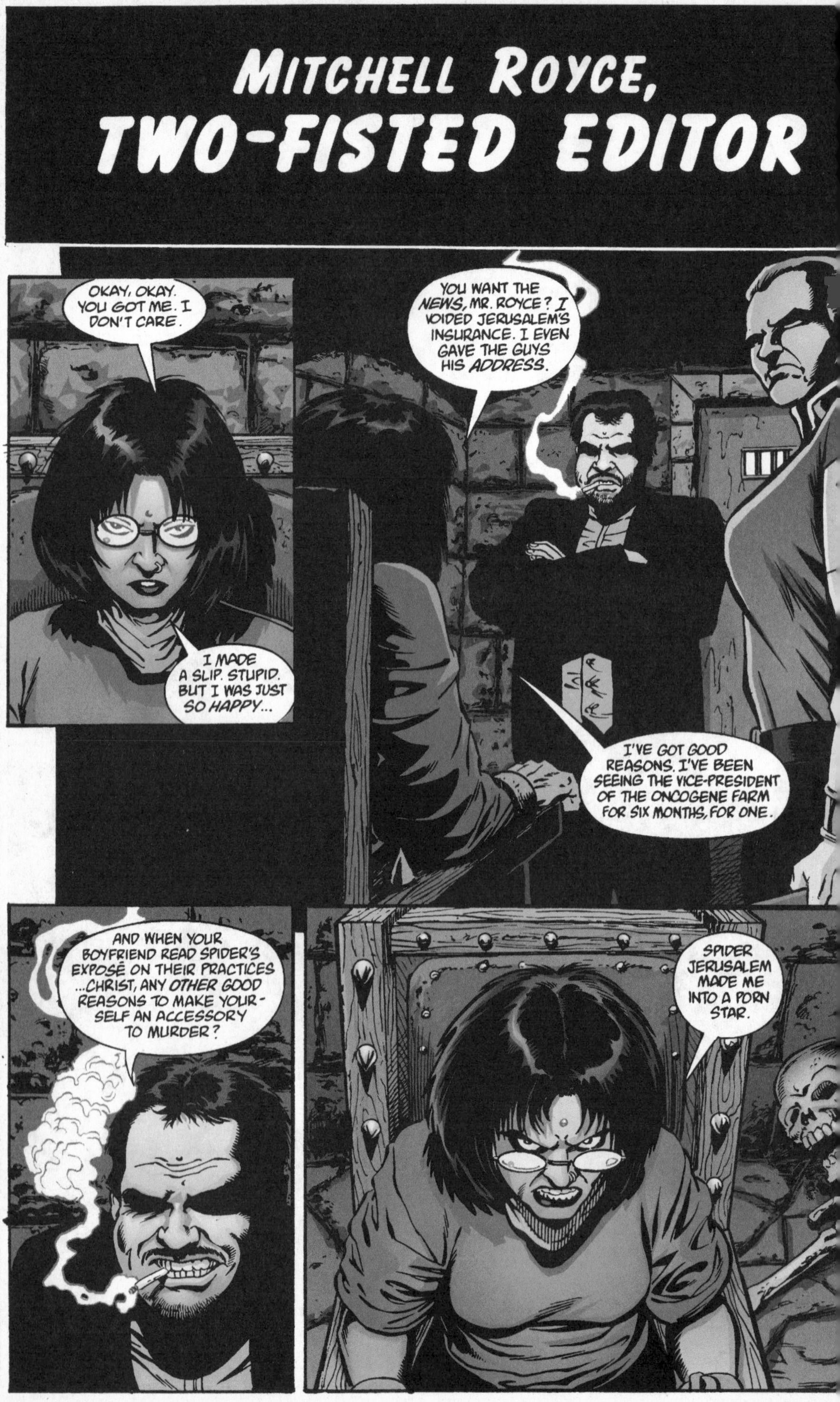
MITCHELL ROYCE, TWO-FISTED EDITOR
OKAY, OKAY. YOU GOT ME. I DON'T CARE.
I MADE A SLIP. STUPID. BUT I WAS JUST SO HAPPY...
YOU WANT THE NEWS, MR. ROYCE? I VOIDED JERUSALEM'S INSURANCE. I EVEN GAVE THE GUYS HIS ADDRESS.
I'VE GOT GOOD REASONS. I'VE BEEN SEEING THE VICE-PRESIDENT OF THE ONCOGENE FARM FOR SIX MONTHS, FOR ONE.
AND WHEN YOUR BOYFRIEND READ SPIDER'S EXPOSÉ ON THEIR PRACTICES ...CHRIST, ANY OTHER GOOD REASONS TO MAKE YOURSELF AN ACCESSORY TO MURDER?
SPIDER JERUSALEM MADE ME INTO A PORN STAR.

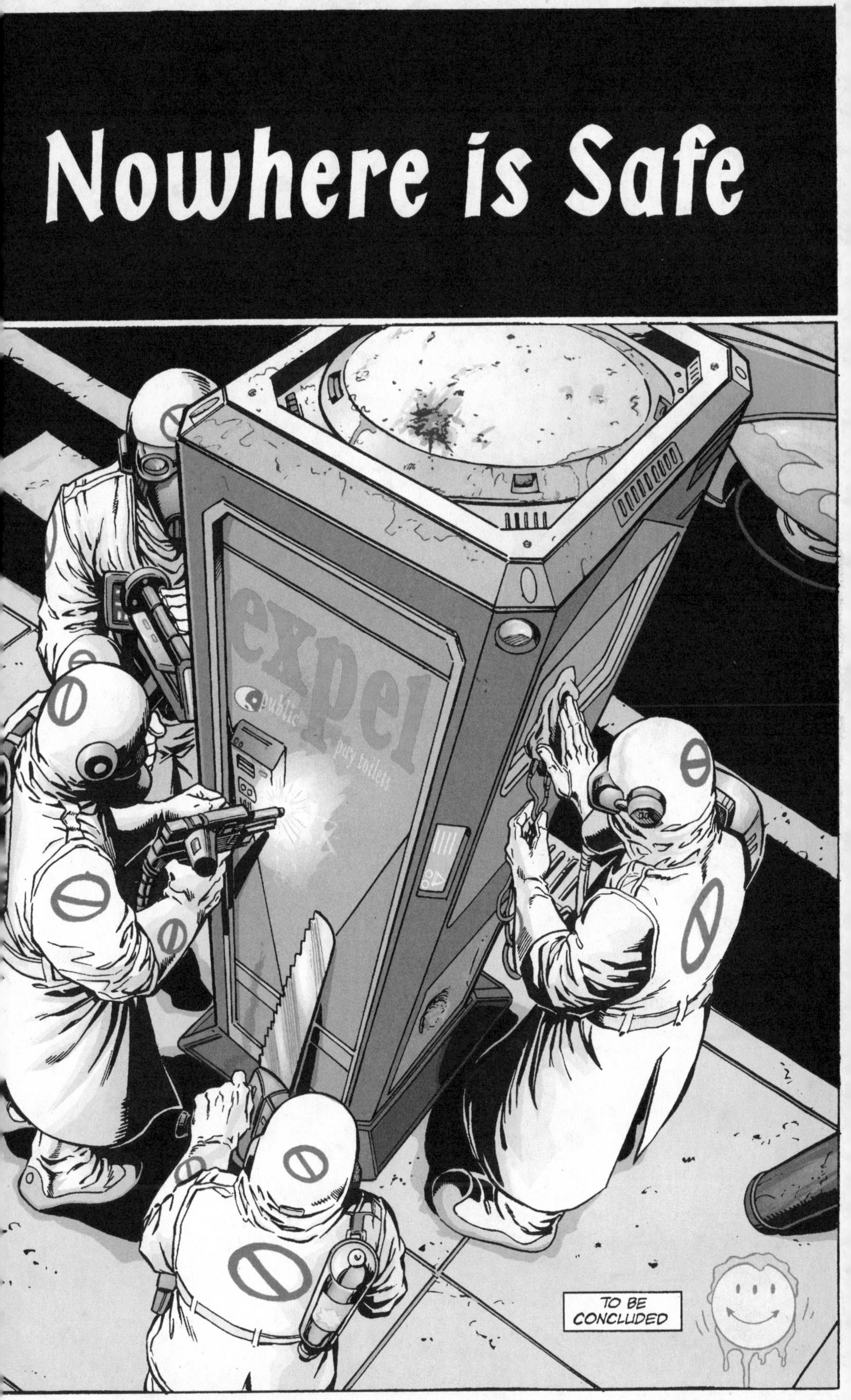
Nowhere is Safe
expel
public pay toilets
TO BE CONCLUDED

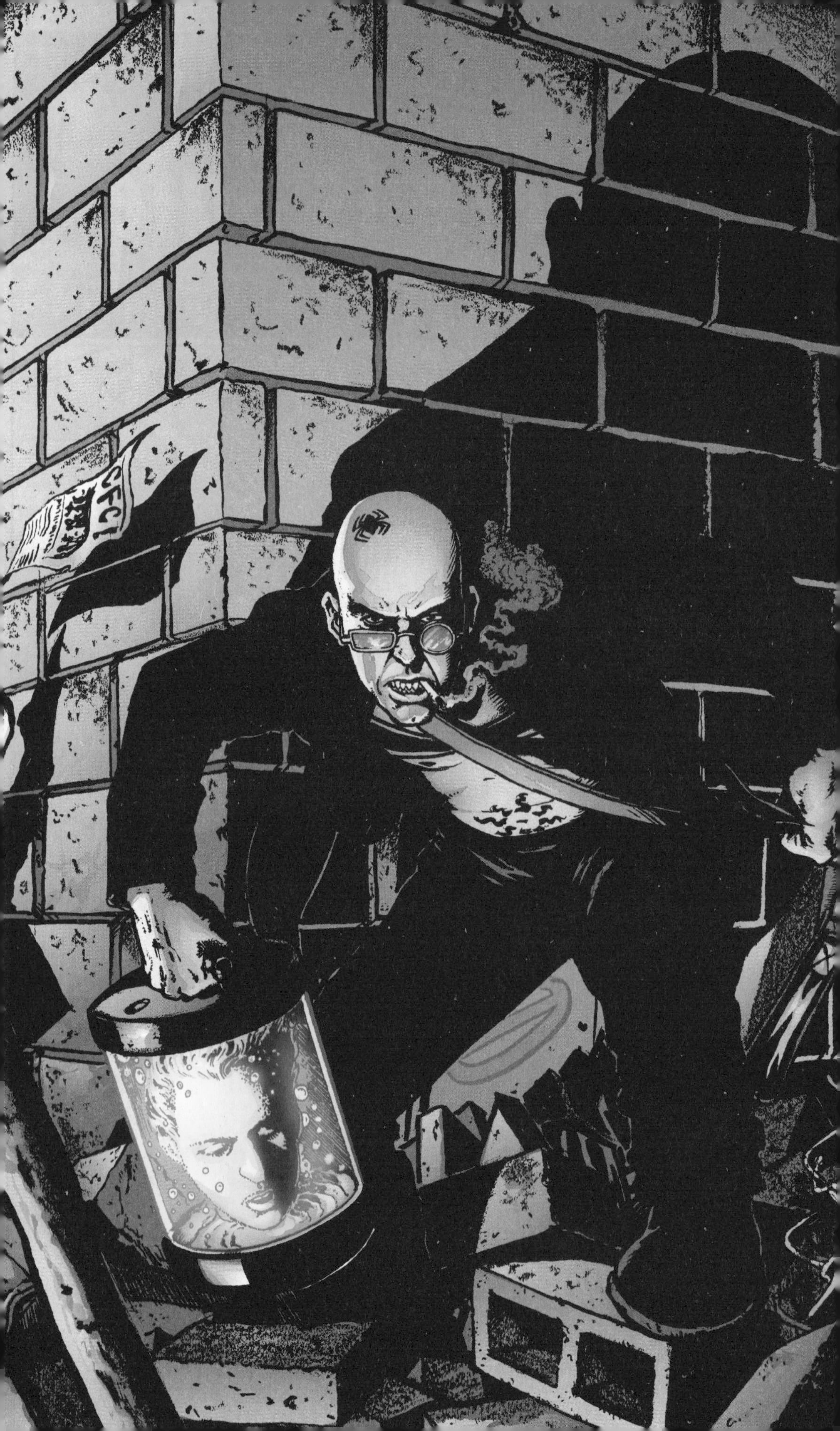
CFC!

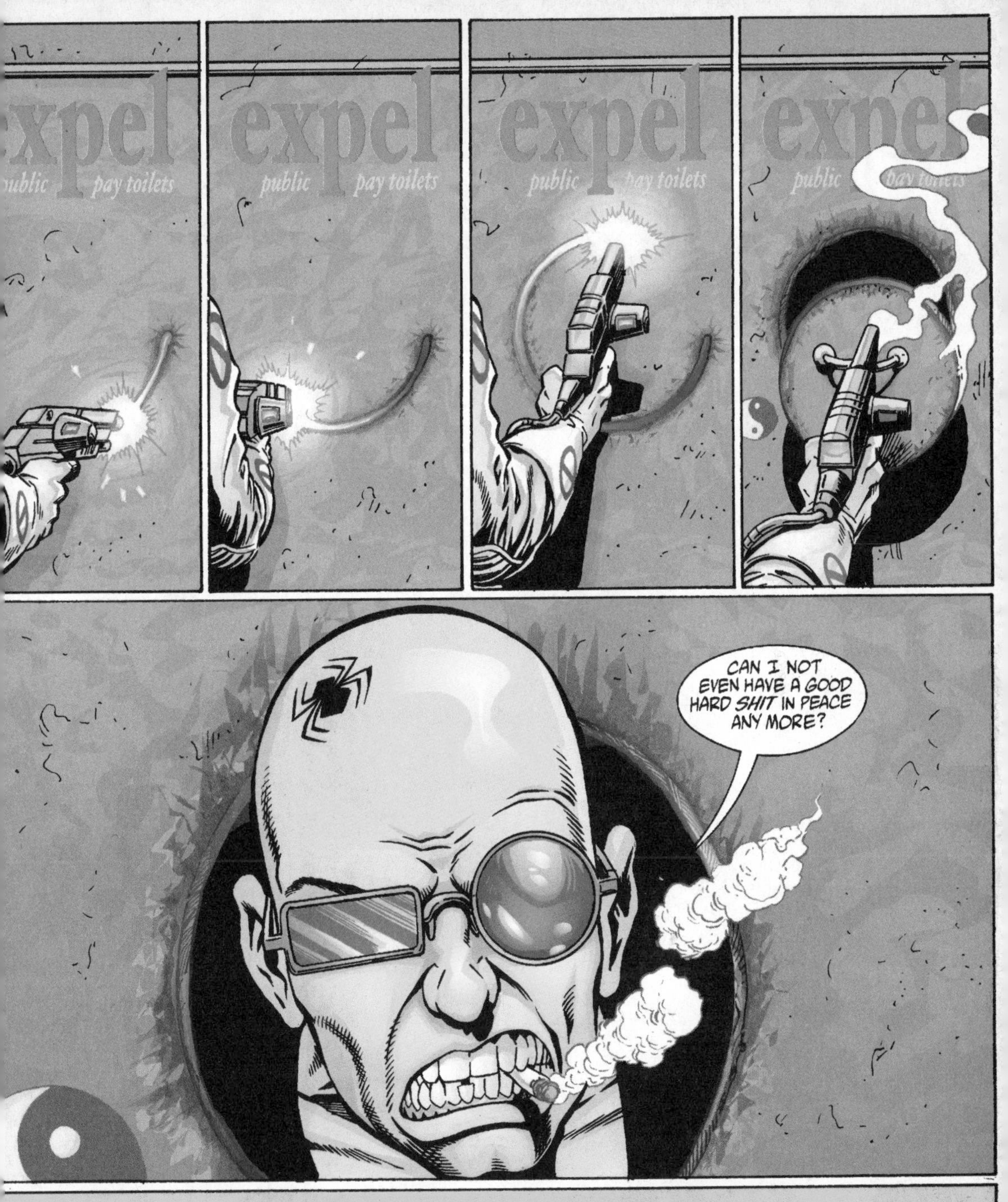
expel
public pay toilets
CAN I NOT EVEN HAVE A GOOD HARD *SHIT* IN PEACE ANY MORE?

WARREN ELLIS writes and DARICK ROBERTSON pencils

FREEZE ME WITH YOUR KISS

PART III OF III

RODNEY RAMOS, inker
NATHAN EYRING, color & separations
CLEM ROBINS, letterer
CLIFF CHIANG, assistant editor
STUART MOORE, editor
TRANSMETROPOLITAN CREATED BY WARREN ELLIS & DARICK ROBERTSON

True Confessions

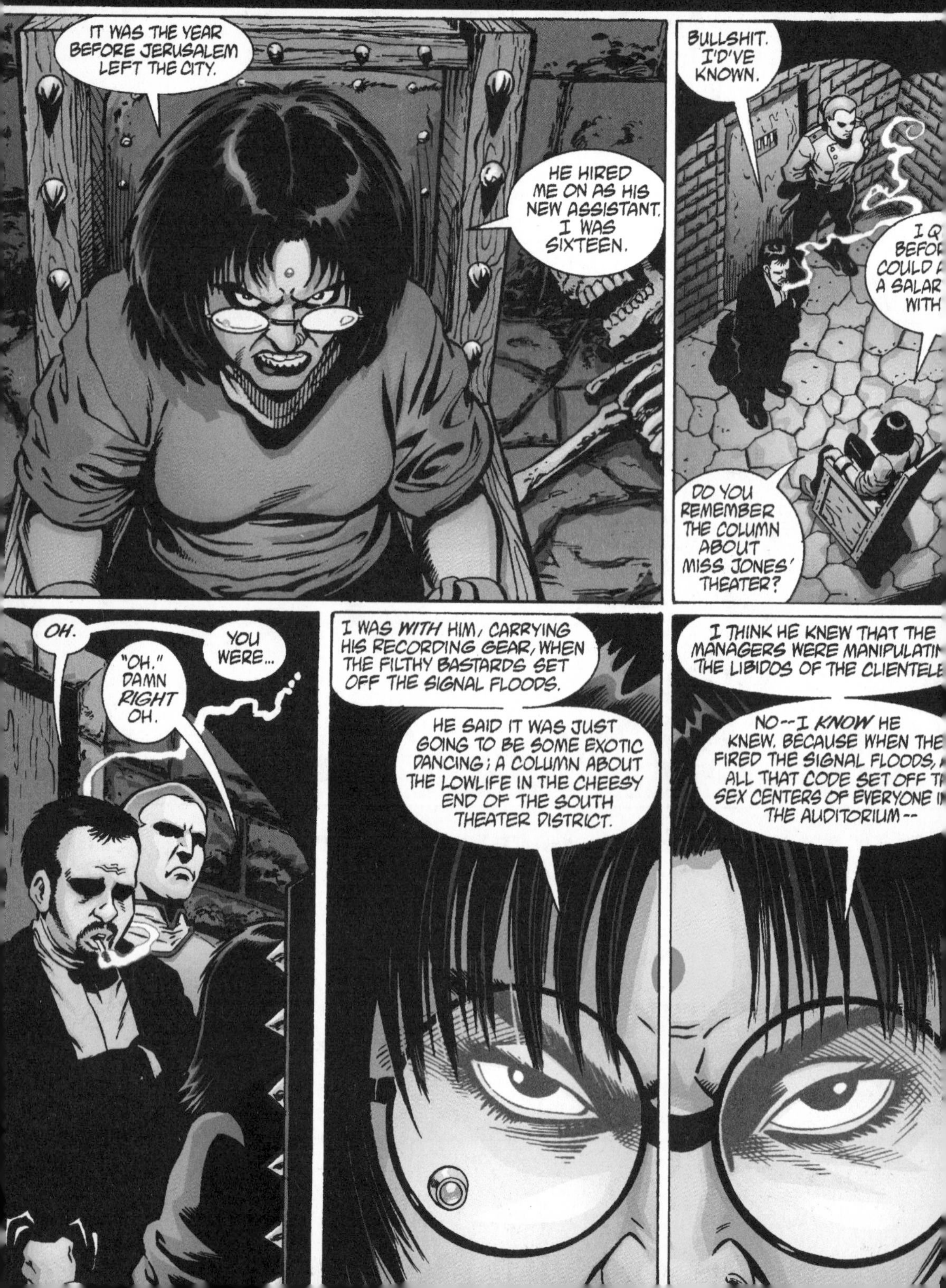
IT WAS THE YEAR BEFORE JERUSALEM LEFT THE CITY.
HE HIRED ME ON AS HIS NEW ASSISTANT. I WAS SIXTEEN.
BULLSHIT. I'D'VE KNOWN.
I Q BEFOR COULD A A SALAR WITH
DO YOU REMEMBER THE COLUMN ABOUT MISS JONES' THEATER?
OH.
YOU WERE...
"OH." DAMN *RIGHT* OH.
I WAS *WITH* HIM, CARRYING HIS RECORDING GEAR, WHEN THE FILTHY BASTARDS SET OFF THE SIGNAL FLOODS.
HE SAID IT WAS JUST GOING TO BE SOME EXOTIC DANCING; A COLUMN ABOUT THE LOWLIFE IN THE CHEESY END OF THE SOUTH THEATER DISTRICT.
I THINK HE KNEW THAT THE MANAGERS WERE MANIPULATIN THE LIBIDOS OF THE CLIENTELE
NO--I *KNOW* HE KNEW. BECAUSE WHEN THE FIRED THE SIGNAL FLOODS, A ALL THAT CODE SET OFF T SEX CENTERS OF EVERYONE I THE AUDITORIUM--

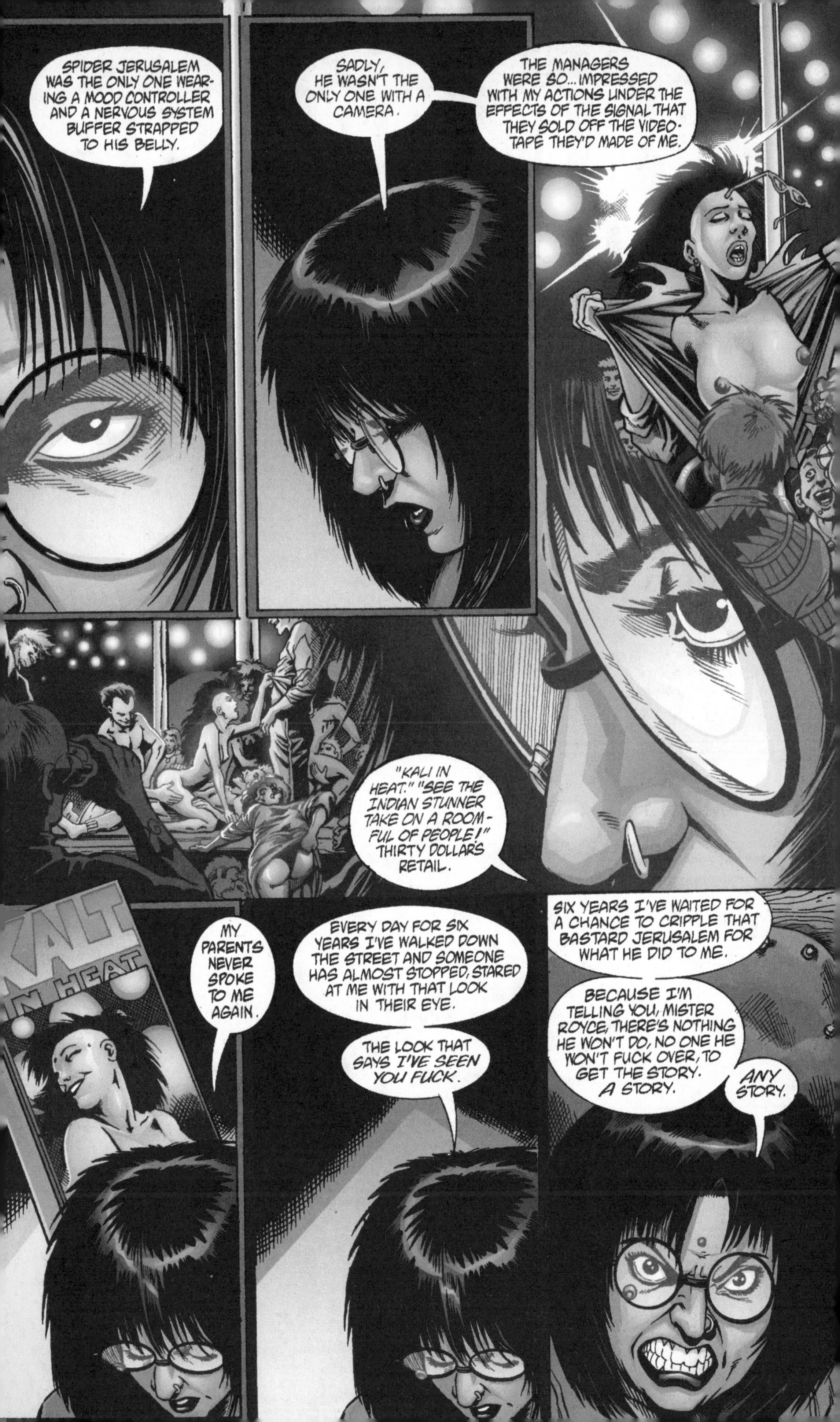
SPIDER JERUSALEM WAS THE ONLY ONE WEARING A MOOD CONTROLLER AND A NERVOUS SYSTEM BUFFER STRAPPED TO HIS BELLY.
SADLY, HE WASN'T THE ONLY ONE WITH A CAMERA.
THE MANAGERS WERE SO... IMPRESSED WITH MY ACTIONS UNDER THE EFFECTS OF THE SIGNAL THAT THEY SOLD OFF THE VIDEOTAPE THEY'D MADE OF ME.
"KALI IN HEAT." "SEE THE INDIAN STUNNER TAKE ON A ROOMFUL OF PEOPLE!" THIRTY DOLLARS RETAIL.
KALI IN HEAT
MY PARENTS NEVER SPOKE TO ME AGAIN.
EVERY DAY FOR SIX YEARS I'VE WALKED DOWN THE STREET AND SOMEONE HAS ALMOST STOPPED, STARED AT ME WITH THAT LOOK IN THEIR EYE.
THE LOOK THAT SAYS *I'VE SEEN YOU FUCK*.
SIX YEARS I'VE WAITED FOR A CHANCE TO CRIPPLE THAT BASTARD JERUSALEM FOR WHAT HE DID TO ME.
BECAUSE I'M TELLING YOU, MISTER ROYCE, THERE'S NOTHING HE WON'T DO, NO ONE HE WON'T FUCK OVER, TO GET THE STORY. A STORY.
ANY STORY.

BAD DOGGIE

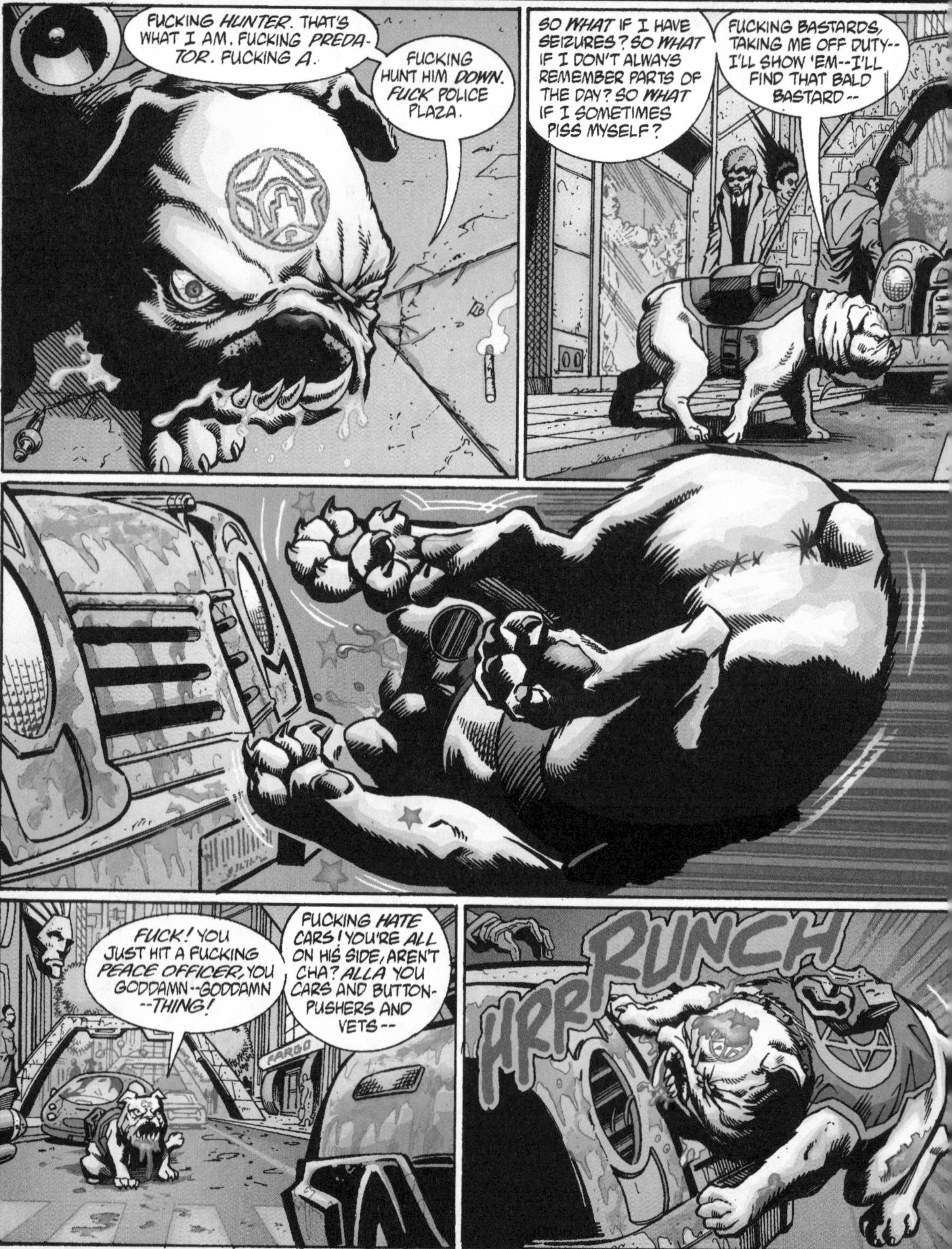

FUCKING HUNTER. THAT'S WHAT I AM. FUCKING PREDATOR. FUCKING A.
FUCKING HUNT HIM DOWN. FUCK POLICE PLAZA.
SO WHAT IF I HAVE SEIZURES? SO WHAT IF I DON'T ALWAYS REMEMBER PARTS OF THE DAY? SO WHAT IF I SOMETIMES PISS MYSELF?
FUCKING BASTARDS, TAKING ME OFF DUTY-- I'LL SHOW 'EM--I'LL FIND THAT BALD BASTARD--
FUCK! YOU JUST HIT A FUCKING PEACE OFFICER, YOU GODDAMN--GODDAMN --THING!
FUCKING HATE CARS! YOU'RE ALL ON HIS SIDE, AREN'T CHA? ALLA YOU CARS AND BUTTON-PUSHERS AND VETS--
FARGO
HRRRUNCH

To Live and Die on a Toilet

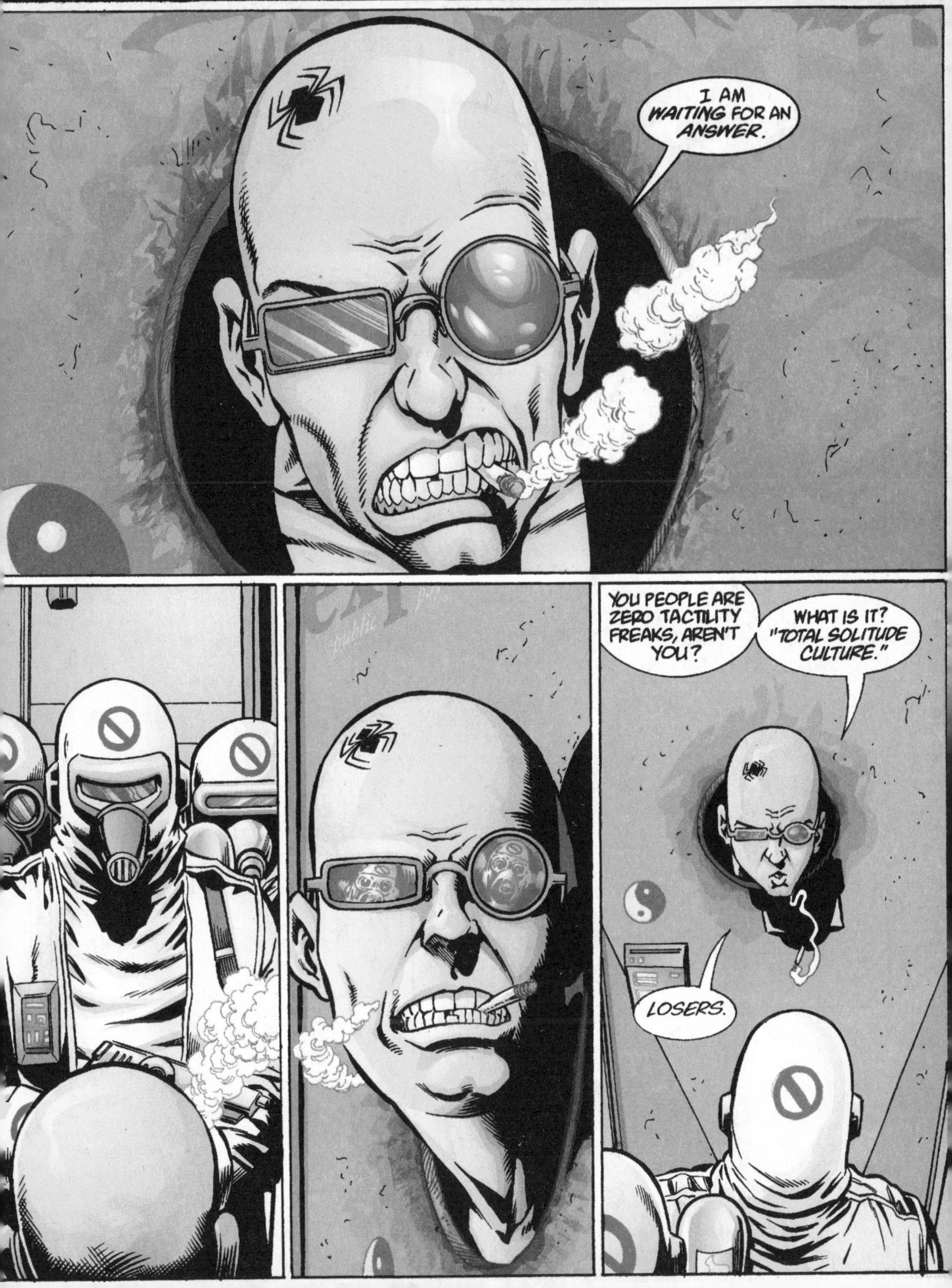

I AM WAITING FOR AN ANSWER.
YOU PEOPLE ARE ZERO TACTILITY FREAKS, AREN'T YOU?
WHAT IS IT? "TOTAL SOLITUDE CULTURE."
LOSERS.

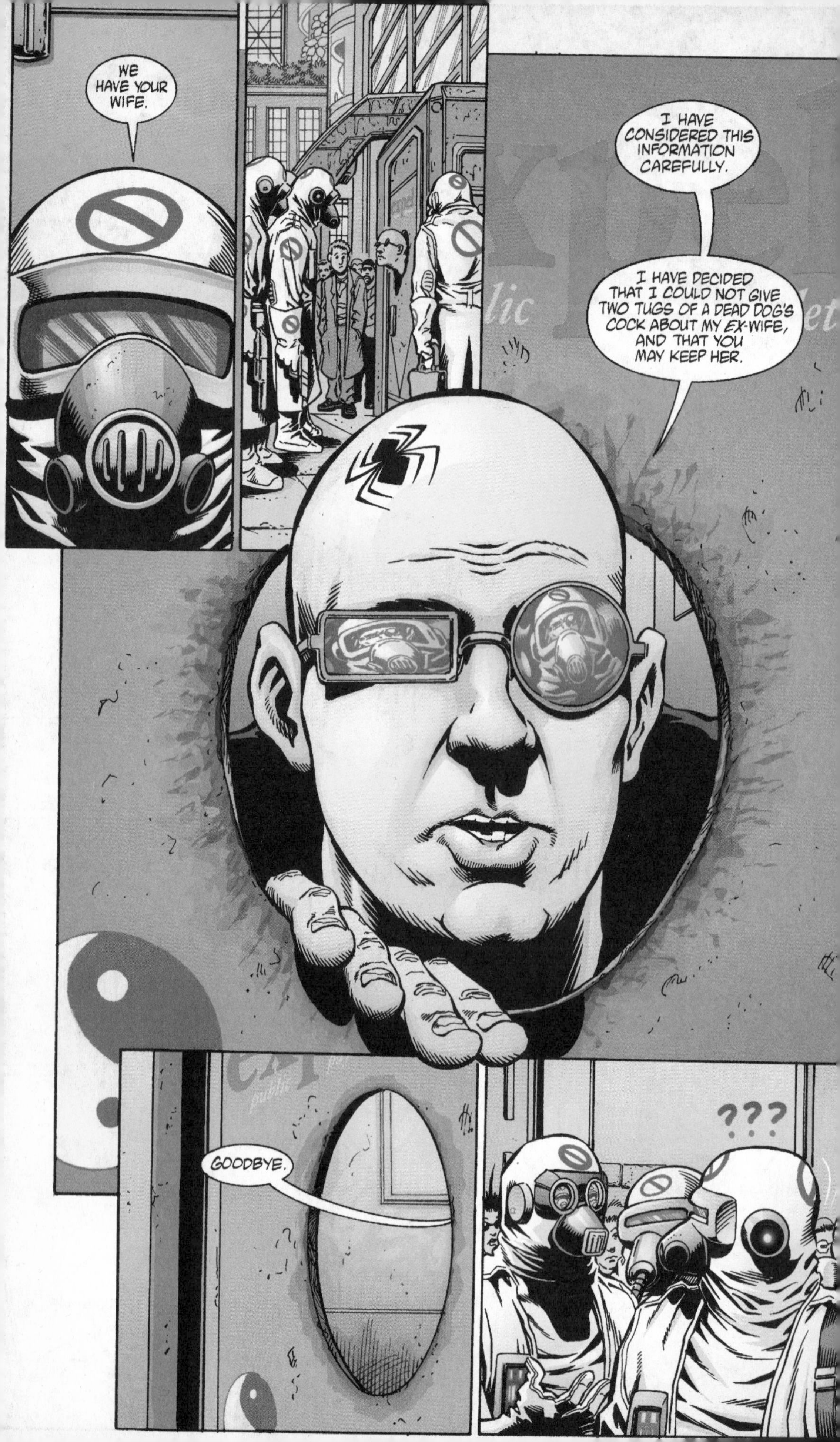
WE HAVE YOUR WIFE.
I HAVE CONSIDERED THIS INFORMATION CAREFULLY.
I HAVE DECIDED THAT I COULD NOT GIVE TWO TUGS OF A DEAD DOG'S COCK ABOUT MY EX-WIFE, AND THAT YOU MAY KEEP HER.
GOODBYE.
???

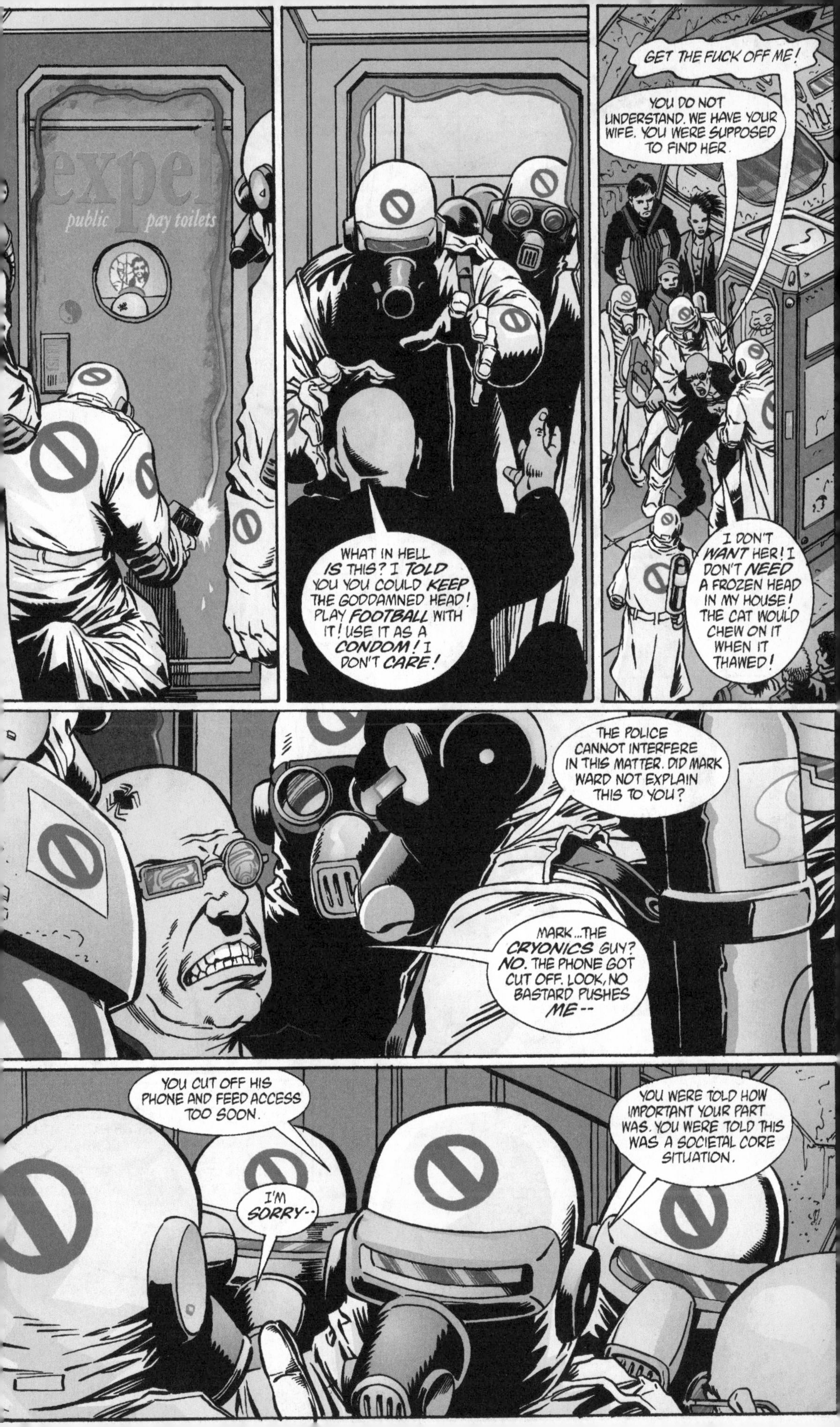
expel
public pay toilets
GET THE FUCK OFF ME!
YOU DO NOT UNDERSTAND. WE HAVE YOUR WIFE. YOU WERE SUPPOSED TO FIND HER.
WHAT IN HELL IS THIS? I TOLD YOU YOU COULD KEEP THE GODDAMNED HEAD! PLAY FOOTBALL WITH IT! USE IT AS A CONDOM! I DON'T CARE!
I DON'T WANT HER! I DON'T NEED A FROZEN HEAD IN MY HOUSE! THE CAT WOULD CHEW ON IT WHEN IT THAWED!
THE POLICE CANNOT INTERFERE IN THIS MATTER. DID MARK WARD NOT EXPLAIN THIS TO YOU?
MARK...THE CRYONICS GUY? NO. THE PHONE GOT CUT OFF. LOOK, NO BASTARD PUSHES ME--
YOU CUT OFF HIS PHONE AND FEED ACCESS TOO SOON.
I'M SORRY--
YOU WERE TOLD HOW IMPORTANT YOUR PART WAS. YOU WERE TOLD THIS WAS A SOCIETAL CORE SITUATION.

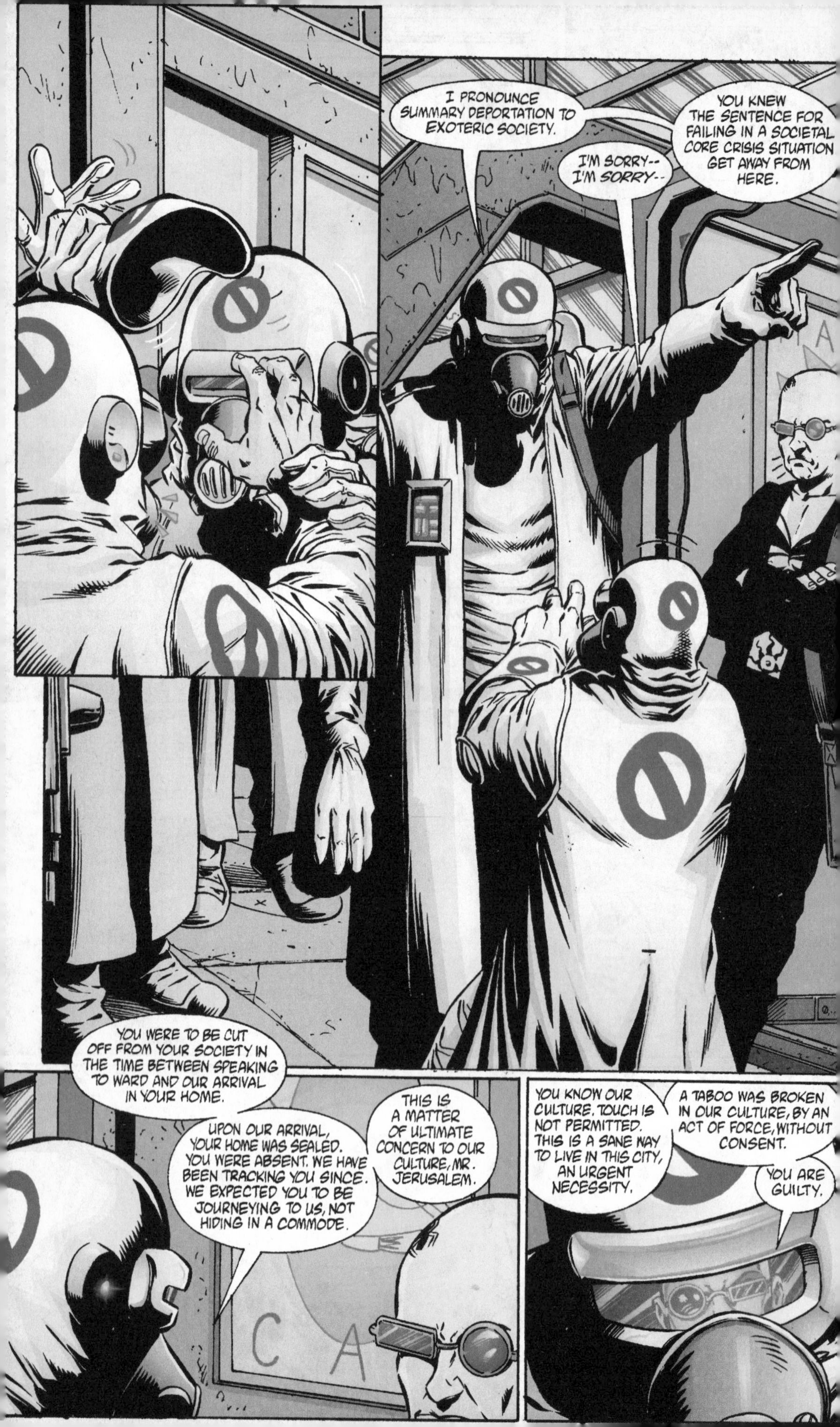
I PRONOUNCE SUMMARY DEPORTATION TO EXOTERIC SOCIETY.
I'M SORRY-- I'M SORRY--
YOU KNEW THE SENTENCE FOR FAILING IN A SOCIETAL CORE CRISIS SITUATION GET AWAY FROM HERE.
YOU WERE TO BE CUT OFF FROM YOUR SOCIETY IN THE TIME BETWEEN SPEAKING TO WARD AND OUR ARRIVAL IN YOUR HOME.
UPON OUR ARRIVAL, YOUR HOME WAS SEALED. YOU WERE ABSENT. WE HAVE BEEN TRACKING YOU SINCE. WE EXPECTED YOU TO BE JOURNEYING TO US, NOT HIDING IN A COMMODE.
THIS IS A MATTER OF ULTIMATE CONCERN TO OUR CULTURE, MR. JERUSALEM.
YOU KNOW OUR CULTURE. TOUCH IS NOT PERMITTED. THIS IS A SANE WAY TO LIVE IN THIS CITY, AN URGENT NECESSITY.
A TABOO WAS BROKEN IN OUR CULTURE, BY AN ACT OF FORCE, WITHOUT CONSENT.
YOU ARE GUILTY.

"TRUTH, JUSTICE, ALL THAT"

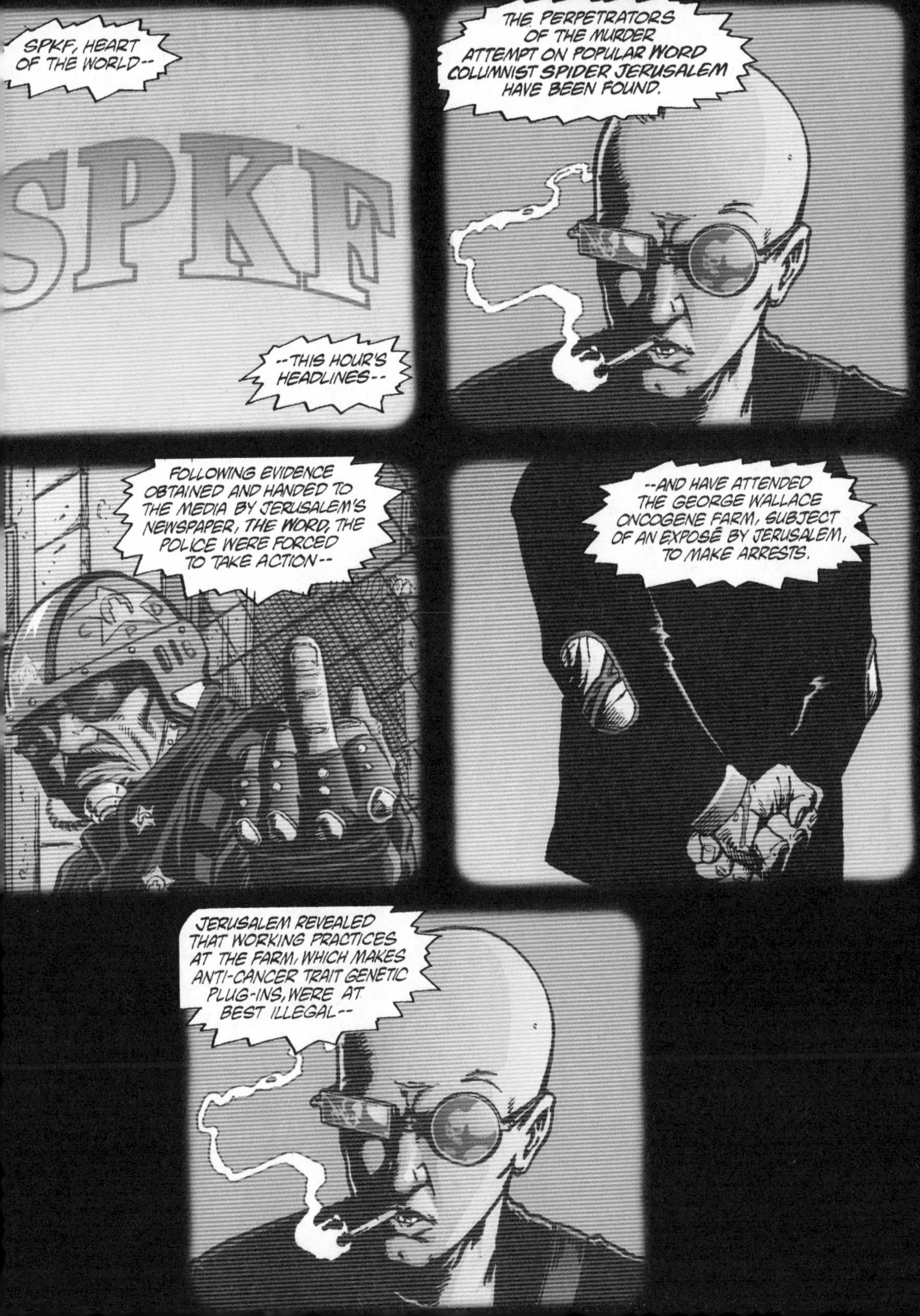
SPKF, HEART OF THE WORLD--
SPKF
--THIS HOUR'S HEADLINES--
THE PERPETRATORS OF THE MURDER ATTEMPT ON POPULAR WORD COLUMNIST SPIDER JERUSALEM HAVE BEEN FOUND.
FOLLOWING EVIDENCE OBTAINED AND HANDED TO THE MEDIA BY JERUSALEM'S NEWSPAPER, THE WORD, THE POLICE WERE FORCED TO TAKE ACTION--
--AND HAVE ATTENDED THE GEORGE WALLACE ONCOGENE FARM, SUBJECT OF AN EXPOSÉ BY JERUSALEM, TO MAKE ARRESTS.
JERUSALEM REVEALED THAT WORKING PRACTICES AT THE FARM, WHICH MAKES ANTI-CANCER TRAIT GENETIC PLUG-INS, WERE AT BEST ILLEGAL--

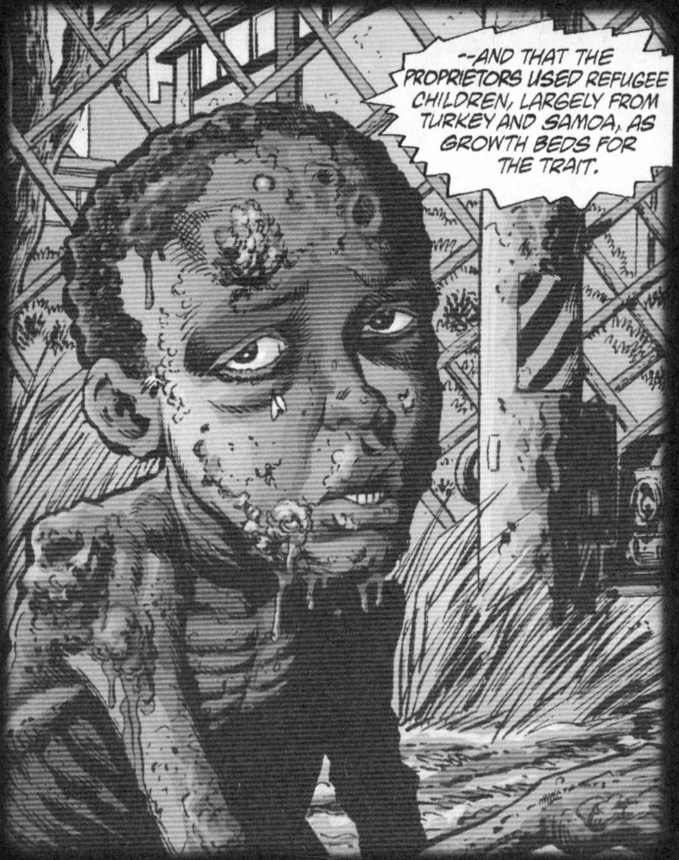
--AND THAT THE PROPRIETORS USED REFUGEE CHILDREN, LARGELY FROM TURKEY AND SAMOA, AS GROWTH BEDS FOR THE TRAIT.

GO TO
THE WORD
FEEDSITE TO READ
THE ARCHIVED
"I HATE IT HERE"
COLUMNS BY
SPIDER JERUSALEM

ALL MAJOR
CREDIT CARDS
ACCEPTED

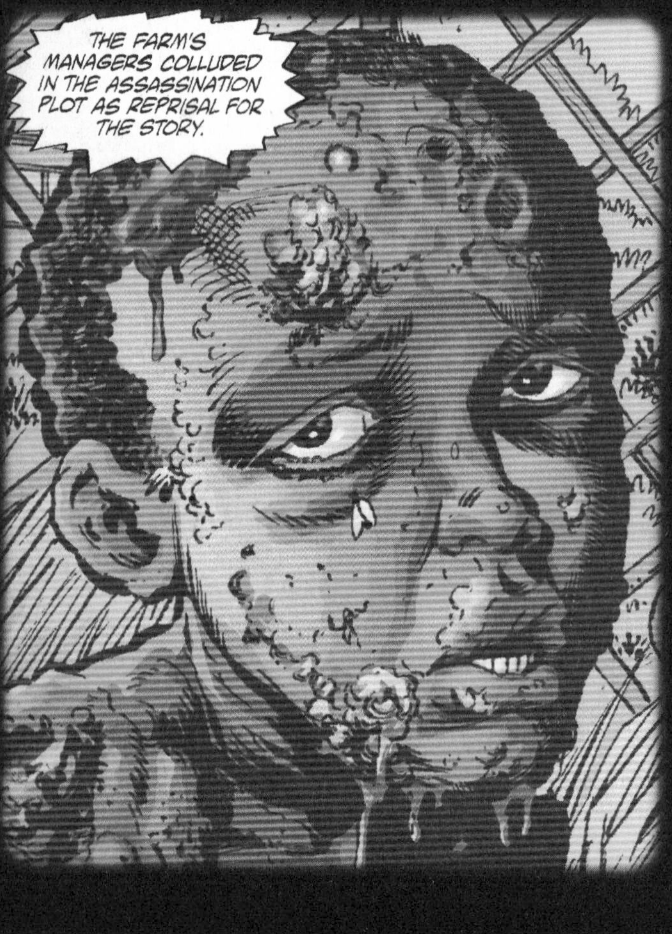
THE FARM'S MANAGERS COLLUDED IN THE ASSASSINATION PLOT AS REPRISAL FOR THE STORY.

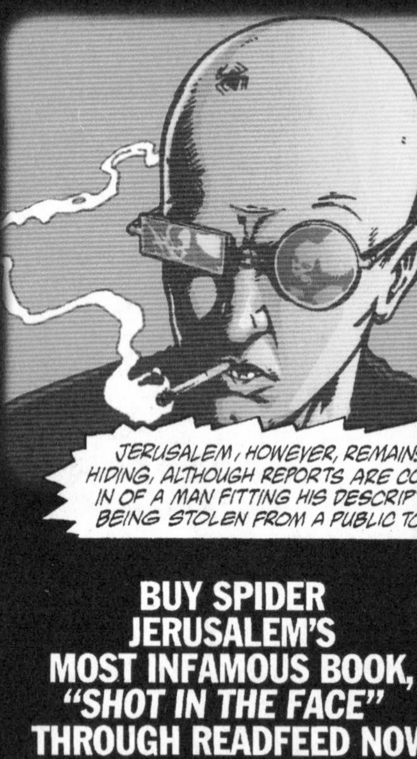
JERUSALEM, HOWEVER, REMAINS
HIDING, ALTHOUGH REPORTS ARE CO
IN OF A MAN FITTING HIS DESCRIP
BEING STOLEN FROM A PUBLIC TO

BUY SPIDER
JERUSALEM'S
MOST INFAMOUS BOOK,
"SHOT IN THE FACE"
THROUGH READFEED NOW

(A division of SPKF)

THE TRUTH ABOUT CATS AND DOGS

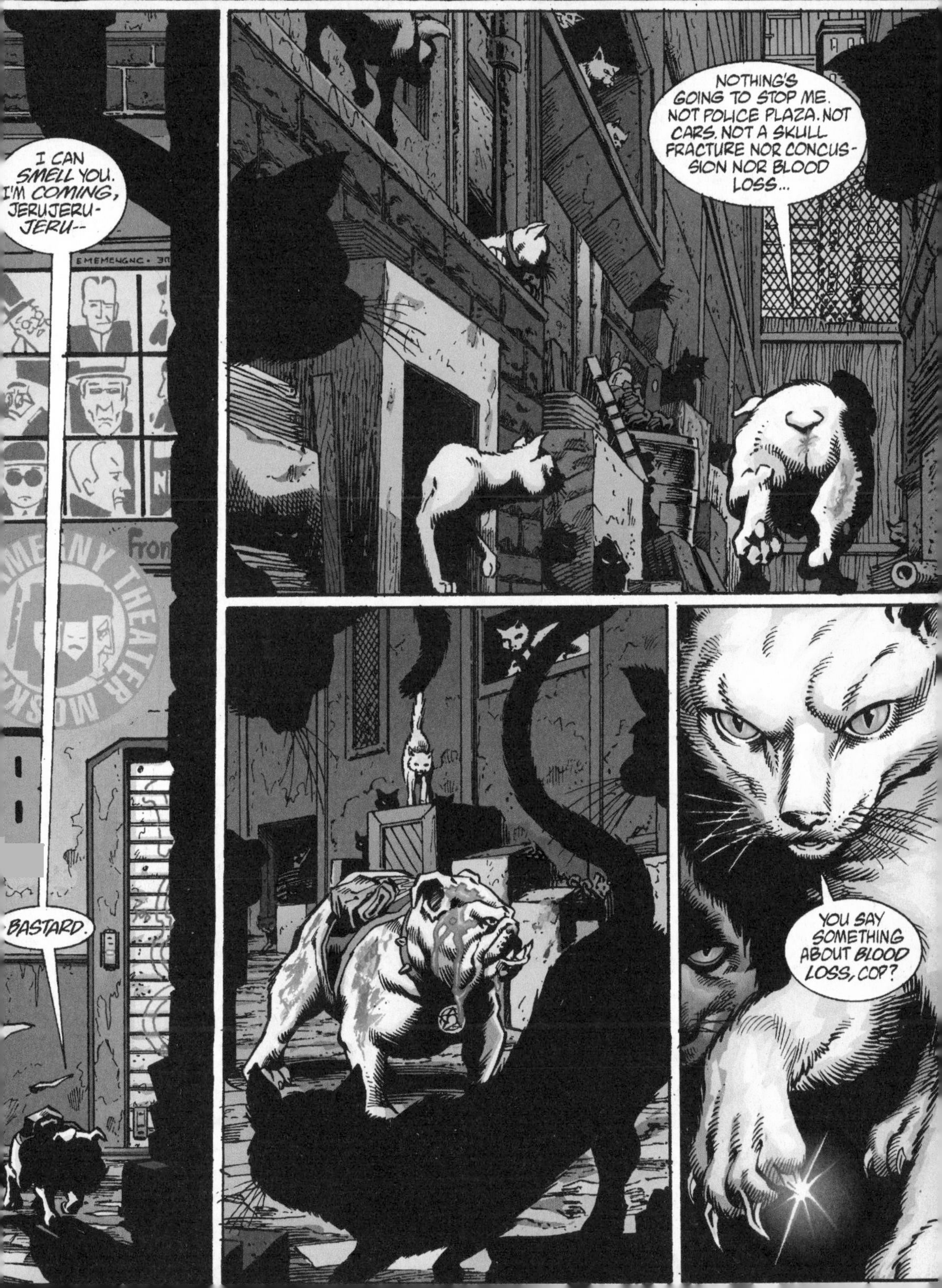

I CAN SMELL YOU. I'M COMING, JERUJERU-JERU--
NOTHING'S GOING TO STOP ME. NOT POLICE PLAZA. NOT CARS. NOT A SKULL FRACTURE NOR CONCUSSION NOR BLOOD LOSS...
BASTARD.
YOU SAY SOMETHING ABOUT BLOOD LOSS, COP?

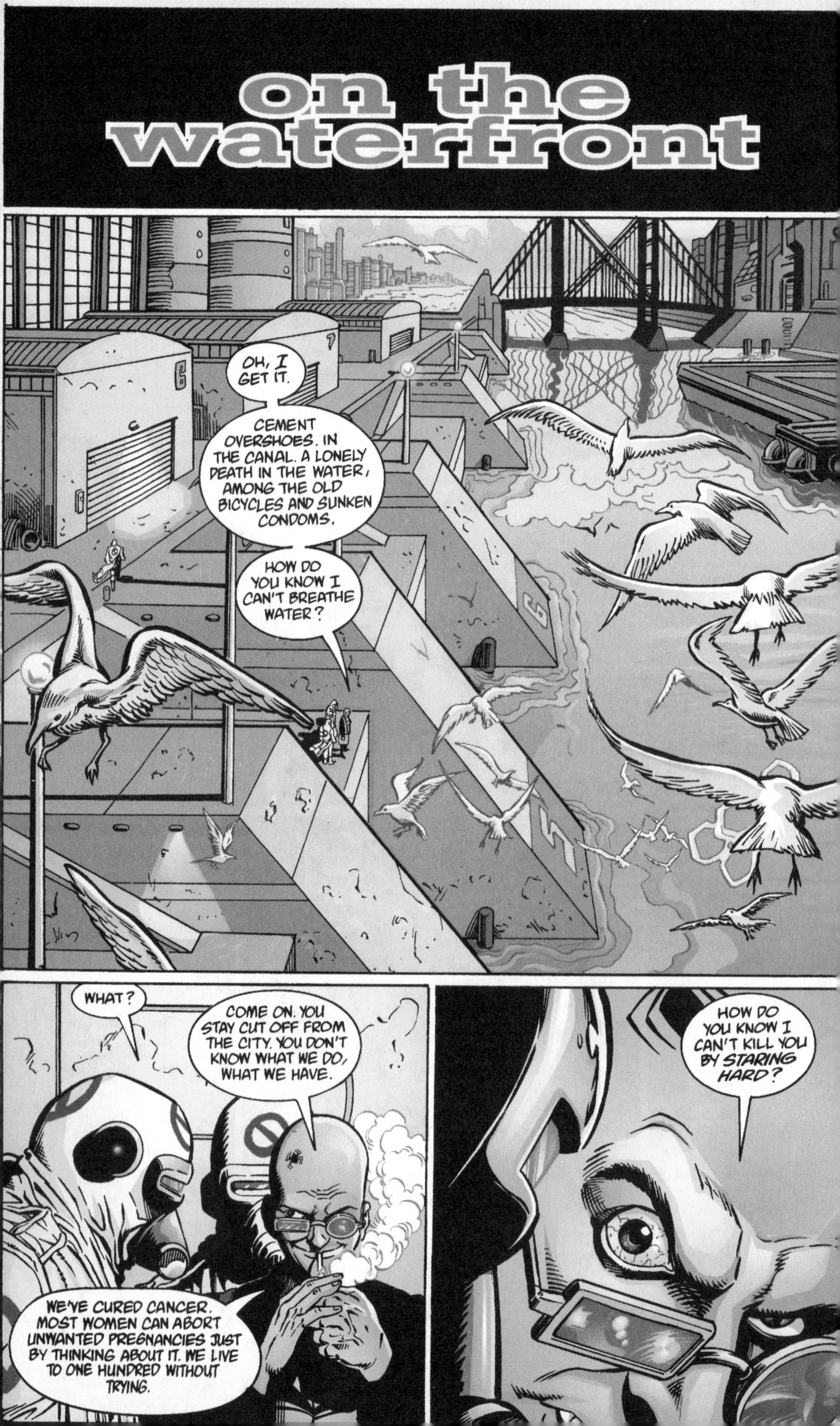
on the waterfront
OH, I GET IT.
CEMENT OVERSHOES. IN THE CANAL. A LONELY DEATH IN THE WATER, AMONG THE OLD BICYCLES AND SUNKEN CONDOMS.
HOW DO YOU KNOW I CAN'T BREATHE WATER?
WHAT?
COME ON. YOU STAY CUT OFF FROM THE CITY. YOU DON'T KNOW WHAT WE DO, WHAT WE HAVE.
WE'VE CURED CANCER. MOST WOMEN CAN ABORT UNWANTED PREGNANCIES JUST BY THINKING ABOUT IT. WE LIVE TO ONE HUNDRED WITHOUT TRYING.
HOW DO YOU KNOW I CAN'T KILL YOU BY *STARING HARD*?

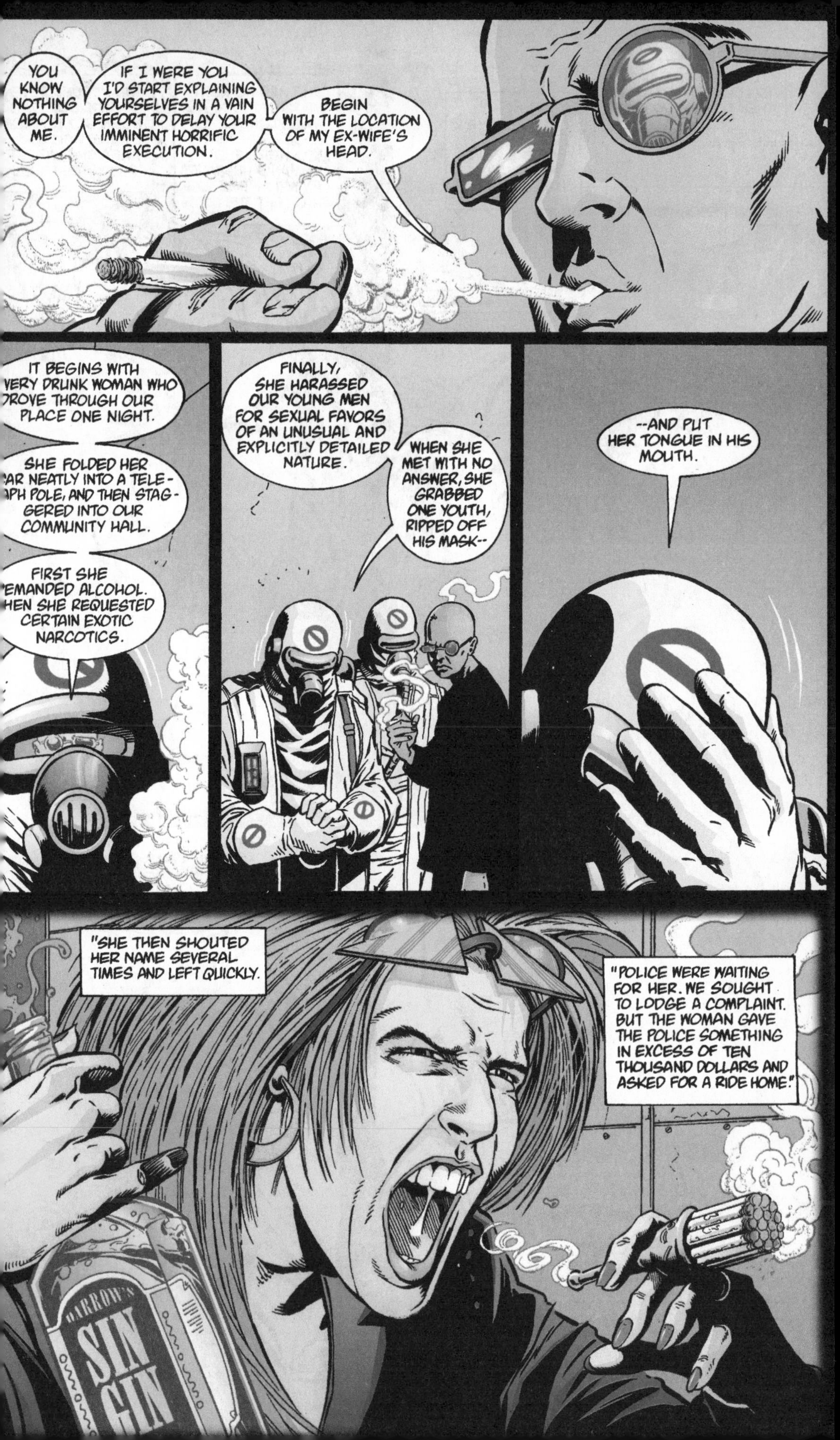

YOU KNOW NOTHING ABOUT ME.
IF I WERE YOU I'D START EXPLAINING YOURSELVES IN A VAIN EFFORT TO DELAY YOUR IMMINENT HORRIFIC EXECUTION.
BEGIN WITH THE LOCATION OF MY EX-WIFE'S HEAD.
IT BEGINS WITH VERY DRUNK WOMAN WHO ROVE THROUGH OUR PLACE ONE NIGHT.
SHE FOLDED HER AR NEATLY INTO A TELE- APH POLE, AND THEN STAG- GERED INTO OUR COMMUNITY HALL.
FIRST SHE EMANDED ALCOHOL. HEN SHE REQUESTED CERTAIN EXOTIC NARCOTICS.
FINALLY, SHE HARASSED OUR YOUNG MEN FOR SEXUAL FAVORS OF AN UNUSUAL AND EXPLICITLY DETAILED NATURE.
WHEN SHE MET WITH NO ANSWER, SHE GRABBED ONE YOUTH, RIPPED OFF HIS MASK--
--AND PUT HER TONGUE IN HIS MOUTH.
"SHE THEN SHOUTED HER NAME SEVERAL TIMES AND LEFT QUICKLY.
"POLICE WERE WAITING FOR HER. WE SOUGHT TO LODGE A COMPLAINT. BUT THE WOMAN GAVE THE POLICE SOMETHING IN EXCESS OF TEN THOUSAND DOLLARS AND ASKED FOR A RIDE HOME."

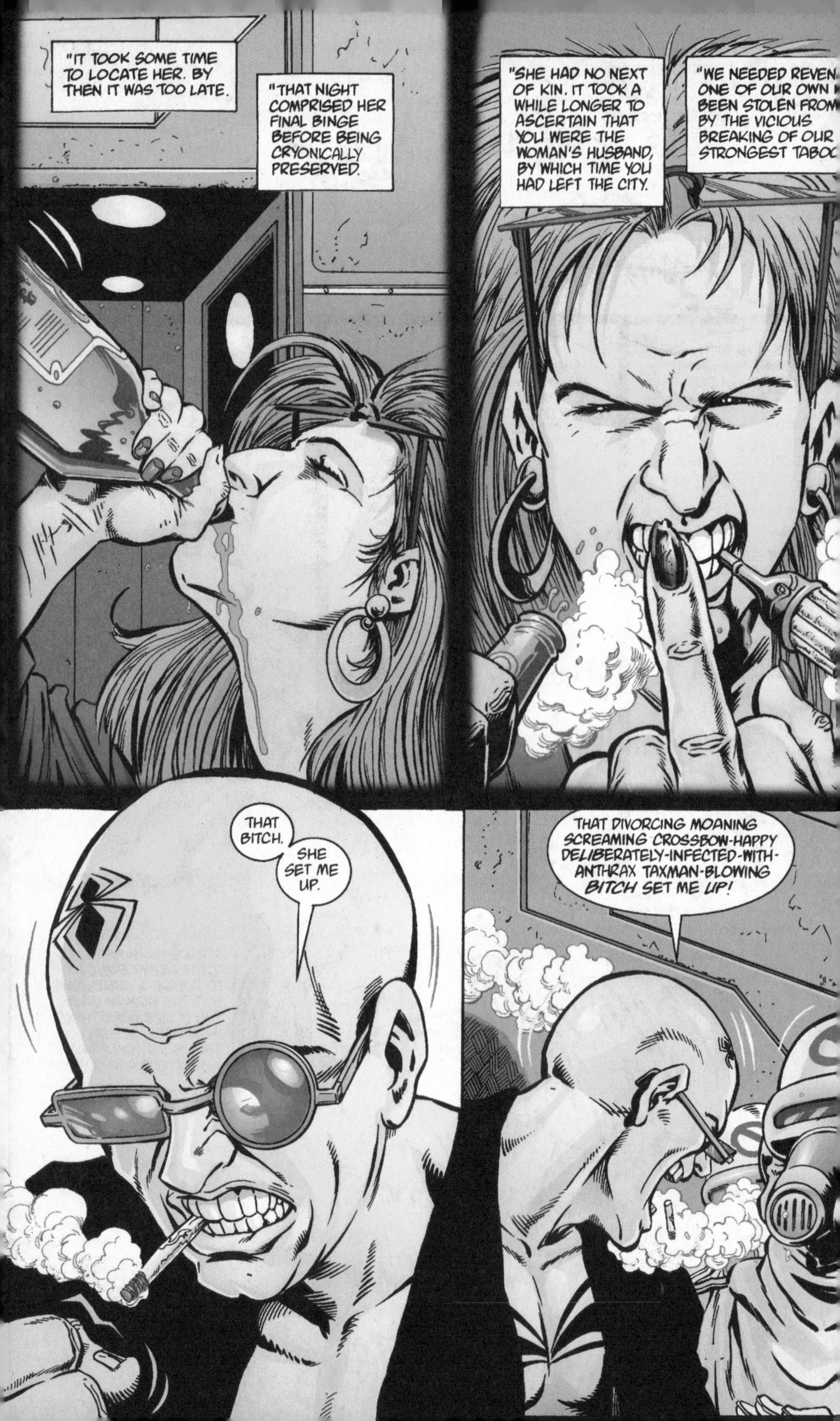
"IT TOOK SOME TIME TO LOCATE HER. BY THEN IT WAS TOO LATE.
"THAT NIGHT COMPRISED HER FINAL BINGE BEFORE BEING CRYONICALLY PRESERVED.
"SHE HAD NO NEXT OF KIN. IT TOOK A WHILE LONGER TO ASCERTAIN THAT YOU WERE THE WOMAN'S HUSBAND, BY WHICH TIME YOU HAD LEFT THE CITY.
"WE NEEDED REVEN ONE OF OUR OWN BEEN STOLEN FROM BY THE VICIOUS BREAKING OF OUR STRONGEST TABOO
THAT BITCH.
SHE SET ME UP.
THAT DIVORCING MOANING SCREAMING CROSSBOW-HAPPY DELIBERATELY-INFECTED-WITH-ANTHRAX TAXMAN-BLOWING *BITCH* SET ME *UP*!

God/Dog

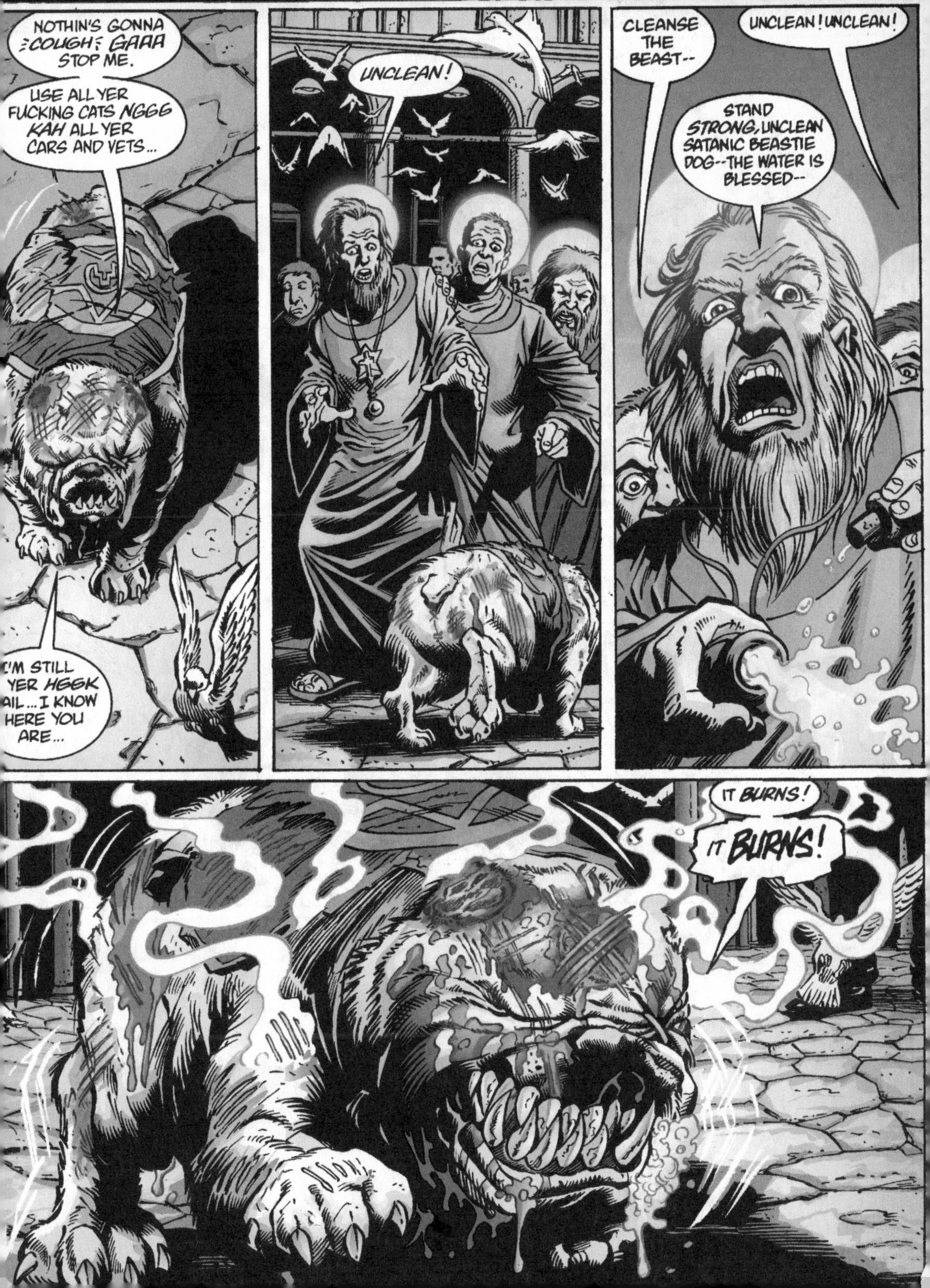
NOTHIN'S GONNA *COUGH* GAAA STOP ME.
USE ALL YER FUCKING CATS NGGG KAH ALL YER CARS AND VETS...
'M STILL YER HGGK AIL... I KNOW HERE YOU ARE...
UNCLEAN!
CLEANSE THE BEAST--
UNCLEAN! UNCLEAN!
STAND STRONG, UNCLEAN SATANIC BEASTIE DOG--THE WATER IS BLESSED--
IT BURNS!
IT BURNS!

spider explains it all

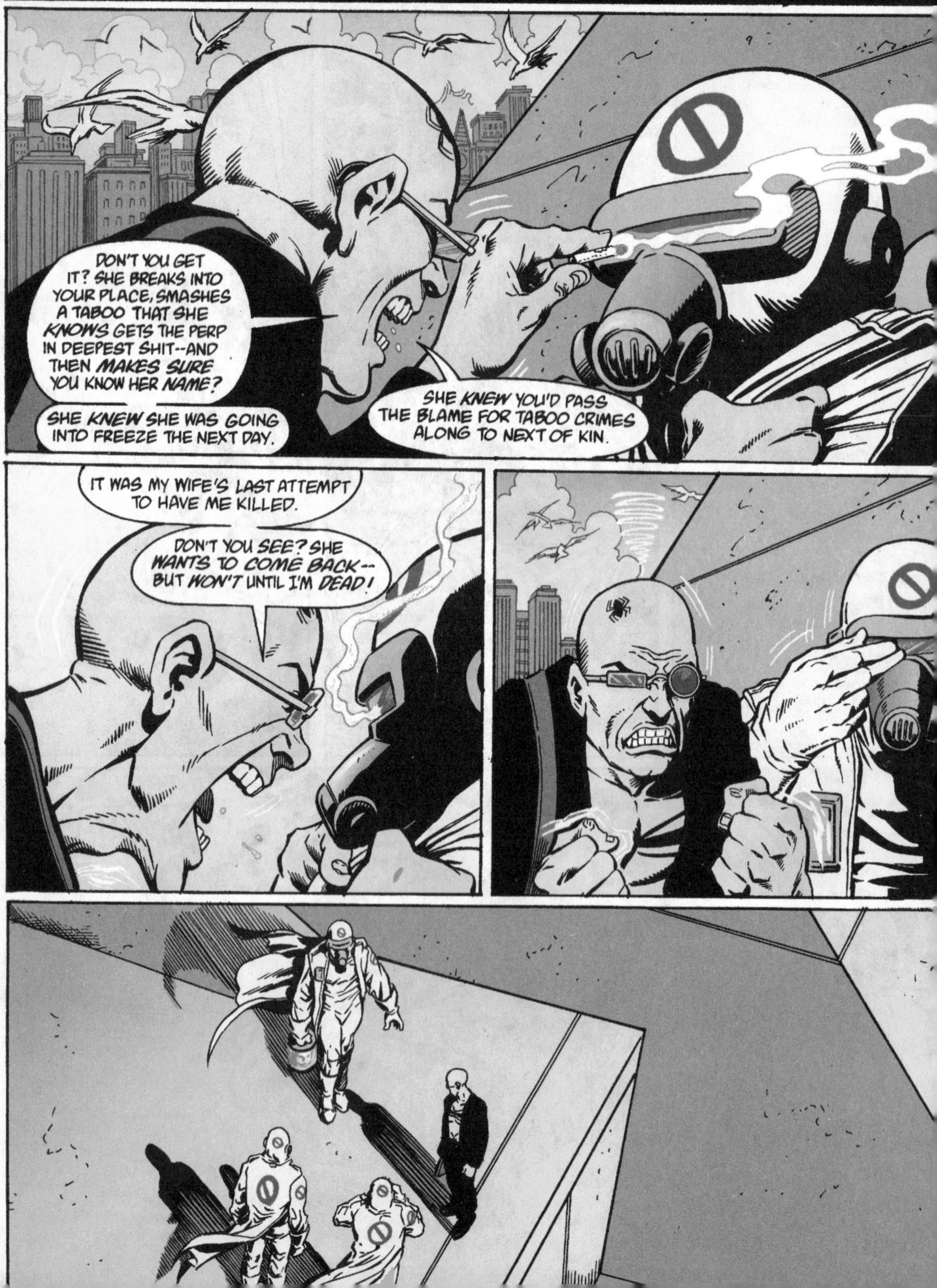
DON'T YOU GET IT? SHE BREAKS INTO YOUR PLACE, SMASHES A TABOO THAT SHE KNOWS GETS THE PERP IN DEEPEST SHIT--AND THEN MAKES SURE YOU KNOW HER NAME?
SHE KNEW SHE WAS GOING INTO FREEZE THE NEXT DAY.
SHE KNEW YOU'D PASS THE BLAME FOR TABOO CRIMES ALONG TO NEXT OF KIN.
IT WAS MY WIFE'S LAST ATTEMPT TO HAVE ME KILLED.
DON'T YOU SEE? SHE WANTS TO COME BACK-- BUT WON'T UNTIL I'M DEAD!

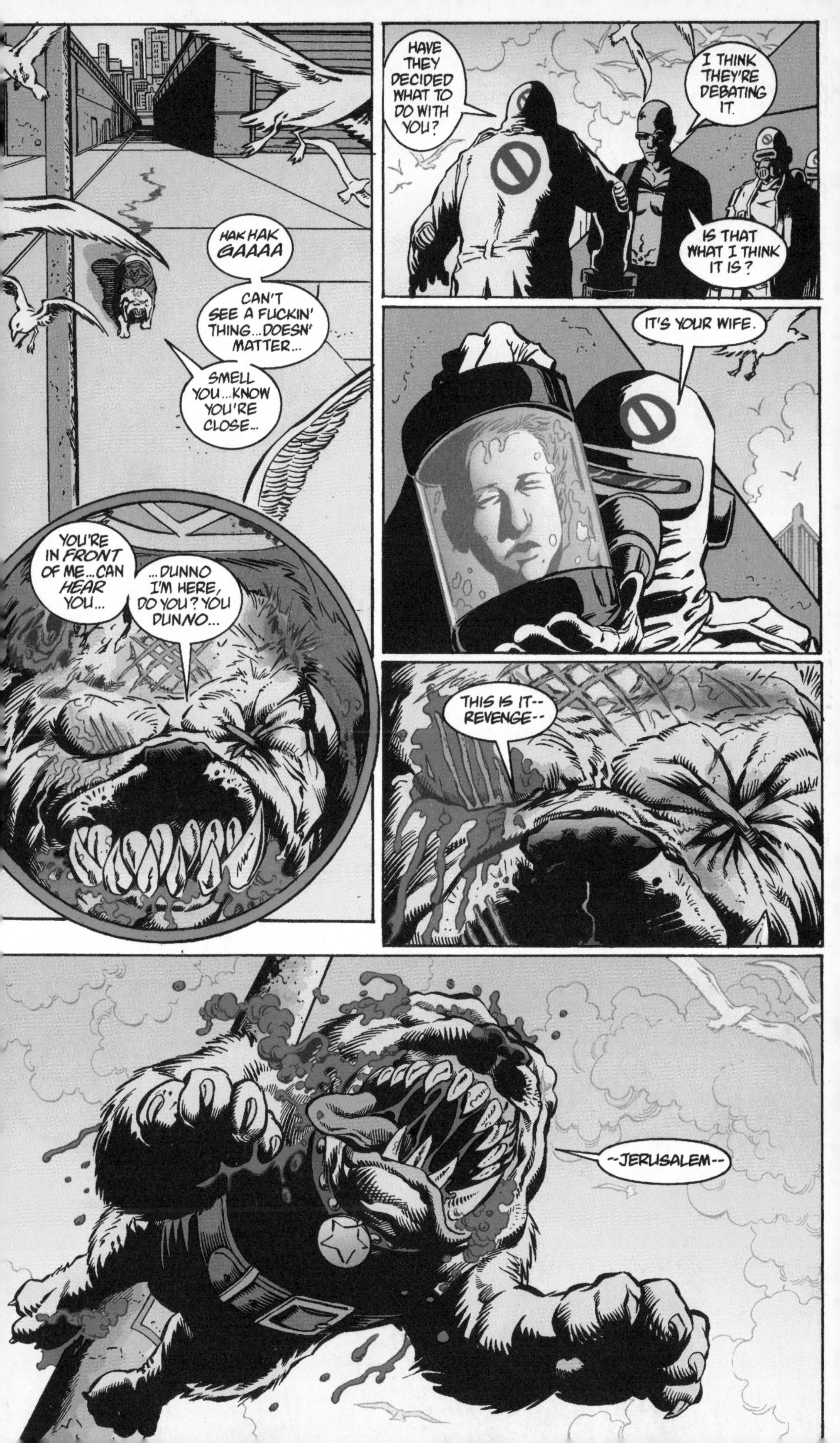
HAK HAK GAAAA
CAN'T SEE A FUCKIN' THING...DOESN' MATTER...
SMELL YOU...KNOW YOU'RE CLOSE...
HAVE THEY DECIDED WHAT TO DO WITH YOU?
I THINK THEY'RE DEBATING IT.
IS THAT WHAT I THINK IT IS?
IT'S YOUR WIFE.
YOU'RE IN FRONT OF ME...CAN HEAR YOU...
...DUNNO I'M HERE, DO YOU? YOU DUNNO...
THIS IS IT-- REVENGE--
--JERUSALEM--

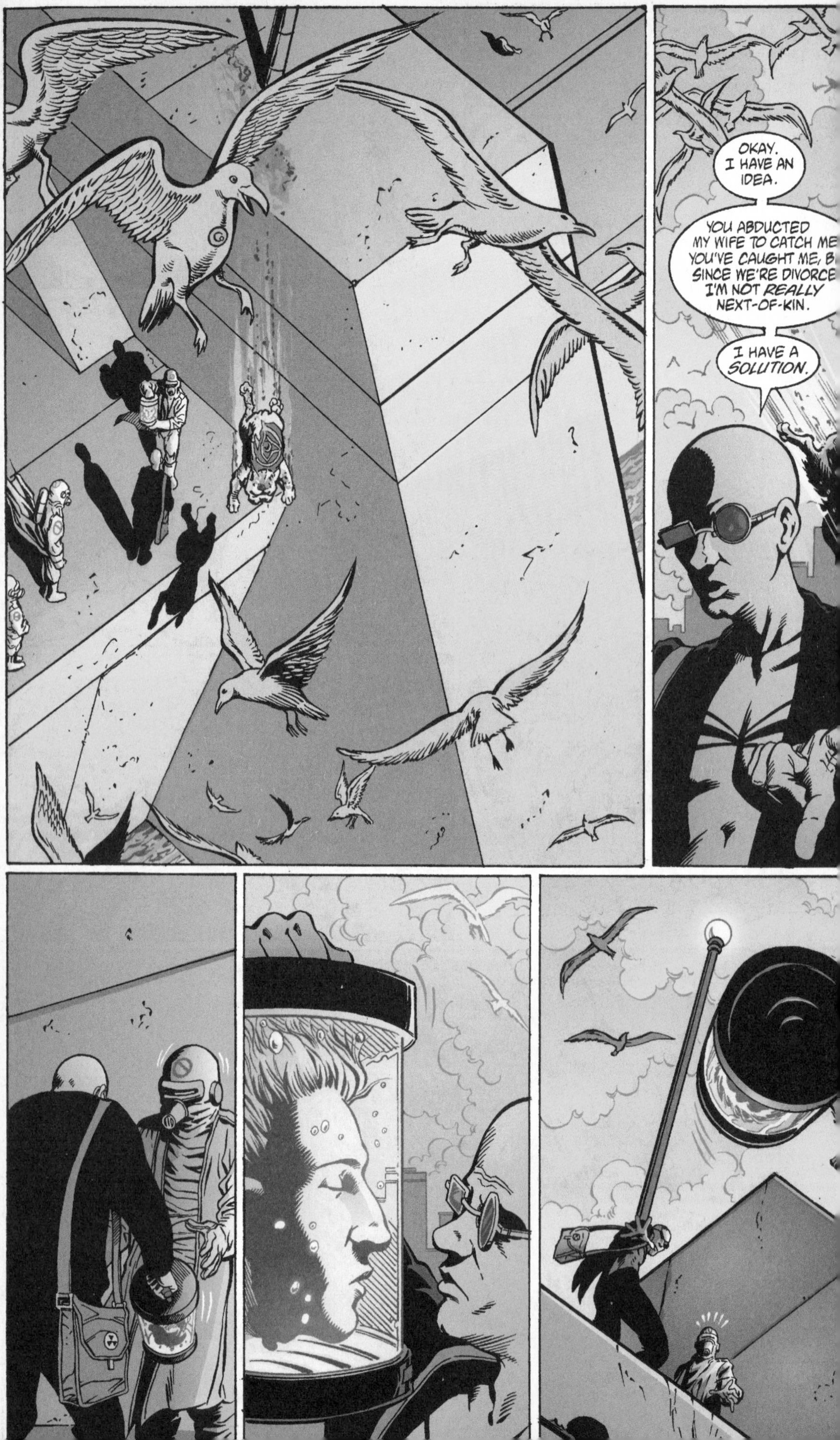
OKAY. I HAVE AN IDEA.
YOU ABDUCTED MY WIFE TO CATCH ME. YOU'VE CAUGHT ME, B
SINCE WE'RE DIVORCE
I'M NOT REALLY NEXT-OF-KIN.
I HAVE A SOLUTION.

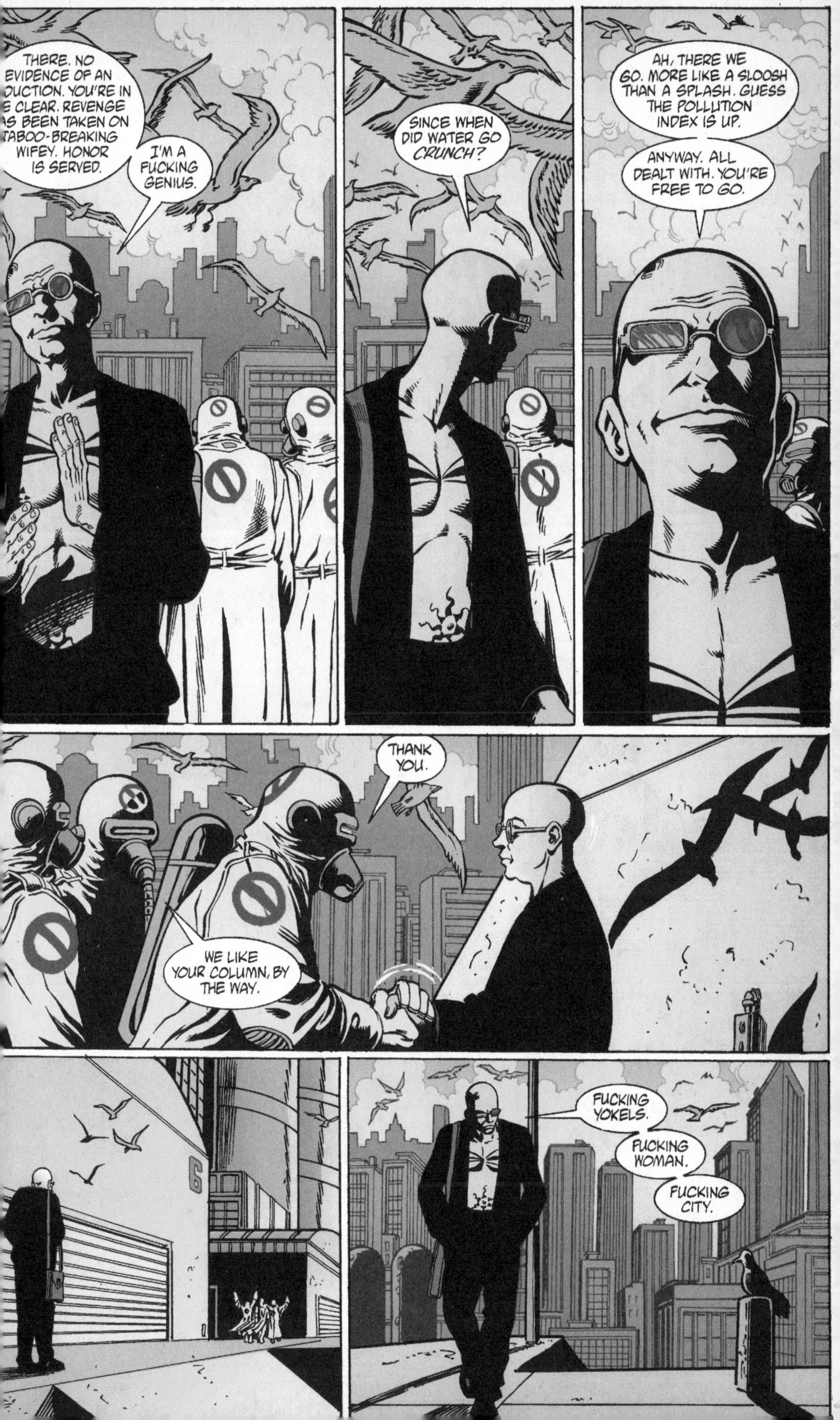
THERE. NO EVIDENCE OF AN DUCTION. YOU'RE IN E CLEAR. REVENGE AS BEEN TAKEN ON TABOO-BREAKING WIFEY. HONOR IS SERVED.
I'M A FUCKING GENIUS.
SINCE WHEN DID WATER GO *CRUNCH?*
AH, THERE WE GO. MORE LIKE A SLOOSH THAN A SPLASH. GUESS THE POLLUTION INDEX IS UP.
ANYWAY. ALL DEALT WITH. YOU'RE FREE TO GO.
THANK YOU.
WE LIKE YOUR COLUMN, BY THE WAY.
6
FUCKING YOKELS.
FUCKING WOMAN.
FUCKING CITY.

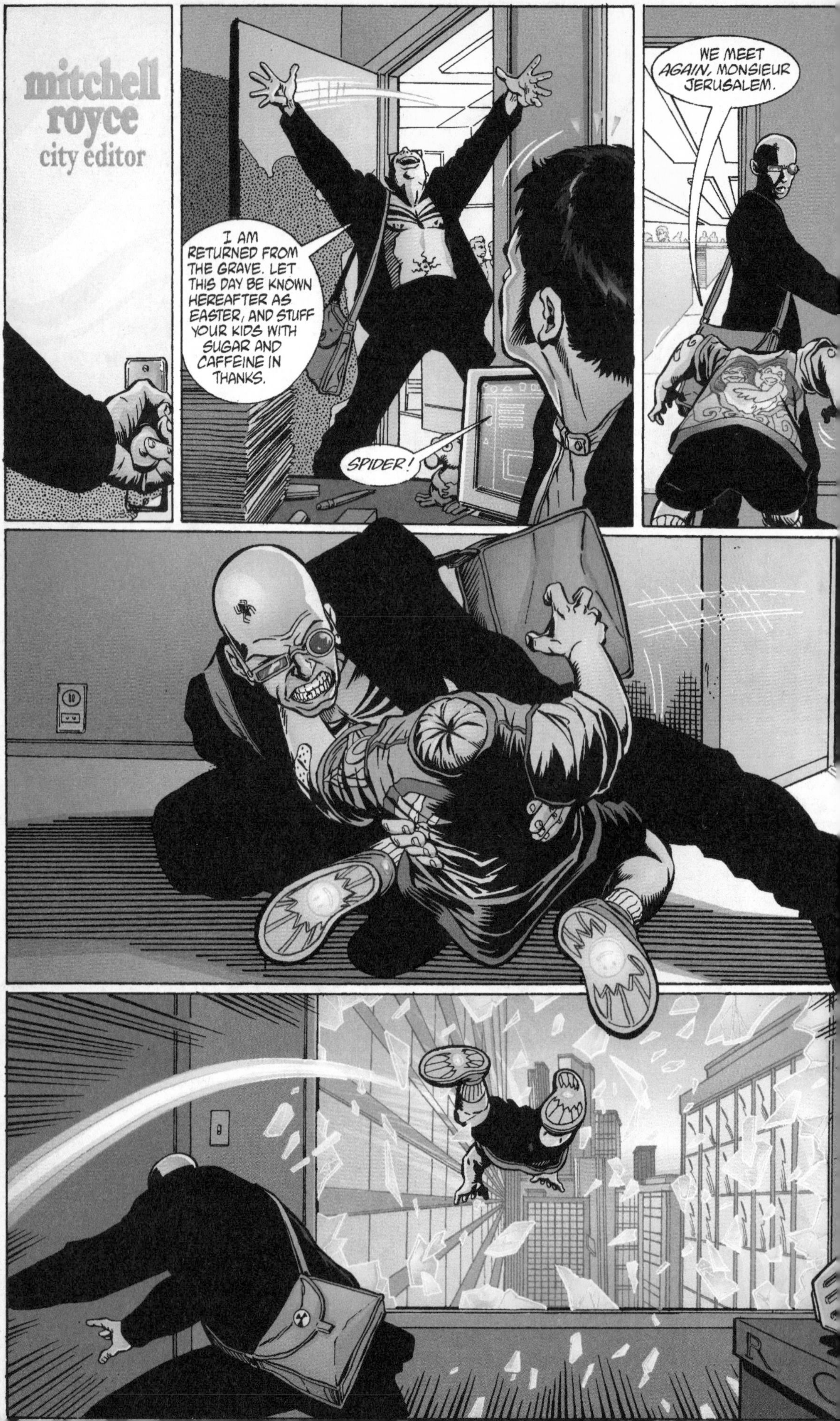
mitchell
royce
city editor
I AM RETURNED FROM THE GRAVE. LET THIS DAY BE KNOWN HEREAFTER AS EASTER, AND STUFF YOUR KIDS WITH SUGAR AND CAFFEINE IN THANKS.
SPIDER!
WE MEET AGAIN, MONSIEUR JERUSALEM.

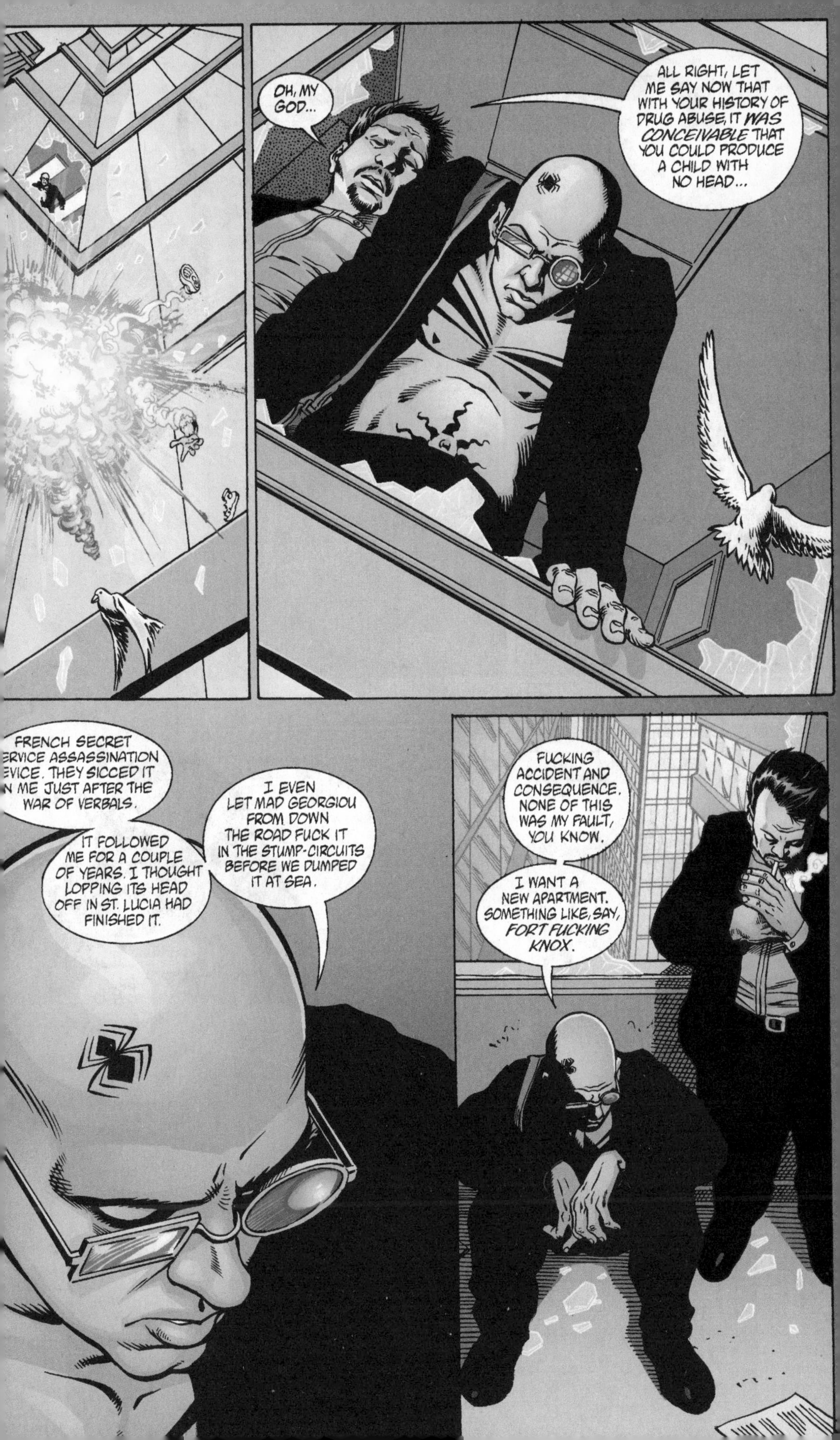
OH, MY GOD...
ALL RIGHT, LET ME SAY NOW THAT WITH YOUR HISTORY OF DRUG ABUSE, IT WAS CONCEIVABLE THAT YOU COULD PRODUCE A CHILD WITH NO HEAD...
FRENCH SECRET ERVICE ASSASSINATION EVICE. THEY SICCED IT N ME JUST AFTER THE WAR OF VERBALS.
IT FOLLOWED ME FOR A COUPLE OF YEARS. I THOUGHT LOPPING ITS HEAD OFF IN ST. LUCIA HAD FINISHED IT.
I EVEN LET MAD GEORGIOU FROM DOWN THE ROAD FUCK IT IN THE STUMP-CIRCUITS BEFORE WE DUMPED IT AT SEA.
FUCKING ACCIDENT AND CONSEQUENCE. NONE OF THIS WAS MY FAULT, YOU KNOW.
I WANT A NEW APARTMENT. SOMETHING LIKE, SAY, FORT FUCKING KNOX.

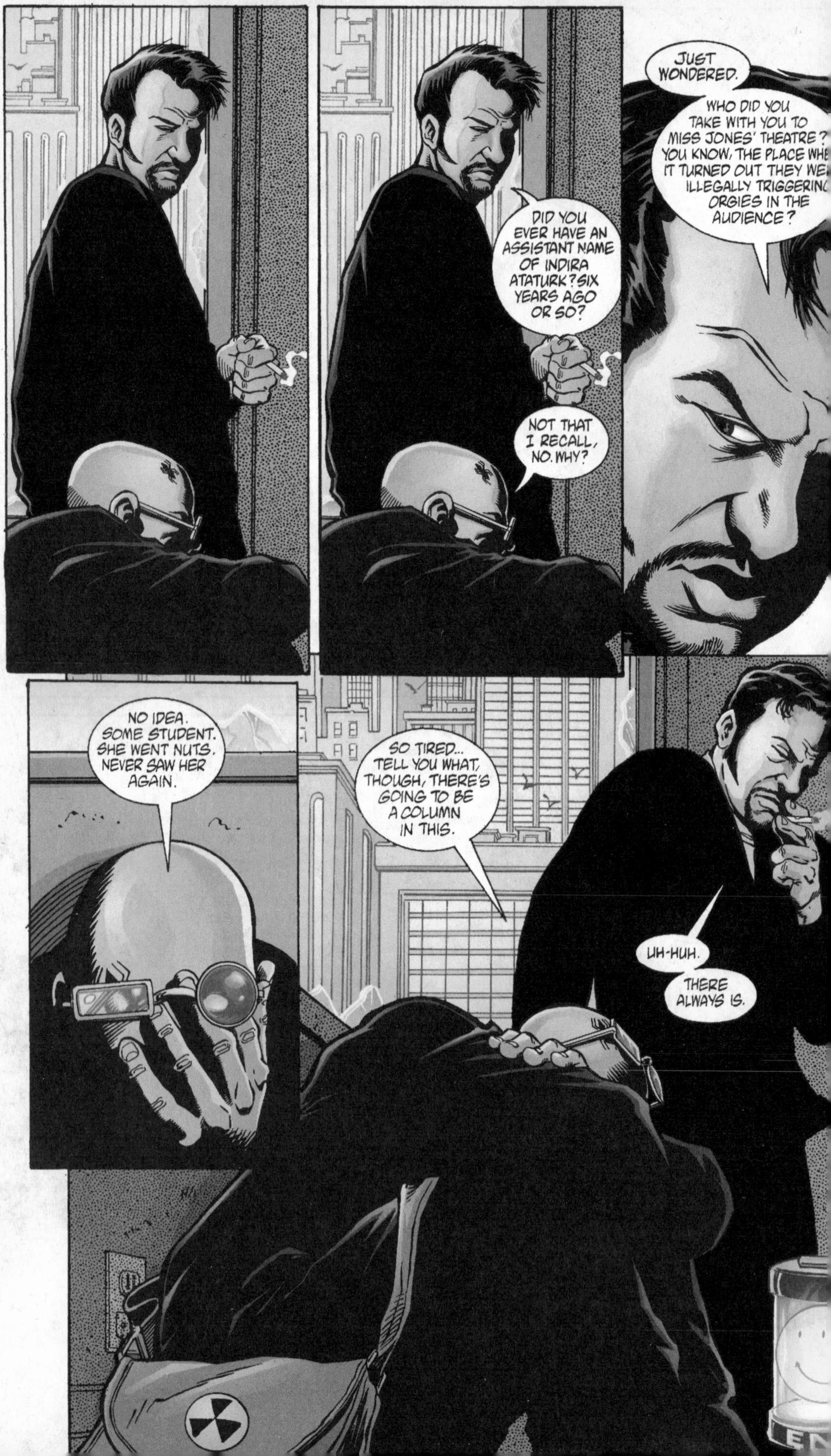
DID YOU EVER HAVE AN ASSISTANT NAME OF INDIRA ATATURK? SIX YEARS AGO OR SO?
NOT THAT I RECALL, NO. WHY?
JUST WONDERED.
WHO DID YOU TAKE WITH YOU TO MISS JONES' THEATRE? YOU KNOW, THE PLACE WHE
IT TURNED OUT THEY WE
ILLEGALLY TRIGGERIN
ORGIES IN THE AUDIENCE?
NO IDEA. SOME STUDENT. SHE WENT NUTS. NEVER SAW HER AGAIN.
SO TIRED... TELL YOU WHAT, THOUGH, THERE'S GOING TO BE A COLUMN IN THIS.
UH-HUH.
THERE ALWAYS IS.